Deep Learning with PyTorch Lightning

Swiftly build high-performance Artificial Intelligence (AI) models using Python

Kunal Sawarkar

BIRMINGHAM—MUMBAI

Deep Learning with PyTorch Lightning

Publishing Product Manager: Sunith Shetty
Senior Editor: Mohammed Yusuf Imaratwale
Content Development Editors: Nazia Shaikh and Joseph Sunil
Technical Editor: Sonam Pandey
Copy Editor: Safis Editing
Language Support Editor: Safis Editing
Project Coordinator: Aparna Ravikumar Nair
Proofreader: Safis Editing
Indexer: Tejal Daruwale Soni
Production Designer: Roshan Kawale
Marketing Coordinator: Abeer Riyaz Dawe

First published: January 2022

Production reference: 3250522

Published by Packt Publishing Ltd.
Livery Place
35 Livery Street
Birmingham
B3 2PB, UK.

ISBN 978-1-80056-161-8

www.packt.com

Thanks to AAI .....

the supernova who formed me … single handedly!!

Kunal ~ Stardust ~

"We are all just stories the end........just make a good one"

Contributors

About the authors

Kunal Sawarkar is a Chief Data Scientist and AI thought leader. He currently leads the worldwide AI Build Labs for crafting innovative products. In the past, he has built multiple AI Product labs from scratch & led products to hyper-growth. He holds a Master's degree from Harvard University with major coursework in Applied Statistics. He has been applying Machine Learning to solve previously unsolved problems in industry & society, with special focus on Deep Learning. He has 20+ patents and published papers in this field. He also serves as an Advisory Board Member and as an Angel Investor focused on Sustainability via AI.

When not diving into data, he enjoys rock climbing and learning to fly apart from continuing his incessant curiosity in astronomy and wildlife.

"What attracted me to Data Science is the poetry of chance & certainty. Building AI is like creating symphony out of chaos."

Shivam R Solanki is a senior data scientist living at the interstice of business, data and technology. He earned his Master's degree from Texas A&M University with a major coursework in Applied Statistics. He is passionate about solving business problems through the application of Statistics, Machine Learning and Deep Learning.

" The reality is unpredictable only as long as we see it without the lens of Statistics. To my family for always supporting me in my endeavors."

Amit Joglekar is an experienced Machine Learning Engineer with strong focus on design. He is passionate about learning new technologies and thoroughly enjoy programming in Cloud Native Technologies and Deep Learning.

"To my parents and brother for encouraging to take up a career in computer science. To my wife & children for support as I continue to explore this new field"

"We would like to pay our respect to Alan Turing for initiating humanity's endeavor towards Turing Machines (what we call Computers today) and for inventing this field by publishing first paper on Artificial Intelligence. Furthermore, Deep Learning would have been impossible without the founding fathers like Yann LeCun and Geoffrey Hinton who brought sea change in the capabilities of AI"

~Authors~

Acknowledgements

Dheeraj Arremsetty

About the reviewers

Aditya Oke is a software engineer and a Deep Learning practitioner. He completed his undergraduate degree in computer science. He is a contributor to the Torchvision and Lightning Bolts libraries. He has experience in computer vision and autonomous vehicles.

I would like to thank my family, especially my parents, for encouraging me. I also extend warm thanks to the PyTorch Lightning team, who have established a great framework and community. I would also like to thank the PyTorch team, which made Deep Learning possible for everyone.

Ashwini Badgujar is a machine learning engineer at Impulselogic Inc. She has been involved in the machine learning domain for the last 3 years. She has research experience in Natural Language Processing and computer vision, specifically neural networks. She has also worked in the earth science domain, working on a number of earth science projects in collaboration with machine learning. She has worked at NASA in data processing and fire project analysis in calculating mixing heights, and at Comcast, where she worked on optimizing machine learning models.

Table of Contents

2

Getting off the Ground with the First Deep Learning Model

3

Transfer Learning Using Pre-Trained Models

4

Ready-to-Cook Models from Lightning Flash

Section 2: Solving using PyTorch Lightning

5

Time Series Models

6
Deep Generative Models

7
Semi-Supervised Learning

8
Self-Supervised Learning

Section 3: Advanced Topics

9
Deploying and Scoring Models

10
Scaling and Managing Training

Index

Other Books You May Enjoy

Preface

Deep Learning (**DL**) is what humanizes machines. Deep Learning makes it possible for machines to see (through vision models), to listen (through voice devices like Alexa) to talk (through chatbots), to write (through generative models like auto-complete or Q&A) and even be an artist by trying to paint (through style transfer models).

PyTorch Lightning lets researchers build their own DL models quickly & easily without having to worry about the complexities. This book will help you maximize productivity for DL projects while ensuring full flexibility from model formulation to implementation.

The book provides a hands-on approach for implementing PyTorch Lightning DL models and associated methodologies that will have you up and running and productive in no time. You'll learn how to configure PyTorch Lightning on a cloud platform, understand the architectural components, and explore how they are configured to build various industry solutions. Next, you'll build a neural network architecture and deploy an application from scratch and see how you can expand it based on your specific needs, beyond what the framework can provide. The book also demonstrates how to implement capabilities to build and train various models like **Convolutional Neural Nets (CNN), Natural Language Processing (NLP), Time Series**, **Self-Supervised Learning**, **Semi-Supervised Learning**, **Generative Adversarial Network** (**GAN**) using PyTorch Lightning.

Who this book is for

If you have always been curious about DL but don't know where to start or feel intimidated by the complexities of large neural networks, then this book is ideal for you! It will make DL feel like a cakewalk!

This *Deep Learning with PyTorch Lightning* book is primarily for citizen data scientists who are beginning their DL journey and need a practical guide to ace their game! It is also beneficial to expert data scientists making the transition from other frameworks to PyTorch Lightning. This book will also appeal to DL researchers who are just getting started with coding for DL models using PyTorch Lightning by serving as a ready reckoner.

Working knowledge of Python programming and an intermediate level understanding of statistics and DL fundamentals is expected.

What this book covers

Chapter 1, PyTorch Lightning Adventure, will start with a brief history of Deep Learning and why PyTorch is the most preferred framework of the community today. We will also see what PyTorch Lightning is, how it is built, and how it differs from PyTorch. We will cover the module structure of PyTorch Lightning and how it makes research more feasible with users putting less effort into engineering and more into modelling.

Chapter 2, Getting off the Ground with the First Deep Learning Model, focuses on how to get started with building models using PyTorch Lightning. As examples, we will build multiple models, ranging from a very simple **Multilayer Perceptron** (**MLP**) to a real-life image recognition model using CNN.

Chapter 3, Transfer Learning Using Pre-Trained Models, mainly focuses on how to customize the models built using pre-trained architecture to achieve great results without large training budgets or time for different datasets. We will walk you through the steps of customizing models using pre-trained models for images and NLP.

Chapter 4, Ready-to-Cook Models from Lightning Flash , mainly focuses on PyTorch Lightning Flash – a state-of-the-art (SOTA) model architecture library. It includes most of the common algorithms or frameworks out of the box, thereby improving the productivity of data scientists by a huge margin for benchmarking & experimentation. This chapter will share various Flash models for video (video classification) and audio (automatic speech recognition) tasks.

Chapter 5, Time Series Models, mainly focuses on the working of time series models, with PyTorch implementation, along with step-by-step working and in-detail examples from basic to advanced time series techniques, such as (Recurrent Neural Networks) RNN and Long Short Term Memory (LSTM) models, along with real-world use cases.

Chapter 6, Deep Generative Models, focuses on the step-by-step, in-detail working and implementation of generative types of DL models, such as Generative Adversarial Networks (GANs), where it will be used to generate new non-existent images.

Chapter 7, Semi-Supervised Learning, mainly focuses on how semi-supervised models work, and how they can be implemented with PyTorch Lightning. We will also cover, in detail, working examples and implementation from basic to advanced semi-supervised models using PyTorch Lightning to handle label propagation and image caption generation using a combination of CNNs and RNNs.

Chapter 8, Self-Supervised Learning, mainly focuses on a new area of Self-Supervised Learning which can work on unlabeled data and explain how self-supervised models can be implemented with PyTorch Lightning. We will also cover working examples of contrastive learning and some techniques like SimCLR architecture.

Chapter 9, Deploying and Scoring Models, will cover, in detail, techniques and ways to deploy a DL model natively as well as in inter-operable formats such as ONNX. It will also cover, in detail, techniques and ways to perform model scoring on massive volumes of data.

Chapter 10, Scaling and Managing Training, will take a nuanced view of the challenges of training a model at scale and managing the training. It will describe some of the common pitfalls and tips and tricks on how to avoid them. It will also describe how to set up your experiments, how to make model training resilient and how to use the hardware to improve training efficiency, among other things.

To get the most out of this book

Getting started with PyTorch Lightning is very easy. You can use the Anaconda distribution to set up your environment locally or use a cloud option such as Google Colab, AWS, Azure, or IBM Watson Studio to get started. (It is recommended that you use a cloud environment with GPU to run some of the more complex models.)

Deep Learning Models in this book are trained using color images. Please also use digital version which has all the color images; to better understand the results.

PyTorch Lightning can be installed using `pip` in your Jupyter Notebook environment:

```
pip install pytorch-lightning
```

In addition to importing PyTorch Lightning (the first `import` statement can be seen as follows), the following `import` block shows statements that are usually part of the code:

```
import pytorch_lightning as pl
import torch
from torch import nn
import torch.nn.functional as F
from torchvision import transforms
```

The import packages and their versions change for each chapter, so please ensure that you are importing correct packages as mentioned on the Technical Requirements sections of the book.

The `torch` package is used for defining tensors and performing mathematical operations on the tensors. The `torch.nn` package is used for constructing neural networks, which is what `nn` stands for. `torch.nn.functional` contains functions including activation and loss functions, whereas `torchvision.transforms` is a separate library that provides common image transformations.

If you are using the digital version of this book, we advise you to type the code yourself or access the code from the book's GitHub repository (a link is available in the next section). Please substitute correct installation & package versions as mentioned in the Technical Requirements sections before running GitHub files. Doing so will help you avoid any potential errors related to the copying and pasting of code.

Download the example code files

You can download the example code files for this book from GitHub at `https://github.com/PacktPublishing/Deep-Learning-with-PyTorch-Lightning`. If there's an update to the code, it will be updated in the GitHub repository.

We also have other code bundles from our rich catalogue of books and videos available at `https://github.com/PacktPublishing/`. Check them out!

Download the colour images

We also provide a PDF file that has colour images of the screenshots and diagrams used in this book. You can download it here: `https://static.packt-cdn.com/downloads/9781800561618_ColorImages.pdf`.

Conventions used

There are a number of text conventions used throughout this book.

`Code in text`: Indicates code words in text, database table names, folder names, filenames, file extensions, pathnames, dummy URLs, user input, and Twitter handles. Here is an example: "You can use the `gpus` argument passed to `Trainer` to specify the number of GPUs."

A block of code is set as follows:

```
import pytorch_lightning as pl
...
# use only 10% of the training data for each epoch
```

```
trainer = pl.Trainer(limit_train_batches=0.1)
# use only 10 batches per epoch
trainer = pl.Trainer(limit_train_batches=10)
```

Any command-line input or output is written as follows:

```
pip install pytorch-lightning
```

Bold: Indicates a new term, an important word, or words that you see onscreen. For instance, words in menus or dialog boxes appear in **bold**. Here is an example: "For example, in Google Colab, you can **Change Runtime Type** to set **Runtime shape** to **High-RAM** instead of **Standard** so that you can increase the value of the `num_workers` argument to `DataLoader` "

> **Tips or Important Notes**
> Appear like this.

Get in touch

Feedback from our readers is always welcome.

General feedback: If you have questions about any aspect of this book, email us at `customercare@packtpub.com` and mention the book title in the subject of your message.

Errata: Although we have taken every care to ensure the accuracy of our content, mistakes do happen. If you have found a mistake in this book, we would be grateful if you would report this to us. Please visit `www.packtpub.com/support/errata` and fill in the form.

Piracy: If you come across any illegal copies of our works in any form on the internet, we would be grateful if you would provide us with the location address or website name. Please contact us at `copyright@packt.com` with a link to the material.

If you are interested in becoming an author: If there is a topic that you have expertise in and you are interested in either writing or contributing to a book, please visit `authors.packtpub.com`.

Share Your Thoughts

Once you've read *Deep Learning with PyTorch Lightning*, we'd love to hear your thoughts! Scan the QR code below to go straight to the Amazon review page for this book and share your feedback.

https://packt.link/r/180056161X

Your review is important to us and the tech community and will help us make sure we're delivering excellent quality content.

Section 1: Kickstarting with PyTorch Lightning

This is the section for beginners that introduces the basics of PyTorch Lightning, starting with how to install it and build simple models. It will also show you how to get going quickly with the library of PyTorch Lightning Flash state-of-the-art models out of the box.

This section comprises the following chapters:

1
PyTorch Lightning Adventure

Welcome to the world of PyTorch Lightning!!

We are witnessing what is popularly referred to as the Fourth Industrial Revolution, driven by **Artificial Intelligence** (**AI**). Since the creation of the steam engine some 350 years ago, which set humanity on the path to industrialization we saw another two industrial revolutions. We saw electricity bringing a sea change roughly 100 years ago, followed by the digital age some 50 years later revolutionizing the way we live our lives today. There is an equally transformative power in AI. Everything that we know about the world is changing fast and will continue to change at a pace that no one imagined before and certainly no one planned for. We are seeing transformational changes in how we contact customer services, with the advent of AI-powered chatbots; in how we watch movies/videos, with AI recommending what we should watch; in how we shop, using algorithms optimized for supply chains; in how cars are driven, using self-driving technology; in how new drugs are developed, by applying AI to complex problems such as protein folding; in how medical diagnoses are being carried out, by finding hidden patterns in massive amounts of data. Underpinning each of the preceding technologies is the power of AI. The impact of AI on our world is more than just the technology that we use; rather, it is much more transformational in terms of how we interact with society, how we work, and how we live. As many have said, AI is the new electricity, powering the engine of the 21st century.

And this monumental impact of AI on our lives and psyche is the result of a recent breakthrough in the field of **Deep Learning** (**DL**). It had long been the dream of scientists to create something that mimics the brain. The brain is a fascinating natural evolutionary phenomenon. A human brain has more Synapses than stars in the universe, and it is those neural connections that make us intelligent and allow us to do things such as think, analyze, recognize objects, reason with logic, and describe our understanding. While **Artificial Neural Networks** (**ANNs**) do not really work in the same way as biological neurons, they do serve as inspiration.

In the evolution of species, the earliest creatures were unicellular (such as amoeba), first appearing around 4 billion years ago, followed by small multi-cellular species that navigated blindly with no sense of direction for about 3.5 billion years. When everyone around you is blind, the first species that developed vision had a significant advantage over all other species by becoming the most intelligent species, and in evolutionary biology, this step (which happened some 500 million years ago) is known as the **Cambrian explosion**. This single event led to remarkable growth in the evolution of species, resulting in everything that we currently see on earth today. In other words, though Earth is about 4.5 billion years old, all the complex forms of life, including human brains, evolved in just the last 500 million years (which is in just 10% of Earth's lifetime), led by that single evolutionary event, which in turn led to the ability of organisms to "see" things.

In fact in humans as much 1/3 of our brain is linked to visual cortex; which is far more than any other senses. Perhaps explaining how our brain evolved to be most intelligence by first mastering "vision" ability.

With DL models of image recognition, we can finally make machines "see" things (Fei Fei Li has described this as the Cambrian explosion of **Machine Learning** (**ML**)), an event that will put AI on a different trajectory altogether, where one day it may really be comparable to human intelligence.

In 2012, a DL model achieved near-human accuracy in image recognition, and since then, numerous frameworks have been created to make it easy for data scientists to train complex models. Creating **Feature Engineering** (**FE**) steps, complex transformations, training feedback loops, and optimization requires a lot of manual coding. Frameworks help to abstract certain modules and make coding easier as well standardized. PyTorch Lightning is not just the newest framework, but it is also arguably the best framework that strikes the perfect balance between the right levels of abstraction and power to perform complex research. It is an ideal framework for a beginner in DL, as well as for professional data scientists looking to productionalize a model. In this chapter, we will see why that is the case and how we can harness the power of PyTorch Lightning to build impactful AI applications quickly and easily.

In this chapter, we will cover the following topics:

- What makes PyTorch Lightning so special?
- `<pip install>`—My Lightning adventure
- Understanding the key components of PyTorch Lightning
- Crafting AI applications using PyTorch Lightning

What makes PyTorch Lightning so special?

So, if you are a novice data scientist, the question on your mind would be this: *Which DL framework should I start with?* And if you are curious about PyTorch Lightning, then you may well be asking yourself: *Why should I learn this rather than something else?* On the other hand, if you are an expert data scientist who has been building DL models for some time, then you will already be familiar with other popular frameworks such as TensorFlow, Keras, and PyTorch. The question then becomes: *If you are already working in this area, why switch to a new framework? Is it worth making the effort to learn something different when you already know another tool?* These are fair questions, and we will try to answer all of them in this section.

Let's start with a brief history of DL frameworks to establish where PyTorch Lightning fits in this context.

The first one....

The first DL model was executed in 1993 in **Massachusetts Institute of Technology** (**MIT**) labs by the godfather of DL, Yann LeCun. This was written in Lisp and, believe it or not, it even contained convolutional layers, just as with modern **Convolutional Neural Network** (**CNN**) models. The network shown in this demo is described in his **Neural Information Processing Systems** (**NIPS**) 1989 paper entitled *Handwritten digit recognition with a backpropagation network.*

The following screenshot shows an extract from this demo:

Figure 1.1 – MIT demo of handwritten digit recognition by Yann LeCun in 1993

Yann LeCun himself described in detail what this first model is in his blog post and this is shown in the following video: `https://www.youtube.com/watch?v=FwFduRA_L6Q`.

As you might have guessed, writing entire CNNs in C wasn't very easy. It took their team years of manual coding effort to achieve this.

The next big breakthrough in DL came in 2012, with the creation of AlexNet, which won the ImageNet competition. The *AlexNet* paper by Geoffrey Hinton et al. is considered the most influential paper, with the largest ever number of citations in the community. AlexNet set a precedent in terms of accuracy, made neural networks cool again, and was a massive network trained on optimized **Graphics Processing Units** (**GPUs**). They also introduced numerous kickass things, like BatchNorm, MaxPool, Dropout, SoftMax, and ReLU, which we will see later in our journey. With network architectures so complicated and massive, there was soon a requirement for a dedicated framework to train them.

So many frameworks?

Theano, Caffe, and Torch can be described as the first wave of DL frameworks that helped data scientists create DL models. While Lua was the preferred option for some as a programming language (Torch was first written in Lua as LuaTorch), many others were C++-based and could help train a model on distributed hardware such as GPUs and manage the optimization process. It was mostly used by ML researchers (typically post-doc) in academia when the field itself was new and unstable. A data scientist was expected to know how to write optimization functions with gradient descent code and make it run on specific hardware while also manipulating memory. Clearly, it was not something that someone in the industry could easily use to train models and take them into production.

Some examples of model-training frameworks are shown here:

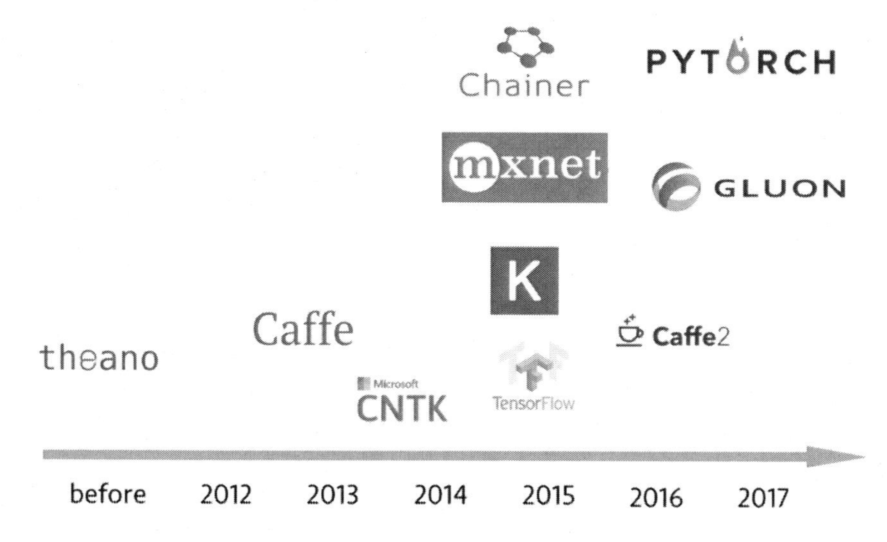

Figure 1.2 – Model-training frameworks

TensorFlow, by Google, became a game-changer in this space by reverting to a Python-based, abstract function-driven framework that a non-researcher could use to experiment with while shielding them from the complexities around running DL code on hardware. Its success was followed by Keras, which simplified DL even further so that anyone with a little knowledge could train a DL model in just four lines of code.

But arguably, TensorFlow didn't parallelize well. It was also harder for it to train effectively in distributed GPU environments, hence the community felt a need for a new framework—something that combined the power of a research-based framework with the ease of Python. And PyTorch was born! This framework has taken the ML world by storm since its debut.

PyTorch versus TensorFlow

Looking on Google Trends at the competition between PyTorch and TensorFlow, you could say that PyTorch has taken over from TensorFlow in recent years and has almost surpassed it.

An extract from Google Trends can be seen here:

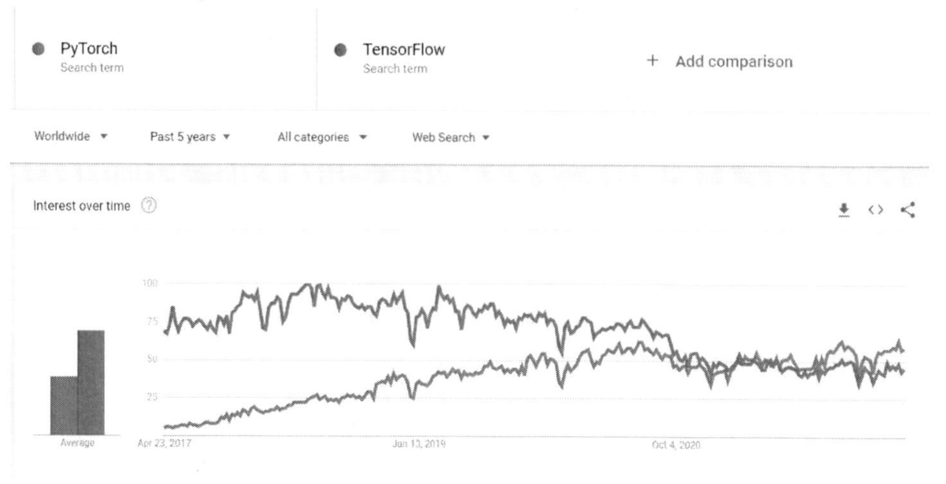

Figure 1.3 – Changes in community interest in PyTorch versus TensorFlow in Google Trends

While some may say that Google Trends is not the most scientific way to judge the pulse of the ML community, you can also look at many influential AI players with massive workloads—such as Facebook, Tesla, and Uber—defaulting to the PyTorch framework to manage their DL workloads and finding significant savings in compute and memory.

In ML research community though, the choice between Tensorflow and PyTorch is quite clear. The winner is hands-down PyTorch!

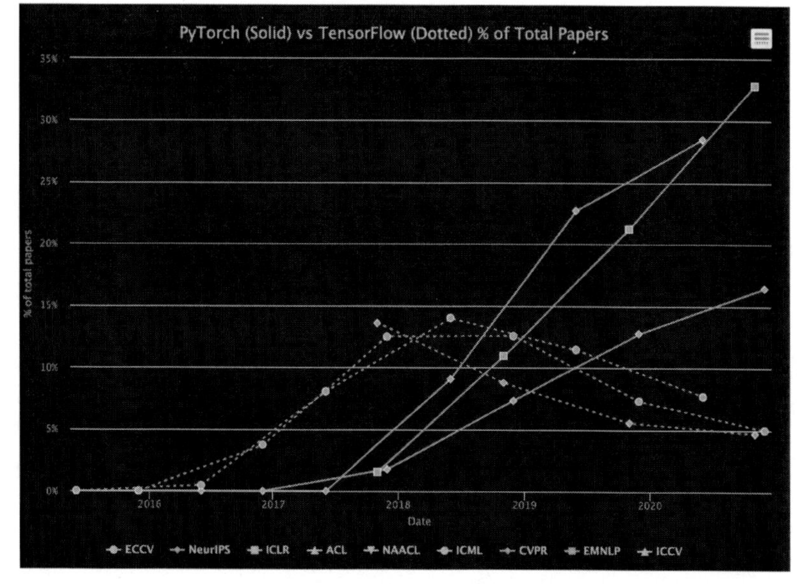

Figure 1.4 – TensorFlow vs PyTorch trends in top AI conferences for papers published

Both frameworks will have their die-hard fans, but PyTorch is reputed to be more efficient in distributed GPU environments given its inherent architecture. Here are a few other things that make PyTorch better than TensorFlow:

- Provides more stability.
- Easy-to-build extensions and wrappers.
- Much more comprehensive domain libraries.
- Static graph representations in TensorFlow weren't very helpful. It wasn't feasible to train networks easily.
- Dynamic Tensors in PyTorch were a game-changer that made it easy to train and scale.

A golden mean – PyTorch Lightning

Rarely do I come across something that I find as exciting as PyTorch Lightning! This framework is a brainchild of William Falcon whose PhD advisor is (guess who)..Yann LeCun! Here's what makes it stand out:

- It's not just cool to code, but it also allows you to do serious ML research (unlike Keras).
- It has better GPU utilization (compared with TensorFlow).
- It has 16-bit precision support (very useful for platforms that don't support **Tensor Processing Units** (**TPUs**), such as IBM Cloud).
- It also has a really good collection of **state-of-the-art** (**SOTA**) model repositories in the form of Lightning Flash.
- It is the first framework with native capability and **Self-Supervised Learning** (**SSL**).

In a nutshell, PyTorch Lightning makes it fun and cool to make DL models and to perform quick experiments, all while not dumbing down the core data science aspect by abstracting it from data scientists, and always leaving a door open to go deep into PyTorch whenever you want to!

I guess it strikes the perfect balance by allowing more capability to do Data Science while automating most of the "engineering" part. Is this the beginning of the end for TensorFlow? For the answer to that question, we will have to wait and see.

<pip install> – My Lightning adventure

Getting started with PyTorch Lightning is very easy. You can use the Anaconda distribution to set up your environment locally or use a cloud option such as **Google Colaboratory** (**Google Colab**), **Amazon Web Services** (**AWS**), Azure, or IBM Watson Studio to get started. (It is recommended that you use a cloud environment to run some of the more complex models.) Most of the code in this book is run on Google Collab or Anaconda using Python 3.6 with Mac OS. Please make appropriate changes to your env on other systems for installation.

PyTorch Lightning can be installed using `pip` in your Jupyter notebook environment, like this:

```
pip install pytorch-lightning
```

In addition to importing PyTorch Lightning (the first `import` statement can be seen in the following code snippet), the following `import` block shows statements that are usually part of the code:

```
import pytorch_lightning as pl
import torch
from torch import nn
import torch.nn.functional as F
from torchvision import transforms
```

The `torch` package is used for defining tensors and for performing mathematical operations on the tensors. The `torch.nn` package is used for constructing neural networks, which is what nn stands for. `torch.nn.functional` contains functions including activation and loss functions, whereas `torchvision.transforms` is a separate library that provides common image transformations. Once the PyTorch Lightning framework and all packages are installed, you should see the completion log, as illustrated in the following screenshot:

```
!pip install pytorch-lightning==1.5.2

Collecting pytorch-lightning==1.5.2
  Downloading pytorch_lightning-1.5.2-py3-none-any.whl (1.0 MB)
     |████████████████████████████████| 1.0 MB 5.3 MB/s
Collecting future>=0.17.1
  Downloading future-0.18.2.tar.gz (829 kB)
     |████████████████████████████████| 829 kB 39.6 MB/s
Requirement already satisfied: torch>=1.6 in /usr/local/lib/python3.7/dist-packages (from pytorch-lightning==1.5.2) (1.10.0+cu111)
Collecting fsspec[http]!=2021.06.0,>=2021.05.0
  Downloading fsspec-2022.2.0-py3-none-any.whl (134 kB)
     |████████████████████████████████| 134 kB 36.7 MB/s
Requirement already satisfied: packaging>=17.0 in /usr/local/lib/python3.7/dist-packages (from pytorch-lightning==1.5.2) (21.3)
Requirement already satisfied: typing-extensions in /usr/local/lib/python3.7/dist-packages (from pytorch-lightning==1.5.2) (3.10.0.2)
Requirement already satisfied: numpy>=1.17.2 in /usr/local/lib/python3.7/dist-packages (from pytorch-lightning==1.5.2) (1.21.5)
Requirement already satisfied: tqdm>=4.41.0 in /usr/local/lib/python3.7/dist-packages (from pytorch-lightning==1.5.2) (4.63.0)
Collecting PyYAML>=5.1
  Downloading PyYAML-6.0-cp37-cp37m-manylinux_2_5_x86_64.manylinux1_x86_64.manylinux_2_12_x86_64.manylinux2010_x86_64.whl (596 kB)
     |████████████████████████████████| 596 kB 36.3 MB/s
Requirement already satisfied: tensorboard>=2.2.0 in /usr/local/lib/python3.7/dist-packages (from pytorch-lightning==1.5.2) (2.8.0)
Collecting pyDeprecate==0.3.1
  Downloading pyDeprecate-0.3.1-py3-none-any.whl (10 kB)
Collecting torchmetrics>=0.4.1
  Downloading torchmetrics-0.7.3-py3-none-any.whl (398 kB)
     |████████████████████████████████| 398 kB 37.5 MB/s
Requirement already satisfied: requests in /usr/local/lib/python3.7/dist-packages (from fsspec[http]!=2021.06.0,>=2021.05.0->pytorch-lightning==1.5.2) (2.23.0)
Collecting aiohttp
  Downloading aiohttp-3.8.1-cp37-cp37m-manylinux_2_5_x86_64.manylinux1_x86_64.manylinux_2_12_x86_64.manylinux2010_x86_64.whl (1.1 MB)
     |████████████████████████████████| 1.1 MB 14.4 MB/s
Requirement already satisfied: pyparsing!=3.0.5,>=2.0.2 in /usr/local/lib/python3.7/dist-packages (from packaging>=17.0->pytorch-lightning==1.5.2) (3.0.7)
Requirement already satisfied: werkzeug>=0.11.15 in /usr/local/lib/python3.7/dist-packages (from tensorboard>=2.2.0->pytorch-lightning==1.5.2) (1.0.1)
Requirement already satisfied: google-auth<3,>=1.6.3 in /usr/local/lib/python3.7/dist-packages (from tensorboard>=2.2.0->pytorch-lightning==1.5.2) (1.35.0)
Requirement already satisfied: protobuf>=3.6.0 in /usr/local/lib/python3.7/dist-packages (from tensorboard>=2.2.0->pytorch-lightning==1.5.2) (3.17.3)
Requirement already satisfied: absl-py>=0.4 in /usr/local/lib/python3.7/dist-packages (from tensorboard>=2.2.0->pytorch-lightning==1.5.2) (1.0.0)
Requirement already satisfied: wheel>=0.26 in /usr/local/lib/python3.7/dist-packages (from tensorboard>=2.2.0->pytorch-lightning==1.5.2) (0.37.1)
Requirement already satisfied: tensorboard-plugin-wit>=1.6.0 in /usr/local/lib/python3.7/dist-packages (from tensorboard>=2.2.0->pytorch-lightning==1.5.2) (1.8.1)
```

Figure 1.5 – Installation result for PyTorch Lightning

Once PyTorch Lightning is installed you can check the version for PyTorch and torch

```
import pytorch_lightning as pl
import torch
print("torch version:",torch.__version__)
print("pytorch ligthening version:",pl.__version__)

torch version: 1.10.0+cu111
pytorch ligthening version: 1.5.2
```

Figure 1.6 – Verifying the installation

That's it! Now, you are all set to begin your Lightning adventure!

Understanding the key components of PyTorch Lightning

Before we jump into building DL models, let's revise a typical pipeline that a Deep Learning project follows.

DL pipeline

Let's revise a typical ML pipeline for a DL network architecture. This is what it looks like:

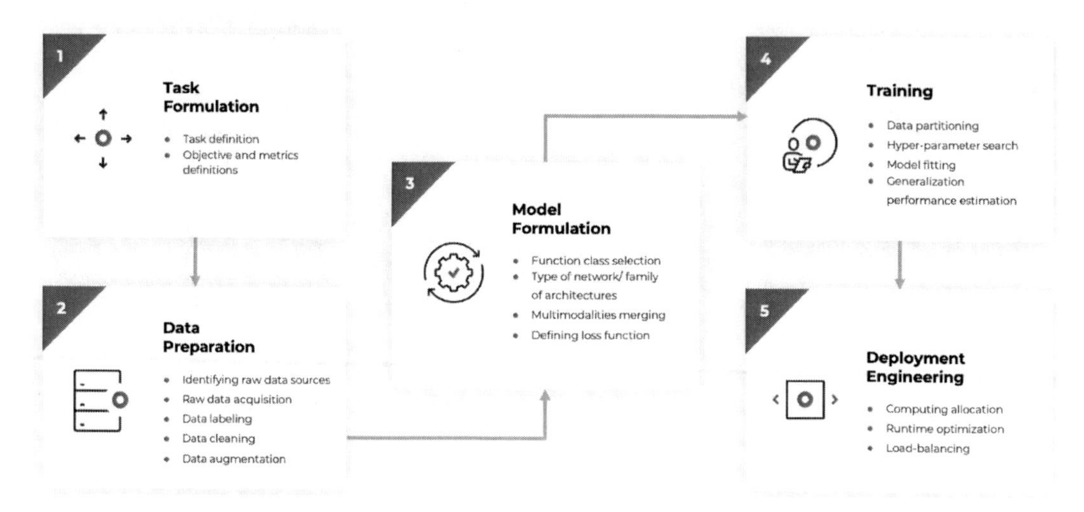

Figure 1.7 – DL pipeline

A DL pipeline typically involves the following steps. We will continue to see them throughout the book, utilizing them for each aspect of problem-solving:

1. **Defining the problem**:
   - Set a clear task and objective of what is expected.
2. **Data preparation**:
   - This step involves finding the right dataset to solve this problem, ingest it, and clean it. For most DL projects, this involves the data engineer working in images, videos, or text corpora to acquire datasets (sometimes by scraping the web), and then cataloging them into sizes.
   - Most DL models require huge amounts of data, while models also need to be resilient to minor changes in images such as cropping. For this purpose, engineers augment the dataset by creating crops of original images or **black and white** (**B/W**) versions, or invert them, and so on.

3. **Modeling**:

    - This would first involve FE and defining what kind of network architecture we want to build.
    - For example, in the case of a data scientist creating new image recognition models, this would involve defining a CNN architecture with three layers of convolution, a step size, slide window, gradient descent optimization, a loss function, and suchlike can be defined.
    - For ML researchers, this step could involve defining new loss functions that measure accuracy in a more useful way or perform some magic by making a model train with a less dense network that gives the same accuracy, or defining a new gradient optimization that distributes well or converges faster.

4. **Training**:

    - Now comes the fun step. After data scientists have defined all the configurations for a DL network architecture, they need to train a model and keep tweaking it until it achieves convergence.
    - For massive datasets (which are the norm in DL), this can be a nightmarish exercise. A data scientist must double up as an ML engineer by writing code to distribute it to the underlying GPU or **central processing unit** (**CPU**) or TPU, manage memory and epochs, and keep iterating the code that fully utilizes compute power. A lower 16-bit precision may help train the model faster, and so data scientists may attempt this.
    - Alternatively, a distributed downpour gradient descent can be used to optimize faster. If you are finding yourself out of breath with some of these terms, then don't worry. Many data scientists experience this, as it has less to do with statistics and more to do with engineering (and this is where we will see how PyTorch Lightning comes to the rescue).
    - Another major challenge in distributed computing is being able to fully utilize all the hardware and accurately compute losses that are distributed in various GPUs. It's not simple either to do data parallelism, (distribute data to different GPUs in batches) or do model parallelism (distribute models to different GPUs).

5. **Deployment engineering**:

    - After the model has been trained, we need to take it to production. **ML operations** (**MLOps**) engineers work by creating deployment-ready format files that can work in their environment.

    - This step also involves creating an **Application Programming Interface** (**API**) to be integrated with the end application for consumption. Occasionally, it can also involve creating infrastructure to score models for incoming traffic sizes if the model is expected to have a massive workload.

PyTorch Lightning abstraction layers

PyTorch Lightning frameworks make it easy to construct entire DL models to aid data scientists. Here's how this is achieved:

- The `LightningModule` class is used to define the model structure, inference logic, optimizer and scheduler details, training and validation logic, and so on.
- A Lightning `Trainer` abstracts the logic needed for loops, hardware interactions, fitting and evaluating the model, and so on.
- You can pass a PyTorch `DataLoader` to the trainer directly, or you can choose to define a `LightningDataModule` for improved shareability and reuse.

Crafting AI applications using PyTorch Lightning

In this book, you will see how we can build various types of AI models effortlessly and efficiently using PyTorch Lightning. With hands-on examples that have industry-wide applications and practical benefits, you will get trained not just in PyTorch Lightning but in the whole gamut of different DL families.

Image recognition models

We will begin our journey by creating our first DL model in the form of an image recognition model in *Chapter 2, Getting off the Ground with the First Deep Learning Model.* Image recognition is the quintessential identity of a DL framework and, by using PyTorch Lightning, we will see how to build an image classification model using CNN..

Transfer learning

DL models are notorious for requiring training over a huge number of epochs before they can converge, thereby consuming tremendous amounts of GPU compute power in the process. In *Chapter 3, Transfer Learning Using Pre-Trained Models*, you will learn a technique known as **Transfer learning** (**TL**), which makes it possible to get good results without much hard work, by transferring knowledge from large pre-trained architectures like ResNet-50 for image classification or BERT for text classification..

NLP Transformer models

We will also look at **Natural Language Processing** (**NLP**) models and see how DL can make text classification possible over gargantuan amounts of text data. You will learn how the famous pre-trained NLP models, including Transformer, can be used in *Chapter 3, Transfer Learning Using Pre-Trained Models*, and adapt to your business needs effortlessly.

Lightning Flash

The creation of DL models also involves a process of fairly complex feature engineering pipelines with equally tedious training and optimization steps. Most data scientists start their journey by adopting SOTA models that have won Kaggle competitions or influential research papers. In *Chapter 4, Ready-to-Cook Models from Lightning Flash*, you will learn how an out-of-the-box utility such as Lightning Flash improves productivity by providing a repository of standard network architecturesfor standard tasks like object detection or classification for text, audio or video. We will build the model for video classification and automatic speech detection for audio files in a jiffy.

Time series models with LSTM

Forecasting and predicting the next event in a time series is an evergreen challenge within the industry. In *Chapter 5, Time Series Models*, you will learn how we can build time series models in PyTorch Lightning using **Reccurent Neural Networks** (**RNN**) with **Long Short Term Memory** (**LSTM**) network architecture.

Generative Adversarial Networks with Autoencoders

Generative Adversarial Network (**GAN**) models are one of the most fascinating aspects of DL applications and can create realistic-looking images of people or places or objects that simply don't exist in real life. In *Chapter 6, Deep Generative Models*, you will learn how, by using PyTorch Lightning, you can easily craft GAN models to create realistic looking fake images of animals, food items, or people.

Self-Supervised models combining CNN and RNN

The application of DL models is not limited to just creating fancy fake images using GANs. We can even ask a machine to describe a scene in a movie or ask informative questions regarding the content of an image (such as who is in the picture or what they are doing). This model architecture is known as a semi-supervised model and, in *Chapter 7, Semi-Supervised Learning*, you will learn a hybrid of CNN-RNN architecture (where **RNN** stands for **Recurrent Neural Network**) that can be utilized to teach a machine how to write situational poetry. In the same chapter, we will also see how to train a model from scratch and speed it up using 16-bit precision and other operational hacks to ensure smooth training.

Self-Supervised models for contrastive learning

If machines can create realistic images or write human-like descriptions, can't they teach themselves? Self-supervised models aim to make machines learn how to perform complex tasks with low or no labels at all, thereby revolutionizing everything that we could do with AI. In *Chapter 8, Self-Supervised Learning*, you will learn how PyTorch Lightning has native support for self-supervised models. You will learn how to teach a machine to perform **Contrastive Learning** (**CL**), which can distinguish images without any labels purely by means of representation learning.

Deploying and scoring models

Every DL model that can ever be trained dreams of one day being productionalized and used for online predictions. This piece of ML engineering requires data scientists to familiarize themselves with various model file formats. In *Chapter 9, Deploying and Scoring Models*, you will learn how to deploy and score models in inter-portable models that can be language-independent and hardware-agnostic in production environments with the help of the Pickle and **Open Neural Network Exchange** (**ONNX**) formats.

Scaling models and productivity tips

Finally, the capabilities of PyTorch Lightning are not just limited to creating new models on defined architectures, but also advance the SOTA using new research. In *Chapter 10, Scaling and Managing Training*, we will see some capabilities that make such new research possible, as well as how to improve productivity by providing troubleshooting tricks and quick tips. We will also focus on various ways to scale the model training.

Further reading

Here are some links for PyTorch Lightning that you will find very useful through the course of this book:

- Official documentation: `https://pytorch-lightning.readthedocs.io/en/latest/?_ga=2.177043429.1358501839.1635911225-879695765.1625671009`.
- GitHub source: `https://github.com/PyTorchLightning/pytorch-lightning`.
- If you face any issues in the code, you can seek help by raising an issue on GitHub. The **Pytorch Lightning** team is normally very responsive: `https://github.com/PyTorchLightning/lightning-flash/issues`.
- You can seek out help on PL community channels. The PyTorch Lightning community is fast growing and very active.

Summary

You may be a beginner exploring the field of DL to see whether it's the right career for you. You may be a student of an advanced degree trying to do your research in ML to complete your thesis or get papers published. Or, you may be an expert data scientist with years of experience in training DL models and taking them to production. PyTorch Lightning has something for everyone to do almost anything in DL.

It combines the raw power of PyTorch, which offers efficiency and rigor, with the simplicity of Python, by providing a wrapper over complexity. You can always go as deep as you want in doing some innovative work (as you will see later in this book), while you can also get numerous out-of-the-box neural network architectures that save you from having to reinvent the wheel (which you will also learn about later). It is fully compatible with PyTorch, and code can easily be refactored. It is also perhaps the first framework that is designed for the persona of *Data Scientist* as opposed to other roles, such as ML researcher, ML-Ops engineer, or data engineer.

We will begin our journey with a simple DL model and will keep expanding our scope to more advanced and complex models with each chapter. You will find that it covers all the famous models, leaving you empowered with Deep Learning skills to make an impact in your organization. So, let's get things moving in our next chapter with your first DL model.

2
Getting off the Ground with the First Deep Learning Model

Deep learning (**DL**) models have gained tremendous popularity in recent times and have caught the attention of data scientists in academia and industry alike. The reason behind their great success is their ability to solve the simplest yet oldest problem in computer science—computer vision. It had long been the dream of computer scientists to find an algorithm that would make machines see like humans do… or at least be able to recognize objects. DL models power not just object recognition but are used in everything, from predicting who is in an image, to **natural language processing** (**NLP**)—where they can be used for predicting and generating text and understanding speech—and even creating deepfakes, such as videos. At their core, all DL models are built using **neural network** (**NN**) algorithms; however, they are much more than just a NN. While NNs have been used since the 1950s, it's only in the last few years that DL has been able to make a big impact on the industry.

NNs were popularized in 1955 with a demonstration from International Business Machines Corporation (IBM) at the World Fair, where a machine made a prediction and the whole world saw the great potential of **Artificial Intelligence** (**AI**) to make machines learn anything and predict anything. That system was a perceptron-based network (a rudimentary cousin of what later became known as **multilayer perceptrons** (**MLPs**), which became the foundation for NNs and DL models).

With the success of NNs, many tried to use them for more advanced problems such as image recognition. The first such formal attempt at computer vision was made by a Massachusetts Institute of Technology (MIT) professor in 1965 (yes—**machine learning** (**ML**) was as big a thing back in the late 1950s and the early 1960s). He gave his students a *summer* assignment to find an algorithm for image recognition. No spoilers for guessing that despite their best efforts and unparalleled smartness, they failed to solve the problem that year. In fact, the problem of computer vision object recognition remained unsolved not just for years but for decades to come, a period popularly called the *AI winter*. The big breakthrough came in the mid-1990s with the invention of **Convolutional Neural Networks** (**CNNs**), a much-evolved form of NN. In 2012, when a more advanced version of a CNN trained at scale won the *ImageNet* competition and achieved accuracy rates as high as humans on the test set, it became the first choice for computer vision problems. After that, CNNs became not just the bedrock of image recognition problems but created a whole branch of ML called Deep Learning. Over the last few years, more advanced forms of CNNs have been devised, and new DL algorithms keep coming every single day that advance the **state of the art** (**SOTA**) and take human mastery of AI to new levels. In this chapter, we will examine the foundations of DL models, which are extremely important to understand, to make the best use of the latest algorithms. It is more than just a practice chapter, as MLPs and CNNs are still extremely useful for the majority of business applications. We will go through the following topics in this chapter:

- Getting started with NNs
- Building a Hello World MLP model
- Building our first DL model
- Working with a CNN model for image recognition

Technical requirements

The code for this chapter has been developed and tested on macOS with Anaconda or in **Google Colaboratory** (**Google Colab**) with Python 3.7. If you are using another environment, please make appropriate changes to your `env` variables.

In this chapter, we will primarily be using the following Python modules, mentioned with their versions:

- PyTorch Lightning (version: 1.5.2)
- Seaborn (version: 0.11.2)
- NumPy (version: 1.21.5)
- Torch (version: 1.10.0)
- pandas (version: 1.3.5)

```
!pip install torch==1.10.0 torchvision==0.11.1
torchtext==0.11.0 torchaudio==0.10.0 --quiet
!pip install pytorch-lightning==1.5.2 --quiet
```

In order to make sure that these modules work together and not go out of sync, we have used the specific version of torch, torchvision, torchtext, torchaudio with PyTorch Lightning 1.5.2. You can also use the latest version of PyTorch Lightning and torch compatible with each other. More details can be found on the GitHub link: `https://github.com/PacktPublishing/Deep-Learning-with-PyTorch-Lightning`

All the aforementioned packages are expected to be imported to Jupyter Notebook. You can refer to *Chapter 1, PyTorch Lightning Adventure* for guidance on importing packages.

You can find working examples of this chapter at the following GitHub link:

`https://github.com/PacktPublishing/Deep-Learning-with-PyTorch-Lightning/tree/main/Chapter02`

Here is the link to the *Histopathologic Cancer Detection* source dataset:

`https://www.kaggle.com/c/histopathologic-cancer-detection`

This dataset contains images of cancer tumors and images labeled with positive and negative identification. It consists of 327,680 color images, each with a size of 96x96 **pixels** (**px**), extracted from scans of lymph nodes. The data is provided under the **Creative Commons** (**CC0**) License. The link to the original dataset is `https://github.com/basveeling/pcam`; however, in this chapter, we will make use of the Kaggle source since it had been de-duplicated from the original set.

Getting started with Neural Networks

In this section, we will begin our journey by understanding the basics of Neural Networks.

Why Neural Networks?

Before we go deep into NNs, it is important to answer a simple question: *Why do we even need a new classification algorithm when there are so many existing classification algorithms, such as decision trees?* The simple answer is that there are some classification problems that decision trees would never be able to solve. As you might be aware, decision trees work by finding a set of objects in one class and then creating splits in the set to continue to create a pure class. This works well when there is a clear distinction between different classes in the dataset, but it fails when they are mixed. One such very basic problem that decision trees cannot ever solve is the XOR problem.

About the XOR operator

The XOR gate/operator is also known as exclusive OR. It is a digital logic in electronics. An XOR gate is a digital logic gate that produces a true output when it has dissimilar inputs. The following diagram shows the **inputs and outputs (I/Os)** generated by an XOR gate:

$$X = A \oplus B$$

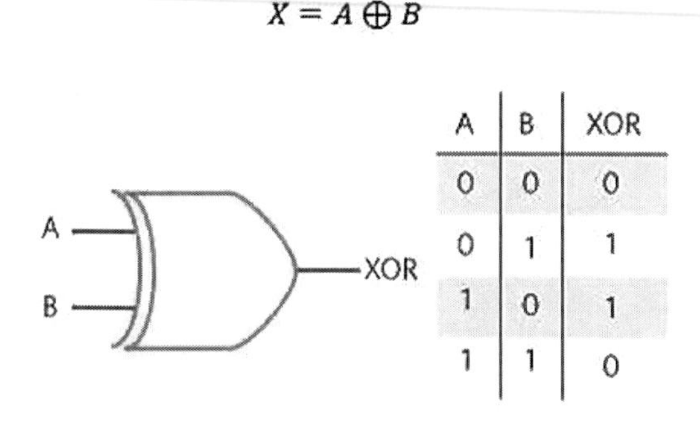

A	B	XOR
0	0	0
0	1	1
1	0	1
1	1	0

Figure 2.1 – XOR gate I/O truth table

In simple words, an XOR gate is a function that takes two inputs—for example, A and B—and generates a single output. From the preceding table, you can see that the XOR gate function gives us the following outputs:

- The output is 1 when the A and B inputs are different.
- The output is 0 when A and B are the same.

As you can see, if we want to build a decision-tree classifier, it will isolate `0` and `1` and will always give a prediction that is 50% wrong. There is no tree structure or logical boundary that can ever differentiate such a weird dataset. In other words, a decision-tree type of algorithm will never be able to solve this kind of classification problem. We need a fundamentally different approach to handle such a challenge.

In order to solve this problem, we need a fundamentally different kind of model that does not train on just input values but by conceptualizing I/O pairs and learning their relationship. That is the basis of the creation of NNs. It is not just another set of classifiers but a classifier that can solve problems others can't.

Neural Networks is an umbrella term for a range of classifiers under it, everything from a perceptron model to a DL model. One such basic yet incredibly powerful algorithm is MLP. The `XOR` problem mentioned here is one of the oldest yet very important problems to understand the origin story of NNs. You can think of `XOR` as a representation of all the problems that a decision-tree-type classifier can never solve since no visible boundary of classification is possible and we have to use a latent model to tackle it.

In this chapter, we will try to build our own simple MLP model to mimic the behavior of an `XOR` gate.

MLP architecture

Let's build an `XOR` NN architecture using the PyTorch Lightning framework. Our goal here is to build a simple MLP model, similar to the one shown in the following diagram:

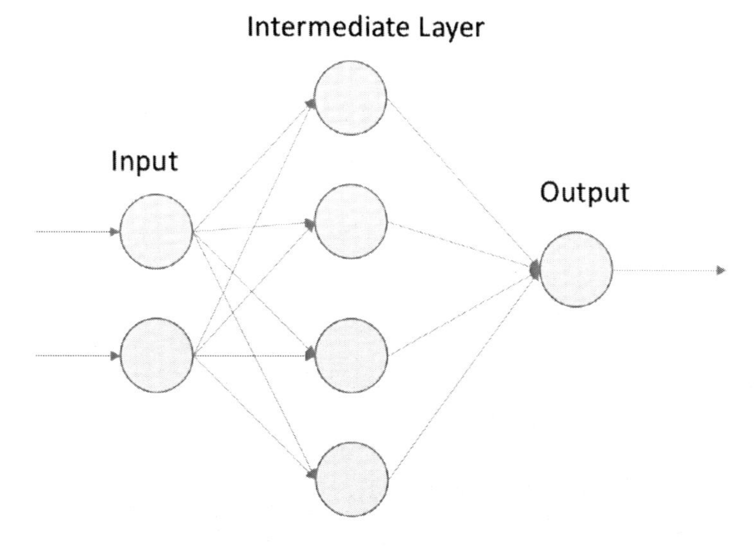

Figure 2.2 – MLP architecture

The preceding NN architecture diagram shows the following:

- An input layer, an intermediate layer, and an output layer.
- This architecture takes two inputs. This is where we pass the `XOR` inputs.
- The intermediate layer has four nodes.
- The final layer has a single node. This is where we expect the output of the `XOR` operation.

This NN that we will be building aims to mimic an `XOR` gate. Now, let's start coding our first PyTorch Lightning model!

Building a Hello World MLP model

Welcome to the world of PyTorch Lightning!

Finally, it's time for us to build our first model using PyTorch Lightning. In this section, we will build a simple MLP model to accomplish the `XOR` operator. This is like a **Hello World** introduction to the world of NNs as well as PyTorch Lightning. We will follow these steps to build our first `XOR` operator:

1. Importing libraries
2. Preparing the data
3. Configuring the model
4. Training the model
5. Loading the model
6. Making predictions

Importing libraries

We begin by first importing the necessary libraries and printing their package versions, as follows:

```
import pytorch_lightning as pl
import torch
from torch import nn, optim
from torch.autograd import Variable
import pytorch_lightning as pl
from pytorch_lightning.callbacks import ModelCheckpoint
```

```
from torch.utils.data import DataLoader

print("torch version:",torch.__version__)
print("pytorch ligthening version:",pl.__version__)

```

This code block should show the following output:

```
torch version: 1.10.0+cu111
pytorch ligthening version: 1.5.2
```

Once you have confirmed that you have the correct version, we are ready to start with the model.

Preparing the data

As you saw in *Figure 2.1*, an `XOR` gate takes two inputs and has four rows of data. In data science terms, we can call columns **A** and **B** our features and the **Out** column our target variable.

Before we start preparing our inputs and target data for `XOR`, it is important to understand that PyTorch Lightning accepts data loaders to train a model. In this section, we will build a simple data loader that has inputs and targets and will use it while training our model. We'll follow these next steps:

1. It's time to build a truth table that matches the `XOR` gate. We will use the variables to create the dataset. The code for creating input features looks like this:

   ```
   xor_inputs = [Variable(torch.Tensor([0, 0])),
                 Variable(torch.Tensor([0, 1])),
                 Variable(torch.Tensor([1, 0])),
                 Variable(torch.Tensor([1, 1]))]
   ```

   Since PyTorch Lightning is built upon the PyTorch framework, all data that is being passed into the model must be in tensor form.

   In the preceding code, we created four tensors, and each tensor had two values—that is, it had two features, `A` and `B`. We are ready with all the input features. A total of four rows are ready to be fed to our `XOR` model.

2. Since the input features are ready, it's time to build our target variables, as shown in the following code snippet:

```
xor_targets = [Variable(torch.Tensor([0])),
               Variable(torch.Tensor([1])),
               Variable(torch.Tensor([1])),
               Variable(torch.Tensor([0]))]
```

   The preceding code for targets is similar to the input features' code. The only difference is that each target variable is a single value.

   Inputs and targets will be ready in the final step of preparing our dataset. It's time to create a data loader. There are different ways in which we can create our dataset and pass it as a data loader to PyTorch Lightning. In the upcoming chapters, we will demonstrate different ways of using data loaders.

3. Here, we will use the simplest way of building a dataset for our `XOR` model. The following code is used to do this:

```
xor_data = list(zip(xor_input, xor_target))
train_loader = DataLoader(xor_data, batch_size=1)
```

   Data loaders in PyTorch Lightning look for two main things—the key and the value, which in our case are the features and target values. We are then using the DataLoader module from torch.utils.data to wrap the xor_data and create a Python iterable over the XOR data.

```
[(tensor([0., 0.]), tensor([0.])),
 (tensor([0., 1.]), tensor([1.])),
 (tensor([1., 0.]), tensor([1.])),
 (tensor([1., 1.]), tensor([0.]))]
```

In the preceding code, we are creating a dataset that is a list of tuples, and each tuple has two values. The first values are the two features/inputs, and the second values are the target values for the given input.

Configuring the model

Finally, it's time to train our first PyTorch Lightning model. Models in PyTorch Lightning are built similarly to how they are built in PyTorch. One added advantage with PyTorch Lightning is that it will make your code more structured with its life cycle methods; most of the model training code is taken care of by the framework, which helps us avoid the boilerplate code.

Also, another great advantage of this framework is that we can easily scale DL models across multiple **graphics processing units** (**GPUs**) and **tensor processing units** (**TPUs**), which we will be using in the upcoming chapters.

Every model we build using PyTorch Lightning must be inherited from a class called `LightningModule`. This is a class that contains the boilerplate code, and this is also where we have Lightning life cycle methods. In simple terms, we can say that `PyTorch LightningModule` is the same as `PyTorch nn.Module` but with added life cycle methods and other operations. If we take a look at the source code, `PyTorch LightningModule` is inherited from `PyTorch nn.Module`. That means most of the functionality in `PyTorch nn.Module` is available in `LightningModule` as well.

Any PyTorch Lightning model needs at least two life cycle methods—one for the training loop to train the model (called `training_step`), and another to configure an optimizer for the model (called `configure_optimizers`). In addition to these two life cycle methods, we also use the `forward` method. This is where we take in the input data and pass it to the model.

Our `XOR` MLP model building follows this process, and we will go over each step in detail, as follows:

1. Initializing the model
2. Mapping inputs to the model
3. Configuring the optimizer
4. Setting up training parameters

Initializing the model

To initialize the model, follow these steps:

1. Begin by creating a class called `XOR` that inherits from `PyTorch LightningModule`, which is shown in the following code snippet:

```
class XORModel(pl.LightningModule)
```

2. We will start creating our layers. This can be initialized in the `__init__` method, as demonstrated in the following code snippet:

```
def __init__(self):

    super(XORModel,self).__init__()

    self.input_layer = nn.Linear(2, 4)
```

```
        self.output_layer = nn.Linear(4,1)

        self.sigmoid = nn.Sigmoid()

        self.loss = nn.MSELoss()

```

In the preceding code snippet, we performed the following actions:

I. Setting up hidden layers, where the first layer takes in two inputs and returns four outputs, and that output becomes our intermediate layer. The intermediate layer merges with the single node, which becomes our output node.

II. Initializing the activation function. Here, we are using the `sigmoid` function to build our `XOR` gate.

III. Initializing the loss function. Here, we are using the **mean squared error** (**MSE**) loss function to build our `XOR` model.

Mapping inputs to the model

This is a simple step where we are using the `forward` method, which takes the inputs and generates the model's output. The following code snippet demonstrates the process:

```
    def forward(self, input):
      #print("INPUT:", input.shape)
      x = self.input_layer(input)
      #print("FIRST:", x.shape)
      x = self.sigmoid(x)
      #print("SECOND:", x.shape)
      output = self.output_layer(x)
      #print("THIRD:", output.shape)
      return output

```

The `forward` method acts as a mapper or medium where data is passed between multiple layers and the activation function. In the preceding `forward` method, it's primarily doing the following operations:

1. It takes the inputs for the `XOR` gate and passes them to our first input layer.
2. Output generated from the first input layer is fed to the `sigmoi` activation function.

3. Output from the `sigmoid` activation function is fed to the final layer, and the same output is being returned by the `forward` method.
4. The commented-out `print` statements are for debugging and explanatory purposes. You can uncomment them and see how tensors are passed to the model and how model training works for deeper understanding.

Configuring the optimizer

All optimizers in PyTorch Lightning can be configured in a life cycle method called `configure_optimizers`. In this method, one or multiple optimizers can be configured. For this example, we can make use of single optimizers, and in future chapters, some models use multiple optimizers.

For our `XOR` model, we will use the `Adam` optimizer, and the following code snippet demonstrates our `configure_optimizers` life cycle methods:

```
def configure_optimizers(self):
params = self.parameters()
optimizer = optim.Adam(params=params, lr = 0.01)
return optimizer
```

All model parameters can be accessed by using the `self` object with the `self.parameters()` method. Here, we are creating an `Adam` optimizer that takes the model parameters with a learning rate (`lr`) of `0.01`, and the same optimizer is being returned.

> **Important Note**
>
> To those who are not familiar with optimizers, it helps with the **stochastic gradient descent** (**SGD**) process and helps the model find global minima. You can learn more about how `Adam` works here: `https://arxiv.org/abs/1412.6980`.

Setting up training parameters

This is where all the model training occurs. Let's try to understand this method in detail. This is the code for `training_step`:

```
    def training_step(self, batch, batch_idx):
      xor_input, xor_target = batch
      #print("XOR INPUT:", xor_input.shape)
      #print("XOR TARGET:", xor_target.shape)
```

```
        outputs = self(xor_input)
        #print("XOR OUTPUT:", outputs.shape)
        loss = self.loss(outputs, xor_target)
        return loss

```

This `training_step` life cycle method takes the following two inputs:

- `batch`: Data that is being passed in the data loader is accessed in batches. This consists of two items: one is the input/features data, and the other item is `targets`.
- `batch_idx`: This is the index number or the sequence number for the batche of data.

In the preceding method, we are accessing our inputs and targets from the batch and then passing the inputs to the `self` method. When the input is passed to the `self` method, that indirectly invokes our `forward` method, which returns the `XOR` multilayer NN output. We are using the `MSE` loss function to calculate the loss and return the loss value for this method.

> **Important Note**
>
> Inputs passed to the `self` method indirectly invoke the `forward` method where the mapping of data happens between layers, and activation functions and output from the model are being generated.

Output from the training step is a single-loss value, whereas, in the upcoming chapter, we will cover different ways and tricks that will help us build and investigate our NN.

There are many other life cycle methods available in PyTorch Lightning. We will cover them in upcoming chapters, depending on the use case and scenario.

We have completed all the steps that are needed to build our first `XOR` MLP model. The complete code block for our `XOR` model looks like this:

```
class XORModel(pl.LightningModule):
    def __init__(self):

        super(XORModel,self).__init__()

        self.input_layer = nn.Linear(2, 4)
        self.output_layer = nn.Linear(4,1)

```

```
        self.sigmoid = nn.Sigmoid()

        self.loss = nn.MSELoss()

    def forward(self, input):
        #print("INPUT:", input.shape)
        x = self.input_layer(input)
        #print("FIRST:", x.shape)
        x = self.sigmoid(x)
        #print("SECOND:", x.shape)
        output = self.output_layer(x)
        #print("THIRD:", output.shape)
        return output

    def configure_optimizers(self):
        params = self.parameters()
        optimizer = optim.Adam(params=params, lr = 0.01)
        return optimizer

    def training_step(self, batch, batch_idx):
        xor_input, xor_target = batch
        #print("XOR INPUT:", xor_input.shape)
        #print("XOR TARGET:", xor_target.shape)
        outputs = self(xor_input)
        #print("XOR OUTPUT:", outputs.shape)
        loss = self.loss(outputs, xor_target)
        return loss
```

To summarize, in the preceding code block, we have the following:

1. The `XOR` model takes in `XOR` inputs of size 2.
2. Data is being passed to the intermediate layer, which has four nodes and returns a single output.
3. In this process, we are using `sigmoid` as our activation function, `MSE` as our loss function, and `Adam` as our optimizer.

If you observe, we have not set up any backpropagation, clearing gradients, or optimizer parameter updates and many other things are taken care of by the PyTorch Lightning framework.

Training the model

All models built in PyTorch Lightning can be trained using a `Trainer` class. Let's learn more about this class now.

The `Trainer` class is an abstraction of some key things, such as looping over the dataset, backpropagation, clearing gradients, and the optimizer step. All the boilerplate code from PyTorch is being taken by the `Trainer` class in PyTorch Lightning. Also, the `Trainer` class supports many other functionalities that help us to build our model easily, and some of those functionalities are various callbacks, model checkpoints, early stopping, dev runs for unit testing, support for GPUs and TPUs, loggers, logs, epochs, and many more. In various chapters in this book, we will try to cover most of the important features supported by the `Trainer` class.

The code for training our `XOR` model looks like this:

```
from pytorch_lightning.utilities.types import TRAIN_DATALOADERS
checkpoint_callback = ModelCheckpoint()
model = XORModel()

trainer = pl.Trainer(max_epochs=100, callbacks=[checkpoint_
callback])
```

In the next step, we are creating a `trainer` object. We are running the model for a maximum of 100 epochs and also passing the model checkpoint as a callback. In the final step, once the model trainer is ready, we invoke the `fit` method by passing model and input data, which is shown in the following code snippet:

```
trainer.fit(model, train_dataloaders=train_loader)
```

In the preceding code snippet, we are training our model for 100 epochs and passing the data using the `train_dataloaders` argument.

We will get the following output after running the model for 100 epochs:

```
GPU available: False, used: False
TPU available: False, using: 0 TPU cores
IPU available: False, using: 0 IPUs

  | Name         | Type    | Params
-----------------------------------------
0 | input_layer  | Linear  | 12
1 | output_layer | Linear  | 5
2 | sigmoid      | Sigmoid | 0
3 | loss         | MSELoss | 0
-----------------------------------------
17        Trainable params
0         Non-trainable params
17        Total params
0.000     Total estimated model params size (MB)
/usr/local/lib/python3.7/dist-packages/pytorch_lightning/trainer/data_loading.py:407: UserWarning: The number of training samples (4) is smaller than the logging
  f"The number of training samples ({self.num_training_batches}) is smaller than the logging interval"
Epoch 99: 100%                                             4/4 [00:00<00:00, 141.04it/s, loss=0.253, v_num=0]
```

Figure 2.3 – Model output after 100 epochs

If we closely observe the progress of model training, at the end, we can see the loss value is being displayed. PyTorch Lightning supports a good and flexible way to configure values to be displayed on the progress bar, which we will cover in upcoming chapters.

To summarize this section, we have created an `XOR` model object and used the `Trainer` class to train the model for 100 epochs.

In PyTorch Lightning, one advantage we see is whenever we train a model multiple times, all the different model versions are saved to disk in a default folder called `lightning_logs`, and once all the models with different versions are made ready, we always have the opportunity to load the different model versions from the files and compare the results. For example, here, we have run the `XOR` model twice, and when we look at the `lightning_logs` folder, we can see two versions of the `XOR` model:

```
ls lightning_logs/
```

This should show the following output:

```
version_0/  version_1/
```

Figure 2.4 – List of files in the lightning_logs folder

Within these version subfolders, we have all the information about the model being trained and built, which can be easily loaded, and predictions can be performed. Files within these folders have some useful information, such as hyperparameters, which are saved as `hparams.yaml`, and we also have a subfolder called `checkpoints`. This is where our `XOR` model is stored in serialized form. Here is a screenshot of all the files within these version folders:

```
ls lightning_logs/*/

lightning_logs/version_0/:
checkpoints/  events.out.tfevents.1615663387.6a881f5bc643.58.0  hparams.yaml

lightning_logs/version_1/:
checkpoints/  events.out.tfevents.1615663398.6a881f5bc643.58.1  hparams.yaml
```

Figure 2.5 – List of subfolders and files within the lightning_logs folder

If you run multiple versions and want to load the latest version of the model from the preceding code snippet, the latest version of the model is stored in the `version_1` folder. We can manually find the path to the latest version of the model or use model checkpoint callbacks.

> **Important Note**
> Please add `!` for the shell commands run inside Colab.

Loading the model

Once we have built the model, the next step is to load that model. As mentioned in the preceding section, identifying the latest version of a model can be done using `checkpoint_callback`, created in the preceding step. Here, we have run two versions of the model to get the path of the latest version of the model, as shown in the following code snippet:

```
print(checkpoint_callback.best_model_path)
```

Here is the output of the preceding code, where the latest file path for the model is displayed. This is later used to load the model back from the checkpoint and make predictions:

```
/content/lightning_logs/version_1/checkpoints/epoch=99-
step=399.ckpt
```

Figure 2.6 – Output of the file path for the latest model version file

Loading the model from the checkpoint can easily be done using the `load_from_checkpoint` method from the model object by passing the model checkpoint path, which is shown in the following code snippet:

```
train_model = model.load_from_checkpoint(checkpoint_callback.
best_model_path)
```

This preceding code will load the model from the checkpoint. In this step, we have built and trained the model for two different versions and loaded the latest model from the checkpoints.

Making predictions

Now that our model is ready, it's time to make some predictions. This process is demonstrated in the following code snippet:

```
test = torch.utils.data.DataLoader(xor_input, batch_size=1)
for val in xor_input:
  _ = train_model(val)
  print([int(val[0]),int(val[1])], int(_.round()))
```

This preceding code is an easy way to make predictions, iterating over our `XOR` dataset, passing the input values to the model, and making the prediction. This is the output of the preceding code snippet:

```
/content/lightning_logs/version_1/checkpoints/epoch=499-step=499.ckpt
[0, 0] 0
[0, 1] 1
[1, 0] 1
[1, 1] 0
```

Figure 2.7 – XOR model output

From the preceding output, we can see that the input model had predicted the correct results. There are different ways and techniques to build a model, which we will cover in the upcoming chapters.

This may seem like a rather simple result but was a breakthrough in ML when it was first accomplished in the 1960s. We could make the machine learn behavior that does not follow a simple sequence of logical breakdowns such as decision trees and encapsulate the knowledge by simply observing I/O values. This core idea of observing I/O values and learning is exactly how an image recognition model using CNN works, whereby it matches an image representation with a label and learns to classify objects.

Building our first Deep Learning model

Now that we have built a basic NN, it's time to use our knowledge of creating an MLP to build a DL model. You will notice that the core framework will remain the same and is built upon the same foundation.

So, what makes it deep?

While the exact origins of who first used DL are often debated, a popular misconception is that DL just involves a really big NN model with hundreds or thousands of layers. While most DL models are big, it is important to understand that the real secret is a concept called **backpropagation**.

As we have seen, NNs such as MLPs have been around for a long time, and by themselves, they could solve previously unsolved classification problems such as `XOR` or give better predictions than traditional classifiers. However, they were still not accurate when dealing with large unstructured data such as images. In order to learn in high-dimensional spaces, a simple method called backpropagation is used, which gives feedback to the system. This feedback makes the model *learn* whether it is doing a good or bad job of predicting, and mistakes are penalized in every iteration of the model. Slowly, over lots of iterations using optimization methods, the system learns to minimize mistakes and achieves convergence. We converge by using the loss function for the feedback loop and continuously reduce the loss, thereby achieving the desired optimization. There are various loss functions available, with popular ones being `log loss` and `cosine loss` functions.

Backpropagation, when coupled with a massive amount of data and the computing power provided by the cloud, can do wonders, and that is what gave rise to the recent renaissance in ML. Since 2012, when a **CNN** architecture won the *ImageNet* competition with subsequent models achieving near-human accuracy, it has only got better. In this section, we will see how to build a CNN model. Let's start with an overview of a CNN architecture.

CNN architecture

As you all know, computers only understand the language of bits, which means they accept input in a numerical form. But how can you convert an image into a number? A CNN architecture is made of various layers that represent convolution. The simple objective of CNNs is to take a high-dimensional object, such as an image, and convert it into a lower-dimensional entity, such as a mathematical form of numbers, which is represented in matrix form (also known as a tensor).

Of course, a CNN does more than convert an image into a tensor. It also learns to recognize that object in an image using backpropagation and optimization methods. Once trained on the number of images, it can easily recognize unseen images accurately. The success of CNNs has been in their flexibility with regard to scale by simply adding more hardware and then giving a stellar performance in terms of accuracy the more they scale.

We will build a CNN model for the *Histopathologic Cancer Detection* dataset to identify metastatic cancer in small image patches taken from larger digital pathology scans. You can see an overview of this here:

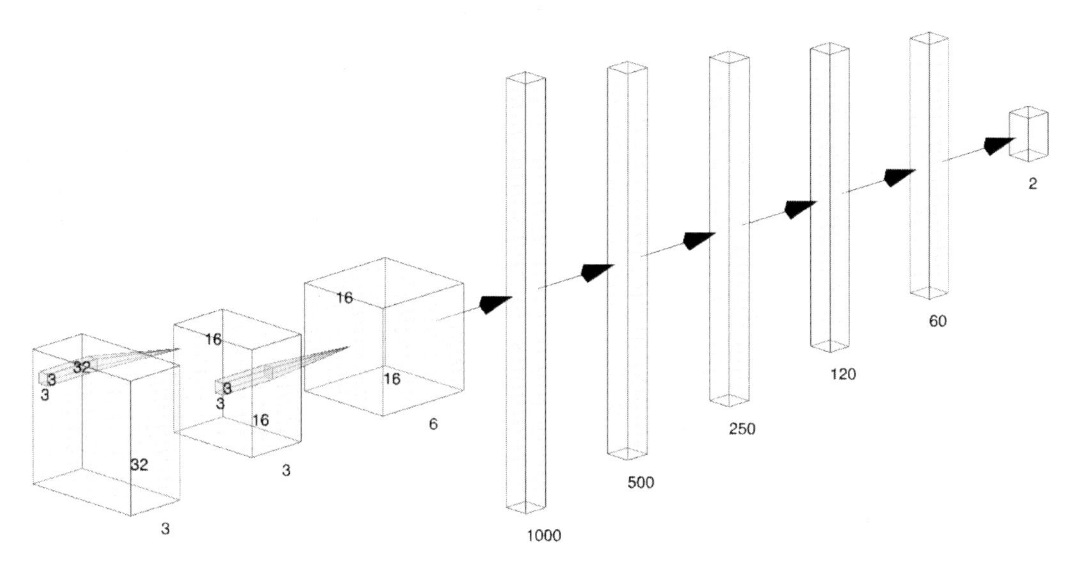

Figure 2.8 – CNN architecture for the Histopathologic Cancer Detection use case

We will use a simple 3 layer CNN architecture for our example.

The source image dataset starts with *96x96* images with *three* color channels. Cancer detection is based on the center 32x32px region if a patch contains at least one pixel of tumor tissue. Tumor tissue in the outer region of the patch does not influence the label. So, the original image is cropped to *32x32* size. We then do the following:

1. We put it through the first convolution with a kernel size of *3* and a stride length of *1*.
2. The first convolution layer is followed by the MaxPool layer, where images are converted to lower-dimensional *16x16* objects.
3. This is followed by another convolutional layer with *six* channels. This convolutional layer is followed by *five* fully connected layers of feature-length *1,000*, *500*, *250*, *120*, and *60* to finally get a SoftMax layer that gives the final predictions.

We will be using `ReLU` as our activation function, `Adam` as our optimizer, and `Cross-Entropy` as our loss function for training this model.

Building a CNN model for image recognition

PyTorch Lightning is a versatile framework, which makes training and scaling DL models easy by focusing on building models than writing complex programs. PyTorch Lightning is bundled with many useful features and options for building DL models. Since it is hard to cover all the topics in a single chapter, we will keep exploring different features of PyTorch Lightning in every chapter.

Here are the steps for building an image classifier using a CNN:

1. Importing the packages
2. Collecting the data
3. Preparing the data
4. Building the model
5. Training the model
6. Evaluating the accuracy of the model

Importing the packages

We will get started using the following steps:

1. First things first– install and load the necessary packages, as follows:

```
!pip install torch==1.10.0 torchvision==0.11.1
torchtext==0.11.0 torchaudio==0.10.0 --quiet
!pip install pytorch-lightning==1.5.2 --quiet
!pip install opendatasets --upgrade --quiet
```

2. Then, please import the following packages before getting started:

```
import os
import shutil
import opendatasets as od
import pandas as pd
import numpy as np
from PIL import Image

```

```
from sklearn.metrics import confusion_matrix
from sklearn.model_selection import train_test_split
import matplotlib.pyplot as plt

import torch
from torch import nn, optim
from torch.utils.data import DataLoader, Dataset
from torch.utils.data.sampler import SubsetRandomSampler
from torchvision.datasets import ImageFolder
import torchvision.transforms as T
from torchvision.utils import make_grid
from torchmetrics.functional import accuracy

import pytorch_lightning as pl
```

3. The following commands should allow us to get started:

```
print("pandas version:",pd.__version__)
print("numpy version:",np.__version__)
#print("seaborn version:",sns.__version__)
print("torch version:",torch.__version__)
print("pytorch ligthening version:",pl.__version__)
```

4. Executing the following code will ensure that you have the correct versions as well:

```
pandas version: 1.3.5
numpy version: 1.21.5
torch version: 1.10.0+cu111
pytorch ligthening version: 1.5.2
```

We can now start building our model by first collecting our data.

Collecting the data

We will now make use of Google Drive to store the dataset as well as to later save the checkpoint. You would need to mount the drive as shown in the GitHub notebook before you complete this step and provide the path where the dataset is downloaded. You can refer to *Chapter 10, Scaling and Managing Training,* on using cloud storage with Colab notebooks.

Firstly, we need to download the dataset from Kaggle, as shown here:

```
dataset_url = 'https://www.kaggle.com/c/histopathologic-cancer-detection'
od.download(dataset_url)
```

Here, we are downloading the PCam dataset from Kaggle using the credentials. You will be prompted to enter your username and key, which can be obtained from Kaggle's website:

```
Please provide your Kaggle credentials to download this dataset. Learn more: http://bit.ly/kaggle-creds
Your Kaggle username: rajsolanki23
Your Kaggle Key: ··········
Downloading histopathologic-cancer-detection.zip to ./histopathologic-cancer-detection
100%|██████████| 6.31G/6.31G [01:43<00:00, 65.7MB/s]

Extracting archive ./histopathologic-cancer-detection/histopathologic-cancer-detection.zip to ./histopathologic-cancer-detection
```

Figure 2.9 – Downloading the dataset from Kaggle

> **Important Note**
>
> To create an **application programming interface** (**API**) key in Kaggle, go to `kaggle.com/` and open your **Account settings** page. Next scroll down to the **API** section and click on the **Create New API Token** button. This will download a file called `Kaggle.json` on your computer from which you can get your username and the key or else upload the `Kaggle.json` file directly to your Google Colab folder to use it in the notebook.

There is a separate file called `train_labels.csv` that contains image **identifiers** (**IDs**) and their respective label/ground truth. So, we will read this file into a pandas DataFrame, as shown here:

```
cancer_labels = pd.read_csv('histopathologic-cancer-detection/train_labels.csv')
cancer_labels.head()
```

	id	label
0	f38a6374c348f90b587e046aac6079959adf3835	0
1	c18f2d887b7ae4f6742ee445113fa1aef383ed77	1
2	755db6279dae599ebb4d39a9123cce439965282d	0
3	bc3f0c64fb968ff4a8bd33af6971ecae77c75e08	0
4	068aba587a4950175d04c680d38943fd488d6a9d	0

Figure 2.10 – Reading the labels file

You can observe from the output shown in *Figure 2.11* that there are two labels for the images, `0` and `1`, so it is a binary classification task.

Preparing the data

The data preparation process will itself consist of multiple steps, as follows:

- Downsampling the data
- Loading the dataset
- Augmenting the dataset

The **PatchCamelyon** (**PCam**) dataset for histopathological cancer detection consists of 327,680 color images extracted from histopathologic scans of lymph nodes. Each image is annotated with a binary label (positive or negative) indicating the presence of metastatic tissue. It has the following subfolders:

```
histopathologic-cancer-detection/train
histopathologic-cancer-detection/test
```

The first path has around 220,000 images of histopathologic scans, while the second path has around 57,000 images of histopathologic scans. The `train_labels.csv` file shown in the following snippet contains the ground truth for the images in the `train` folder:

```
histopathologic-cancer-detection/train_labels.csv
```

Here are some example images of histopathological scans:

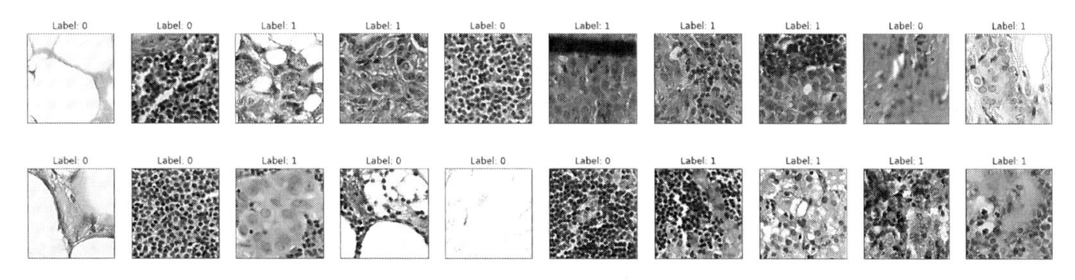

Figure 2.11 – Sample images of histopathological scans

Downsampling the dataset

A positive label indicates that the center 32x32 px region of a patch contains at least one px of tumor tissue. There are 130,908 normal cases (0) and 89,117 abnormal (or cancerous) tissue images (1). This is a huge dataset that will require a lot of time and compute resources to train on a full dataset, thus for the purpose of learning our first image classification model, we will downsample the 220,000 images in the train folder to 10,000 images and then split them into training and testing datasets, as shown in the following code block:

```
np.random.seed(0)
train_imgs_orig = os.listdir("histopathologic-cancer-detection/
train")
selected_image_list = []
for img in np.random.choice(train_imgs_orig, 10000):
  selected_image_list.append(img)
len(selected_image_list)
```

In the preceding code snippet, we are first setting the seed to make the results reproducible (feel free to use any number in the `random.seed()` method). Then, we are randomly selecting 10,000 images names (or IDs) from the `train` folder and storing them in `selected_image_list`. Once the 10,000 images are selected, we will split the data into train and test data, as shown here:

```
np.random.seed(0)
np.random.shuffle(selected_image_list)
cancer_train_idx = selected_image_list[:8000]
cancer_test_idx = selected_image_list[8000:]
print("Number of images in the downsampled training dataset: ",
len(cancer_train_idx))
print("Number of images in the downsampled testing dataset: ",
len(cancer_test_idx))
```

In the preceding code snippet, we are again setting the seed to make the results reproducible. Then, we are shuffling the image list and selecting 8000 image names (or IDs) that are stored in `cancer_train_idx` and the remaining 2000 image names in `cancer_test_idx`. The output is shown here:

```
Number of images in the downsampled training dataset:  8000
Number of images in the downsampled testing dataset:  2000
```

Figure 2.12 – Number of train and test images

Once the train and test image names are stored in `cancer_train_idx` and `cancer_test_idx` respectively, we need to store those 8,000 and 2,000 images on persistent storage on Google Drive so that we don't have to redo all of this during the model improvement exercise or when debugging the code. You can mount the persistent storage using the following code:

```
from google.colab import drive
drive.mount('/content/gdrive')
```

This results in the following output:

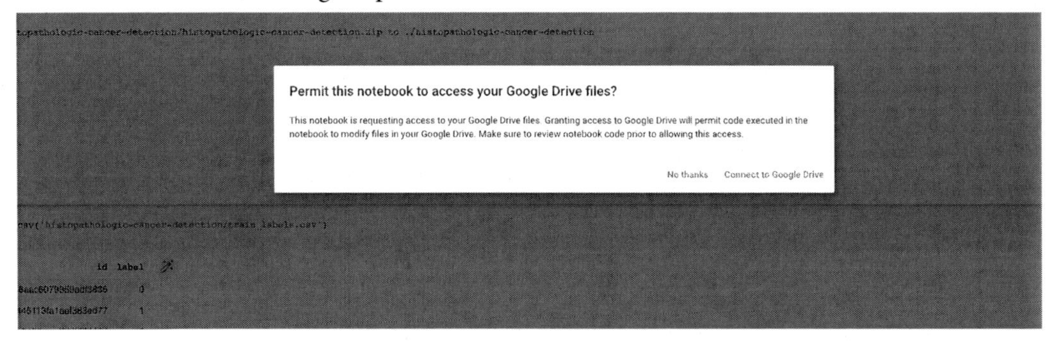
Permit this notebook to access your Google Drive files?
This notebook is requesting access to your Google Drive files. Granting access to Google Drive will permit code executed in the notebook to modify files in your Google Drive. Make sure to review notebook code prior to allowing this access.
No thanks
Connect to Google Drive

Figure 2.13 – Allowing access to Google Drive

You will be prompted to allow access to your drive; once you accept it, your drive will be mounted and you can access any of the data stored on persistent storage even after the session expires, and you can resume your work without having to download, downsample, and split the data again. The code for storing the images on persistent storage is shown here:

```
os.mkdir('/content/gdrive/My Drive/Colab Notebooks/
histopathologic-cancer-detection/train_dataset/')
for fname in cancer_train_idx:
  src = os.path.join('histopathologic-cancer-detection/train',
fname)
  dst = os.path.join('/content/gdrive/My Drive/Colab Notebooks/
histopathologic-cancer-detection/train_dataset/', fname)
  shutil.copyfile(src, dst)
```

In the preceding code snippet, we are first creating a folder called `train_dataset` on the following path:

```
content/gdrive/My Drive/Colab Notebooks/histopathologic-cancer-
detection/
```

Then, we are looping over `cancer_train_idx` to get image names for the training data and copying all the files from local storage in the machine allotted to us at the time we created a notebook to persistent storage on our Google Drive using the `shutils` Python module. We will also repeat this exercise for the test dataset. The code is illustrated in the following snippet:

```
os.mkdir('/content/histopathologic-cancer-detection/test_dataset/')
for fname in test_idx:
    src = os.path.join('histopathologic-cancer-detection/train', fname)
    dst = os.path.join('/content/histopathologic-cancer-detection/test_dataset/', fname)
    shutil.copyfile(src, dst)
print('No. of images in downsampled testing dataset: ', len(os.listdir("/content/histopathologic-cancer-detection/test_dataset/")))
```

As shown in the preceding code snippet, we are saving the training and testing dataset in the persistent storage on Google Drive for further use and to help in tuning the image classification model.

The labels for the images that were selected in the downsampled data will be extracted in a list that will be used for training and evaluating the image classification model, as shown here:

```
selected_image_labels = pd.DataFrame()
id_list = []
label_list = []

for img in selected_image_list:
    label_tuple = df_labels.loc[df_labels['id'] == img.split('.')[0]]
    id_list.append(label_tuple['id'].values[0])
    label_list.append(label_tuple['label'].values[0])
```

Loading the dataset

PyTorch Lightning expects data to be in folders with the classes. So, we cannot use the `DataLoader` module directly when all train/test images are in one folder without subfolders. Therefore, we will write our custom class for loading the data, as follows:

```
class LoadCancerDataset(Dataset):
    def __init__(self, data_folder,
                 transform = T.Compose([T.CenterCrop(32),T.
ToTensor()]), dict_labels={}):
        self.data_folder = data_folder
        self.list_image_files = [s for s in os.listdir(data_
folder)]
        self.transform = transform
        self.dict_labels = dict_labels
        self.labels = [dict_labels[i.split('.')[0]] for i in
self.list_image_files]

    def __len__(self):
        return len(self.list_image_files)

    def __getitem__(self, idx):
        img_name = os.path.join(self.data_folder, self.list_
image_files[idx])
        image = Image.open(img_name)
        image = self.transform(image)
        img_name_short = self.list_image_files[idx].split('.')
[0]

        label = self.dict_labels[img_name_short]
        return image, label
```

In the preceding code block, we have defined a custom data loader.

The custom class defined earlier inherits from the `torch.utils.data.Dataset` module. The `LoadCancerDataset` custom class is initialized in the `__init__` method and accepts three arguments: the path to the data folder, the transformer with a default value of cropping the image to size 32 and transforming it to a tensor, and a dictionary with the labels and IDs of the dataset.

The LoadCancerDataset class reads all the images in the folder and extracts the image name from the filename, which is also the ID for the images. This image name is then matched with the label in the dictionary with the labels and IDs.

The LoadCancerDataset class returns the images and their labels, which can then be used in the DataLoader module of the torch.utils.data library as it can now read the images with their corresponding label.

Now we need to create a dictionary with labels and IDs that will be used in our LoadCancerDataset class:

```
img_class_dict = {k:v for k, v in zip(selected_image_labels.id,
selected_image_labels.label)}
```

The preceding code extracts the ID and labels from the selected_image_labels data frame and stores them in the img_class_dict dictionary.

Augmenting the dataset

Now that we have loaded the data, we will start the process of data preprocessing by augmenting the images, as follows:

```
data_T_train = T.Compose([
    T.CenterCrop(32),
    T.RandomHorizontalFlip(),
    T.RandomVerticalFlip(),
    T.ToTensor(),
    ])
data_T_test = T.Compose([
    T.CenterCrop(32),
    T.ToTensor(),
    ])
```

In the preceding code block, we have used transformations to crop the image to 32x32 by using Torchvision's built-in libraries. We then also augmented the data by flipping it horizontally and vertically, thereby creating two additional copies from the original image.

Now, we will call our LoadCancerDataset custom class with the path to the data folder, transformer, and the image label dictionary to convert it to the format accepted by the torch.utils.data.DataLoader module. The code to achieve this is illustrated in the following snippet:

```
train_set = LoadCancerDataset(data_folder='/content/gdrive/My
Drive/Colab Notebooks/histopathologic-cancer-detection/train_
dataset/',
```

```
                              # datatype='train',
                              transform=data_T_train, dict_
labels=img_label_dict)
```

This will be repeated for the test data as well, and then, in the final step, we will create `train_dataloader` and `test_dataloader` data loaders using the output from our `LoadCancerDataset` custom class by leveraging the `DataLoader` module from the `torch.utils.data` library. The code to do so is illustrated in the following snippet:

```
batch_size = 256
train_dataloader = DataLoader(dataset, batch_size, num_
workers=2, pin_memory=True, shuffle=True)
test_dataloader = DataLoader(test_set, batch_size, num_
workers=2, pin_memory=True)
```

In the preceding code snippet, we have the following:

1. We started with the original data without the subfolders as expected by the PyTorch Lightning module. The data was downsampled and saved on Google Drive's persistent storage.
2. Using the `LoadCancerDataset` custom class, we created two datasets `train_set` and `test_set`, by reading images and their labels.
3. In the process of creating datasets, we also used the Torchvision `transform` module to crop the images to the center, that is, converting images to the square of *32 x 32* px and also converting images to tensors.
4. In the final step, the two `train_set` and `test_set` datasets that were created are used to create two `train_dataloader` and `test_dataloader` data loaders for them.

At this point, we are ready with our `train_dataloader` data loader with around *8,000* images, and `test_dataloader` with around *2,000* images. All the images are of size *32 x 32*, converted to tensor form, and served in batches of *256* images. We will use the train data loader to train our model and the test data loader to measure our model's accuracy.

Building the model

To build our CNN image classifier, let's divide the process into multiple steps, as follows:

1. Initializing the model
2. Configuring the optimizer
3. Configuring training and testing

Initializing the model

Similar to the `XOR` model, we will begin by creating a class called `CNNImageClassifier` that inherits from the `PyTorch LightningModule` class, as shown in the following code snippet:

```
class CNNImageClassifier(pl.LightningModule)
```

> **Important Note**
>
> Every model that is built in a **PyTorch Lightning** (**PL**) must inherit from `PyTorch LightningModule`, as we will see throughout this book.

1. Let's start by setting up our CNN `ImageClassifier` class. This can be initialized in the `__init__` method, as shown in the following code snippet. We will break this method into chunks to make it easier for you to understand:

```
def __init__(self, learning_rate = 0.001):
    super().__init__()

    self.learning_rate = learning_rate

```

In the preceding code snippet, the CNN `ImageClassifier` class accepts a single parameter—the learning rate, with a default value of `0.001`.

> **Important Note**
>
> The learning rate determines "how well" and "how fast" an ML algorithm "learns". This job of optimizing the learning path is performed by an optimizer (`Adam`, in this case). There is often a trade-off between accuracy and speed. A very low learning rate may learn well but it may take too long and get stuck in local minima. A very high learning rate may reduce loss initially but then never converge. In reality, this is a hyperparameter setting that needs to be tuned for each model.

2. Next, we will build two convolution layers. Here is the code for building two convolution layers, along with max pooling and activation functions:

```
#Input size (256, 3, 32, 32)
    self.conv_layer1 = nn.Conv2d(in_channels=3,out_
channels=3,kernel_size=3,stride=1,padding=1)
    #output_shape: (256, 3, 32, 32)
```

```
        self.relu1=nn.ReLU()
        #output_shape: (256, 3, 32, 32)

        self.pool=nn.MaxPool2d(kernel_size=2)
        #output_shape: (256, 3, 16, 16)

        self.conv_layer2 = nn.Conv2d(in_channels=3,out_
    channels=6,kernel_size=3,stride=1,padding=1)
        #output_shape: (256, 3, 16, 16)

        self.relu2=nn.ReLU()
        #output_shape: (256, 6, 16, 16)

```

In the preceding code snippet, we primarily built two convolutional layers—`conv_layer1` and `conv_layer2`. Our images from the data loaders are in batches of 256, which are colored, and thus it has *three* input channels (**red-green-blue**, or **RGB**) with a size of *32 x 32*.

Our first convolution layer, called `conv_layer1`, takes an input of size `(256, 3, 32, 32)`, which is *256* images with *three* channels (RGB) of size *32* in width and height. If we look at `conv_layer1`, it is a **two-dimensional** (**2D**) CNN that takes *three* input channels and outputs *three* channels, with a kernel size of *3* and a stride and padding of *1* px. We also initialized max pooling with a kernel size of *2*.

The second convolution layer, `conv_layer2`, takes *three* input channels as input and outputs *six* channels with a kernel size of *3* and a stride and padding of *1*. Here, we are using two `ReLU` activation functions initialized in variables as `relu1` and `relu2`. In the next section, we will cover how we pass data over these layers.

3. In the following snippet, we will build six fully connected linear layers followed by a loss function. The code for six fully linear layers along with the loss function looks like this:

```
    self.fully_connected_1 =nn.Linear(in_features=16 * 16 *
    6,out_features=1000)
    self.fully_connected_2 =nn.Linear(in_features=1000,out_
    features=500)
    self.fully_connected_3 =nn.Linear(in_features=500,out_
    features=250)
    self.fully_connected_4 =nn.Linear(in_features=250,out_
```

```
features=120)
self.fully_connected_5 =nn.Linear(in_features=120,out_
features=60)
self.fully_connected_6 =nn.Linear(in_features=60,out_
features=2)
self.loss = nn.CrossEntropyLoss()
```

In the preceding code snippet, we had six fully connected linear layers, as follows:

- The first linear layer—that is, `self.fully_connected_1`—takes the input, which is the output generated from `conv_layer2`, and this `self.fully_connected_1` layer outputs 1,000 nodes.
- The second linear layer—that is, `self.fully_connected_2`—takes the output from the first linear layer and outputs 500 nodes.
- Similarly, the third linear layer—that is, `self.fully_connected_3`—takes the output from the second linear layer and outputs 250 nodes.
- Then, the fourth linear layer—that is, `self.fully_connected_4`—takes the output from the third linear layer and outputs 120 nodes.
- Subsequently, the fifth linear layer—that is, `self.fully_connected_5`—takes the output from the fourth linear layer and outputs 60 nodes.
- The final layer—that is, `self.fully_connected_6`—takes the output from the fifth layer and outputs two nodes.

Since this is a binary classification, the output of this NN architecture should be the probability for the two classes. Finally, we will initialize the loss function, which is cross-entropy loss.

> **Important Note – Loss Function**
>
> A loss function is a method by which we measure how well our model is converging. As the model is trained through various epochs, the loss should tend toward zero (though it may not or never should reach zero). The cross-entropy loss function is one of the many loss functions available in DL models and is a good choice for image recognition models. You can read about the theory of the cross-entropy loss function here: `https://en.wikipedia.org/wiki/Cross_entropy`.

4. Our NN architecture is defined as a combination of CNN and fully connected linear networks, so it's time to pass in the data from the different layers and the activation functions. We will do this with the help of the `forward` method:

```
def forward(self, input):
output=self.conv_layer1(input)
output=self.relu1(output)
output=self.pool(output)

output=self.conv_layer2(output)
output=self.relu2(output)

output=output.view(-1, 6*16*16)
output = self.fully_connected_1(output)
output = self.fully_connected_2(output)
output = self.fully_connected_3(output)
output = self.fully_connected_4(output)
output = self.fully_connected_5(output)
output = self.fully_connected_6(output)

return output
```

In the preceding code block, we have used the `forward` method. To summarize, in the `forward` method, the input image data is first passed over the two convolution layers, and then the output from the convolution layers is passed over six fully connected layers. Finally, the output is returned. Let's understand this step by step, as follows:

I. The data is passed to our first convolution layer (`conv_layer1`). The output from `conv_layer1` is passed to the `ReLU` activation function, and the output from `ReLU` is passed to the max-pooling layer.

II. Once the input data is being processed by the first convolution layer, the activation function undergoes the max-pooling layer.

III. Then, the output is passed to our second convolution layer (`conv_layer2`), and the output from the second convolution layer is passed to our second `ReLU` activation function.

IV. Data is passed through the convolution layer, and the output from these layers, is multidimensional. To pass the output to our linear layers, it is converted to a single-dimensional form, which can be achieved using the tensor `view` method.

V. Once the data is ready in single-dimensional form, it is passed over six fully connected layers and the final output is returned.

> **Important Note**
>
> Hyperparameters can be saved using a method called `save_hyperparameters()`. This technique will be covered in upcoming chapters.

Configuring the optimizer

We have seen earlier that we will be using the `Adam` optimizer in this architecture to minimize our loss and converge the model. In order to do so, we need to configure optimizers that are available as one of the life cycle methods in PyTorch Lightning work.

The code for the `configure_optimizers` life cycle method for our `CNNImageClassifier` model looks like this:

```
def configure_optimizers(self):
params = self.parameters()
optimizer = optim.Adam(params=params, lr = self.learning_rate)
return optimizer
```

In the preceding code snippet, we are using the `Adam` optimizer with a learning rate that has been initialized in the `__init__()` method, and we then return the optimizer from this method.

The `configure_optimizers` method can return up to six different outputs. As in the preceding example, it can also return a single list/tuple object. With multiple optimizers, it can return two separate lists: one for the optimizers, and a second consisting of the learning-rate scheduler.

> **Important Note**
>
> `configure_optimizers` can return six different outputs. We will not cover all the cases in this book, but some of them have been used in our upcoming chapters on advanced topics.
>
> For example, when we build some complex NN architectures, such as **generative adversarial network** (**GAN**) models, there may be a need for multiple optimizers, and in some cases, we may need a learning rate scheduler along with optimizers. This can be addressed by configuring optimizers in a life cycle method.

Configuring the training and testing steps

In the `XOR` model we have covered, one of the life cycle methods that helps us to train our model on the training dataset is `training_step`. Similarly, if we want to test our model on the `test` dataset, we have a life cycle method called `test_step`.

For our `CNNImageClassifier` model, we have used the life cycle methods for training and also for testing.

The code for the PyTorch Lightning `training_step` life cycle method looks like this:

```
def training_step(self, batch, batch_idx):
    inputs, targets = batch
    outputs = self(inputs)
    train_accuracy = accuracy(outputs, targets)
    loss = self.loss(outputs, targets)
    self.log('train_accuracy', train_accuracy, prog_bar=True)
    self.log('train_loss', loss)
    return {"loss":loss, "train_accuracy": train_accuracy }
```

In the preceding code block, we have the following:

1. In the `training_step` life cycle method, batches of data are accessed a input parameters and input data is passed to the model.
2. We then calculate loss using the `self.loss` function.
3. The next step is to calculate accuracy. For this, we use a utility function called `accuracy()` from the `torchmetrics.functional` module. This method takes in the actual targets and the predicted output of the model as input and calculates the accuracy. The complete code for the `accuracy` method is available using the GitHub link for the book.

We will perform some additional steps here that were not done in our XOR model. We will use the self.log function and log some of the additional metrics. The following code will help us log our train_accuracy and also train_loss metrics:

```
self.log('train_accuracy', train_accuracy, prog_bar=True)
self.log('train_loss', loss)
```

In the preceding code snippet, the self.log method accepts the key/name of the metrics as the first parameter, the second parameter is the value for the metric, and the third parameter that we passed is prog_bar by default, which is always set to false.

We are logging accuracy and loss for our train dataset. These logged values can be later used for plotting our charts or for further investigation and will help us to tune the model. By setting the prog_bar parameter to true, it will display the train_accuracy metric on the progress bar for each epoch while training the model.

This life cycle method can return a dictionary as output with loss and test accuracy.

The code for the test_step life cycle method looks like this:

```
def test_step(self, batch, batch_idx):
    inputs, targets = batch
    outputs = self.forward(inputs)
    test_accuracy = self.binary_accuracy(outputs,targets)
    loss = self.loss(outputs, targets)
    self.log('test_accuracy', test_accuracy)
    return {"test_loss":loss, "test_accuracy": test_accuracy }
```

The code for the test_step life cycle method is similar to the training_step life cycle method; the only difference is that the data being passed to this method is the test dataset. We will see how this method is being triggered in the next section of this chapter.

In this model, we will focus on logging some additional metrics and also display some metrics on the progress bar while training the model.

Training the model

One of the key features of the PyTorch Lightning framework is the simplicity with which we can train the model. The trainer class comes in handy for doing training along with easy-to-use options such as picking the hardware (cpu/gpu/tpu), controlling training epochs, and all other nice things.

In PyTorch Lightning, to train the model, we first initialize the `trainer` class and then invoke the `fit` method to actually train the model. The code snippet for training our `CNNImageClassifier` model is shown here:

```
model = CNNImageClassifier()
trainer = pl.Trainer(max_epochs=500, progress_bar_refresh_
rate=50, gpus=-1)
trainer.fit(model, train_dataloader=train_dataloader)
```

In the preceding code snippet, we started by initializing our `CNNImageClassifier` model with a default learning rate of `0.001`.

Then, we initialized the `trainer` class object from the PyTorch Lightning framework with `500` epochs, making use of all the available GPUs and setting the progress bar rate to `50`.

We ran our model, which is making use of the GPU for computation and running for a total of `500` epochs, which reduces the training time to 20 minutes. The results for both the 100-epochs run and 500-epochs run are captured.

Whenever we train any PyTorch Lightning model, mainly on Jupyter Notebook, the progress of training for each epoch is visualized in a progress bar. This parameter helps us to control the speed to update this progress bar. The `fit` method is where we are passing our model and the train data loader, which we created earlier in the previous section. The data from the train data loader is accessed in batches in our `training_step` life cycle method, and that is where we train and calculate the loss. The process is illustrated in the following screenshot:

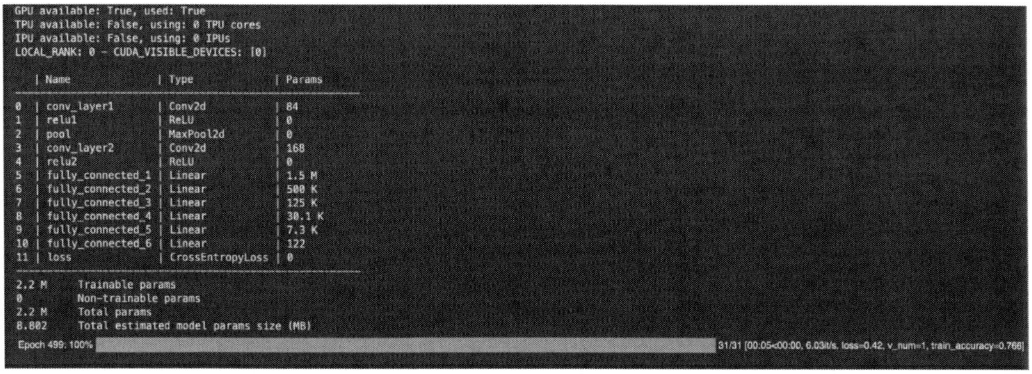

```
GPU available: True, used: True
TPU available: False, using: 0 TPU cores
IPU available: False, using: 0 IPUs
LOCAL_RANK: 0 - CUDA_VISIBLE_DEVICES: [0]

   | Name               | Type             | Params
---------------------------------------------------------
0  | conv_layer1        | Conv2d           | 84
1  | relu1              | ReLU             | 0
2  | pool               | MaxPool2d        | 0
3  | conv_layer2        | Conv2d           | 168
4  | relu2              | ReLU             | 0
5  | fully_connected_1  | Linear           | 1.5 M
6  | fully_connected_2  | Linear           | 500 K
7  | fully_connected_3  | Linear           | 125 K
8  | fully_connected_4  | Linear           | 30.1 K
9  | fully_connected_5  | Linear           | 7.3 K
10 | fully_connected_6  | Linear           | 122
11 | loss               | CrossEntropyLoss | 0
---------------------------------------------------------
2.2 M     Trainable params
0         Non-trainable params
2.2 M     Total params
8.802     Total estimated model params size (MB)
Epoch 499: 100% 31/31 [00:05<00:00, 6.03it/s, loss=0.42, v_num=1, train_accuracy=0.766]
```

Figure 2.14 – Training image classifier for 500 epochs

The preceding screenshot shows the metrics used for training. You can see in the result set that two convolution layers followed by six fully connected layers' parameters are listed, and a cross-entropy loss is calculated.

In `training_step`, we logged the `train_accuracy` metric and set the `prog_bar` value to `true`. This enables the `train_accuracy` metric to be displayed on the progress bar for every epoch, as shown in the preceding results.

At this point, we have trained our model on the training dataset for `100` epochs and, as per the `train_accuracy` metric displayed on the progress bar, the training accuracy is 76%.

While the model is performing relatively well on the training dataset, it is important to check how well our model performs on the test dataset. The performance on the test dataset is an indication of how reliable the model will be in detecting unseen or new cancer-tissue images.

Evaluating the accuracy of the model

To calculate the accuracy of the model, we need to pass test data into our test data loader and check the accuracy on the `test` dataset. The following code snippet shows how to do this:

```
trainer.test(test_dataloaders=test_dataloader)
```

In the preceding code snippet, we are calling the `test` method from the `trainer` object and passing in the test data loader. When we do this, PyTorch Lightning internally invokes our `test_step` life cycle method and passes in the data in batches.

The output of the preceding code gives us the test accuracy, as shown here:

```
[ ] trainer.test(test_dataloaders=test_dataloader)

/usr/local/lib/python3.7/dist-packages/pytorch_lightning/trainer/trainer.py:902: LightningDeprecationWarning: `trainer.test(test_dataloaders)` is deprecated in v1.
  "`trainer.test(test_dataloaders)` is deprecated in v1.4 and will be removed in v1.6."
/usr/local/lib/python3.7/dist-packages/pytorch_lightning/trainer/trainer.py:1394: UserWarning: `.test(ckpt_path=None)` was called without a model. The best model c
  f"`.{fn}(ckpt_path=None)` was called without a model."
Restoring states from the checkpoint path at /content/gdrive/MyDrive/Colab Notebooks/cnn/lightning_logs/version_1/checkpoints/epoch=499-step=15499.ckpt
LOCAL_RANK: 0 - CUDA_VISIBLE_DEVICES: [0]
Loaded model weights from checkpoint at /content/gdrive/MyDrive/Colab Notebooks/cnn/lightning_logs/version_1/checkpoints/epoch=499-step=15499.ckpt
Testing: 100%                                                    8/8 [00:01<00:00, 5.82it/
--------------------------------------------------------------------------------
DATALOADER:0 TEST RESULTS
{'test_accuracy': 0.7797888517379761}
--------------------------------------------------------------------------------
[{'test_accuracy': 0.7797888517379761}]
```

Figure 2.15 – Output of the test method

From the preceding output, our `ImageClassifier` model gives us an accuracy of 78% on our test dataset. This means that our model is performing really well on the test dataset as well, and we can use this model to correctly diagnose 8 of 10 cases of cancer tissues based on their image scans.

You may be wondering how this model actually gets deployed so that we can pass an unseen image scan of tissue and a user gets a prediction as to whether that image is cancerous or not. That process is called "scoring a model" and needs the deployment of an ML model—we will cover that in *Chapter 9, Deploying and Scoring Models*.

> **Important Note - Overfitting**
>
> You may have noticed that our model has really good accuracy on the `train` dataset as well as quite a good accuracy on the `test` dataset. This is a sign of a well-trained model. If you observe that accuracy between train and test scores is widely off (such as very good accuracy on the train set but very poor accuracy on the test set) then such behavior is normally known as *overfitting*. This typically happens when the model memorizes a training set while not generalizing on an unseen dataset. There are various methods to make models perform better on a test dataset, and such methods are called *regularization* methods. Batch normalization, dropout, and so on can be useful in regularizing the model. You can try them, and you will see improvement in test accuracy. We will also use them in future chapters.

Model improvement exercises

So, our first DL model is ready and is performing really well, considering the fact that we have trained it on just a sample set of a larger set. It was also relatively smooth to create this model using PyTorch Lightning, which made coding for CNN so straightforward. You can further try some of the following exercises to make this even better:

- Try running the model for more epochs and see how the accuracy improves. We have downsampled 10,000 images from the larger set. A DL model typically performs much better with larger datasets. You can try running it over a larger set and see the difference in accuracy (more GPU power may be needed).
- Try adjusting the batch size and see the results. A lower batch size can provide interesting results in some situations.
- You can also try changing the learning rate for the optimizer, or even using a different optimizer, such as `AdaGrad`, to see whether there is a change in performance. Typically, a lower learning rate means a longer time to train but avoids false convergences.

- We have tried two data augmentation methods in this model. You can also try different augmentation methods, such as `T.RandomRotate()`, color distortion or blurriness, and so on. Data augmentation methods create new entries to train a set from original images by modifying images. Such additional variations of the original images make a model learn better and improve its accuracy on unseen images. Adding `T.HorizontalFlip()` and `T.VerticalFlip()` methods increases the testing accuracy to 80% in the case of the preceding model, thus making the classifier more robust to unseen data as there is hardly any overfitting after augmenting the data.
- Later, you can try adding a third layer of convolution or an additional fully connected layer to see the impact on the model's accuracy. A boilerplate is shared here for your reference:

```
        self.conv_layer1 = nn.Conv2d(3, 16, 3, padding=1)
        self.conv_layer2 = nn.Conv2d(16, 32, 3,
padding=1)
        self.conv_layers3 = nn.Conv2d(32, 64, 3,
padding=1)
        self.pool = nn.MaxPool2d(2, 2)
        self.relu = nn.ReLU(
        self.fully_connected_1 = nn.Linear(64 * 4 * 4,
512)
        self. fully_connected_2  = nn.Linear(512, 256)
        self. fully_connected_3  = nn.Linear(256, 2)
        self.dropout = nn.Dropout(0.2)
        self.sig = nn.Sigmoid()

    def forward(self, output):
        output = self.pool(self.relu self. conv_
layer1(output)))
        output = self.pool(self.relu (self. conv_
layer2(output)))
        output = self.pool(self.relu (self. conv_
layer3(output)))
        output = output.view(-1, 64 * 4 * 4)
        output = self.relu (fully_connected_1(output))
        output = self.dropout(output)
        output = self.relu (fully_connected_2(output))
```

```
        output = self.sig(fully_connected_3(output))
        return output
```

This architecture can lead up to 81% test accuracy when combined with data augmentation techniques. All these changes will improve the model. You may need to increase the number of GPUs enabled as well, as it may need more compute power.

Summary

We got a taste of basic MLPs and CNNs in this chapter, which are the building blocks of DL. We learned that by using the PyTorch Lightning framework, we can easily build our models. While MLPs and CNNs may sound like basic models, they are quite advanced in terms of business applications, and many companies are just warming up to their industrial use. Neural Networks are used very widely as classifiers on structured data for predicting users' likes or propensity to respond to an offer or for marketing campaign optimization, among many other things. CNNs are also widely used in many industrial applications, such as counting the number of objects in an image, recognizing car dents for insurance claims, facial recognition to identify criminals, and so on.

In this chapter, we saw how to build the simplest yet most important `XOR` operator using an MLP model. We further extended the concept of MLPs to build our first CNN DL model to recognize images. Using PyTorch Lightning, we saw how to build DL models with minimal coding and built-in functions.

While DL models are extremely powerful, they are also very compute-hungry. To achieve the accuracy rates that are normally seen in research papers, we need to scale the model for a massive volume of data and train it for thousands of epochs, which in turn requires a massive amount of investment in hardware or a shocking bill for cloud-compute usage. One way to get around this problem is to not train DL models from scratch rather use information from models trained by these big models and transfer it to our model. This method, also known as **Transfer Learning** (**TL**), is very popular in the domain as it helps save time and money.

In the next chapter, we will see how we can use TL to get really good results in a fraction of the epochs without the headache of full training from scratch.

3
Transfer Learning Using Pre-Trained Models

Deep learning models become more accurate the more data they have for training. The most spectacular Deep Learning models, such as ImageNet, are trained on millions of images and often require a massive amount of computing power. To put things into perspective, the amount of power used to train OpenAI's GPT3 model could power an entire city. Unsurprisingly, the cost of training such Deep Learning models from scratch is prohibitive for most projects.

This begs the question: do we really need to train a Deep Learning model from scratch each time? One way of getting around this problem, rather than training Deep Learning models from scratch, is to borrow representations from an already trained model for a similar subject. For example, if you wanted to train an image recognition model to detect faces, you *could* train your **Convolutional Neural Network** (**CNN**) to learn *all* the representations for each of the layers – or you might think, "All faces in the world have similar representations, so why not borrow representations from some other model that has already been trained on millions of faces and apply it directly to my dataset?" This simple idea is called **Transfer Learning**.

Transfer learning is a technique that helps us to make use of knowledge acquired from a previously built model that was designed for a similar task to ours. For example, to learn how to ride a mountain bike, you could utilize the knowledge you acquired previously when learning how to ride a bicycle. Transfer learning works not just for transferring learned representations from one set of images to another, but for language models as well.

In the machine learning community, there are various pre-built models whose weights are shared by their authors. By re-using those trained model weights, you can avoid longer training durations and save on computing costs.

In this chapter, we will try to make use of existing pre-trained models to build our image classifier and text classifier. We will use a popular CNN architecture known as ResNet-50 to build our image classifier and then use another blockbuster transformer architecture known as BERT to build a text classifier. This chapter will show you how to make use of PyTorch Lightning life cycle methods and how to build models using transfer learning techniques.

In this chapter, we will cover the following topics:

- Getting started with transfer learning
- An image classifier using a pre-trained ResNet-50 architecture
- Text classification using BERT transformers

Technical requirements

The code for this chapter has been developed and tested on macOS with Anaconda or in Google Colab with Python 3.6. If you are using another environment, please make the appropriate changes to your `env` variables.

In this chapter, we will primarily be using the following Python modules, mentioned with their versions:

- PyTorch Lightning (version: 1.5.2)
- Seaborn (version: 0.11.2)
- NumPy (version: 1.21.5)
- Torch (version: 1.10.0)
- pandas (version: 1.3.5)

Please import all these modules into your Jupyter environment. In order to make sure that these modules work together and not go out of sync, we have used the specific version of torch, torchvision, torchtext, torchaudio with PyTorch Lightning 1.5.2. You can also use the latest version of PyTorch Lightning and torch compatible with each other. More details can be found on the GitHub link: `https://github.com/PacktPublishing/Deep-Learning-with-PyTorch-Lightning`

```
!pip install torch==1.10.0 torchvision==0.11.1
torchtext==0.11.0 torchaudio==0.10.0 --quiet
!pip install pytorch-lightning==1.5.2 --quiet
```

You can refer to *Chapter 1, PyTorch Lightning Adventure*, if you need any help regarding the importing of packages.

The working examples for this chapter can be found at this GitHub link: `https://github.com/PacktPublishing/Deep-Learning-with-PyTorch-Lightning/tree/main/Chapter03` Here are links to the source datasets:

1. For image classification, we will use the same dataset that we used in *Chapter 2, Getting off the Ground with the First Deep Learning Model*. You can download the dataset from Kaggle or directly from the PCam website: `https://www.kaggle.com/c/histopathologic-cancer-detection`.
2. For the text classification case, we will make use of the public health claims dataset. This dataset is made available under an MIT license: `https://huggingface.co/datasets/health_fact`.

This dataset consists of a collection of 12,288 posts from various fact-checking, news review, and news websites.

Getting started with transfer learning

Transfer learning has many interesting applications, with one of the most fascinating being converting an image into the style of a famous painter, such as Van Gogh or Picasso.

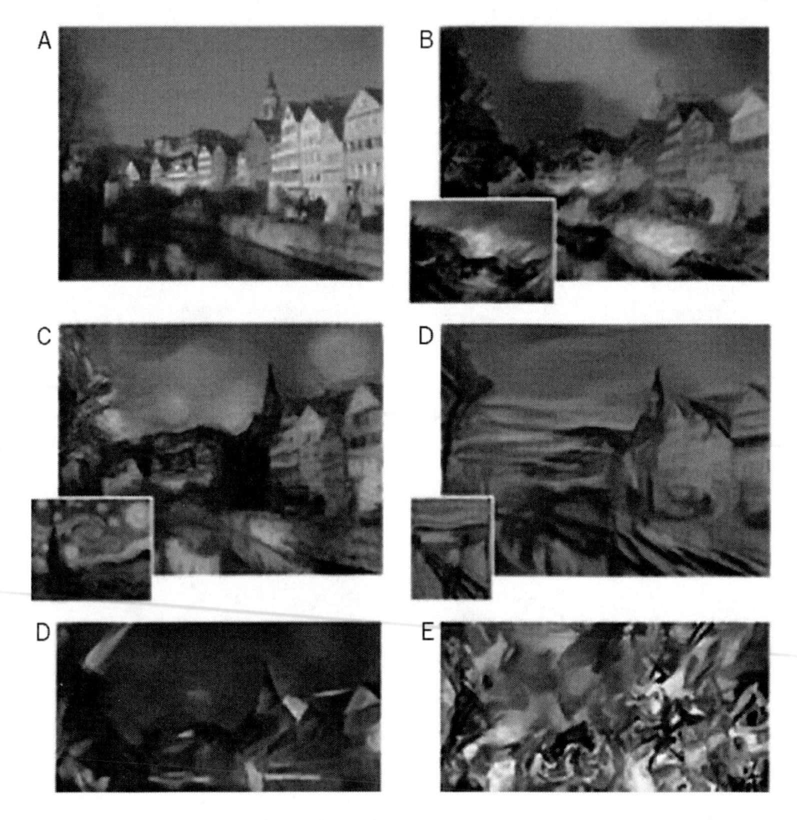

Figure 3.1 – Image credit: A neural algorithm of artistic style (https://arxiv.org/pdf/1508.06576v2.pdf)

The preceding example is also known as **Style Transfer**. There are many specialized algorithms for accomplishing this task, and VGG-16, ResNet, and AlexNet are some of the more popular architectures.

In this chapter, we will start with the creation of a simple image classification model using ResNet-50 architecture on the PCam dataset, which contains image scans of cancer tissues. Later, we will build a text classification model that uses **Bi-directional Encoder Representations from Transformers** (**BERT**).

In both examples in this chapter, we will make use of a pre-trained model and its weights and fine-tune the model to make it work for our dataset. One great advantage of a pre-trained model is that since it has already been trained on a vast dataset, we can get good results in a smaller number of epochs.

Any model that uses transfer learning typically follows this structure:

1. Access the pre-trained model.
2. Configure the pre-trained model.
3. Build the model.
4. Train the model.
5. Evaluate the model's performance.

If you have previously worked with `torch` and have built Deep Learning models using transfer learning, you will see the similarities to working with PyTorch Lightning. The only difference is that we will make use of PyTorch Lightning life cycle methods, which make things even simpler and easier.

An image classifier using a pre-trained ResNet-50 architecture

ResNet-50 stands for **Residual Network**, which is a type of CNN architecture that was first published in a computer vision research paper entitled *Deep Residual Learning for Image Recognition*, by Kaiming He, Xiangyu Zhang, Shaoqing Ren, and Jian Sun, in 2015.

ResNet is currently the most popular architecture for image-related tasks. While it certainly works great on image classification problems (which we will see as follows), it works equally great as an encoder to learn image representations for more complex tasks such as Self-Supervised Learning. There are multiple variations of ResNet architecture, including ResNet-18, ResNet-34, ResNet-50, and ResNet-152 based on the number of deep layers it has.

The ResNet-50 architecture has 50 deep layers and is trained on the ImageNet dataset, which has 14 million images belonging to 1,000 different classes, including animals, cars, keyboards, mice, pens, and pencils. The following is the architecture for ResNet-50:

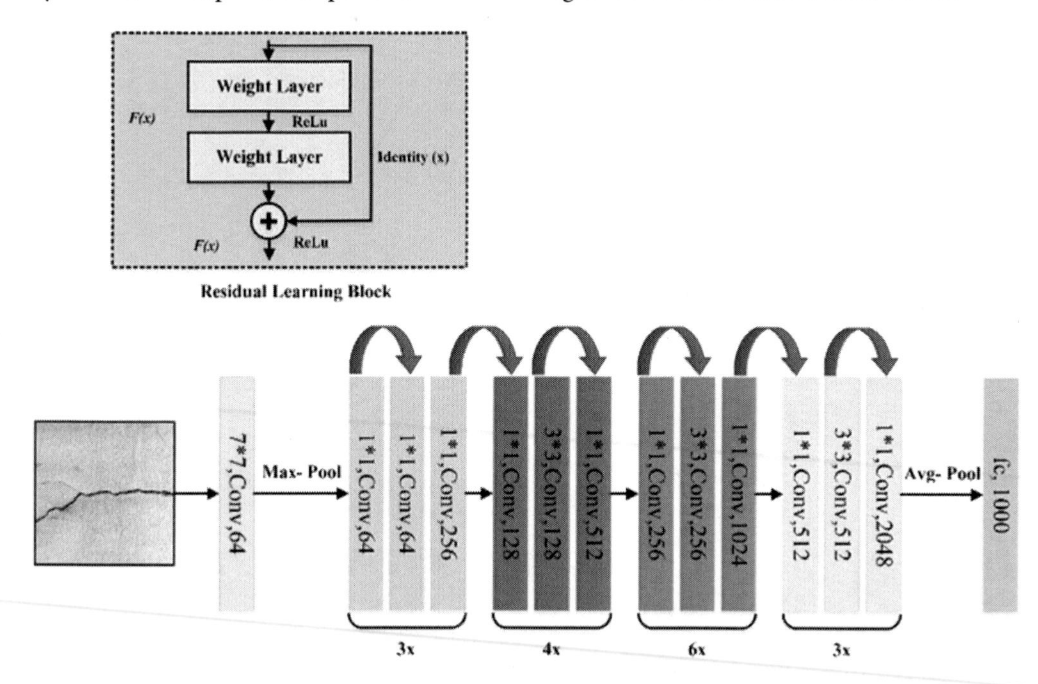

Figure 3.2 – VGG-16 architecture (Image credit: VGG-16 paper)

In the ResNet-50 model architecture, there are 48 convolution layers along with 1 AvgPool layer and 1 MaxPool layer.

The ResNet-50 model on ImageNet has been trained for several weeks in its compute process. Again, a fantastic benefit of transfer learning, as mentioned in the introduction, is that we don't need to train the model from scratch; rather, we can simply use the weights of the model and bootstrap the whole process.

In this section, we will use the ResNet-50 pre-trained model. We will configure it to process and train our PCam image dataset. Building our image classifier using the pre-trained ResNet-50 model will essentially entail the same basic steps that were detailed previously:

1. Preparing the data
2. Building the model
3. Training the model
4. Evaluating the accuracy of the model

Let's go through these steps in the following sub-sections. Before executing any code, please install the correct version of PyTorch Lightning and `opendatasets` (for instructions, refer to *Chapter 2, Getting off the Ground with the First Deep Learning Model*, in the *Collecting the dataset* section).

Preparing the data

There are different ways to handle and process datasets in PyTorch Lightning. One way is to use PyTorch Lightning's `DataModule`. Now, `DataModule` is a good way of processing and structuring data. You can create `DataModule` by inheriting the `DataModule` class from the PyTorch Lightning module. One advantage of using this module is that it comes with some life cycle methods. These can help us with different phases of data preparation, such as loading the data, processing it, and setting up the training, validation, and test `DataLoader` instances.

PyTorch Lightning's DataLoader expects the images to be in their respective subfolders, so we need to pre-process the data before feeding it into the `DataLoader` instances. We will create a custom `LoadCancerDataset` for the purpose of pre-processing the dataset, which we will see in a later section.

Extracting the dataset

Here, we are again using the PCam dataset for histopathological cancer detection that we used in *Chapter 2, Getting off the Ground with the First Deep Learning Model*. The **PatchCamelyon (PCam)** dataset for histopathological cancer detection consists of 327,680 color images (96 x 96px) extracted from histopathological scans of lymph node sections. Each image is annotated with a binary label indicating the presence of metastatic tissue. More information about the dataset can be found here: `https://www.kaggle.com/c/histopathologic-cancer-detection`.

The following are some sample images from the PCam dataset:

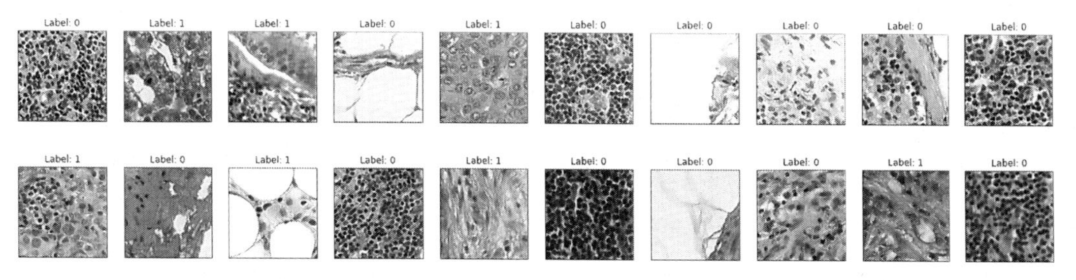

Figure 3.3 – 20 sample images with labels from the PCam dataset

We are going to re-use the code from *Chapter 2, Getting off the Ground with the First Deep Learning Model*, to load the dataset. Please refer to the *Collecting the dataset* section for instructions on how to collect the dataset.

Once the dataset is collected, we can start the process of loading the dataset.

We first need to extract the labels for the images that were selected in the down-sampled data, as shown here:

```
selected_image_labels = pd.DataFrame()
id_list = []
label_list = []

for img in selected_image_list:
  label_tuple = cancer_labels.loc[cancer_labels['id'] == img.
split('.')[0]]
  id_list.append(label_tuple['id'].values[0])
  label_list.append(label_tuple['label'].values[0])
```

In the preceding code, we are creating an empty data frame called `selected_image_labels` and two empty lists called `id_list` and `image_list` to store the image ID and corresponding labels. We are then looping over `selected_image_list` and adding the image ID to `id_list` as well as the label to `label_list`. Finally, we will add the two lists, `id_list` and `label_list`, as columns to the `selected_image_labels` data frame, as shown here:

```
selected_image_labels['id'] = id_list
selected_image_labels['label'] = label_list
selected_image_labels.head()
```

	id	label
0	a31e99f1b06d1ed5f9f0306a1d453385659ab32b	0
1	c8d9799680419ede996570d7610da43136da6e7d	1
2	568b66ad4616f94d204b6df2ab15289b4af76976	1
3	f3509bad70373d29ec2c4d7221d4e7ef4f0f97a5	0
4	ee33ffaf0ec4d1a3c71d92a7d926266cc56c5180	1

Figure 3.4 – Image label verification

The dataset is now ready to be loaded into the Dataloader.

Pre-processing the dataset

Now we need to create a dictionary with labels and IDs that will be used in our `LoadCancerDataset` class:

```
img_class_dict = {k:v for k, v in zip(selected_image_labels.id,
selected_image_labels.label)}
```

The preceding code extracts the ID and labels from the `selected_image_labels` data frame and stores them in the `img_class_dict` dictionary.

The final step before creating our custom `LoadCancerDataset` class is to define the transformer, as shown here:

```
data_T_train = T.Compose([
    T.Resize(224),
    T.RandomHorizontalFlip(),
    T.ToTensor()
    ])
data_T_test = T.Compose([
    T.Resize(224),
    T.ToTensor()
    ])
```

In the preceding code, we are defining train and test transformers using the `torchvision transform` module. The `data_T_train` transformer resizes the train images to 224 pixels from the original size of 96 pixels since the ResNet-50 model expects the images to be 224 pixels. We are also augmenting the training images by using the `RandomHorizontalFlip` function, which adds an additional image to the training dataset. Finally, the transformer is converting the image to tensors. The `data_T_test` transformer carries out a similar transformation for the test dataset.

The dataset is now ready to be loaded into the Dataloader.

Loading the dataset

After completing all the data pre-processing steps, we are ready to create our custom `LoadCancerDataset` class for preparing the data to be loaded using the DataLoader instances:

```
class LoadCancerDataset(Dataset):
    def __init__(self, datafolder,
```

```
                 transform = T.Compose([T.CenterCrop(32),T.
ToTensor()]), labels_dict={}):
        self.datafolder = datafolder
        self.image_files_list = [s for s in
os.listdir(datafolder)]
        self.transform = transform
        self.labels_dict = labels_dict
        self.labels = [labels_dict[i.split('.')[0]] for i in
self.image_files_list]

    def __len__(self):
        return len(self.image_files_list)

    def __getitem__(self, idx):
        img_name = os.path.join(self.datafolder, self.image_
files_list[idx])
        image = Image.open(img_name)
        image = self.transform(image)
        img_name_short = self.image_files_list[idx].split('.')
[0]

        label = self.labels_dict[img_name_short]
        return image, label
```

In the preceding code, we have the following:

- The custom class defined here inherits from the `torch.utils.data.Dataset` module. The custom `LoadCancerDataset` class is initialized in `the __init__` method and accepts three arguments: the path to the `data` folder, the transformer with a default value of cropping the image to size 32, and transforming it to a tensor and a dictionary with the labels and IDs of the dataset.
- `LoadCancerDataset` reads all the images in the folder and extracts the image name from the filename, which is also the ID for the images.
- This image name is then matched with the label in the dictionary with the labels and IDs. `LoadCancerDataset` returns the images and their labels, which can then be used in the `DataLoader` module of `torch.utils.data` as it can now read the images with their corresponding labels.

We will now call instances of `LoadCancerDataset` to load the training and test datasets, as shown here:

```
cancer_train_set = LoadCancerDataset(datafolder='/
content/gdrive/My Drive/Colab Notebooks/histopathologic-
cancer-detection/train_dataset/',
                                transform=data_T_train, labels_
dict=img_class_dict)
cancer_test_set = LoadCancerDataset(datafolder='/content/
gdrive/My Drive/Colab Notebooks/histopathologic-cancer-
detection/test_dataset/',
                                transform=data_T_test, labels_
dict=img_class_dict)
```

We are passing the three required arguments to our `LoadCancerDataset` class to create `cancer_train_set` and `cancer_test_set`. The first argument is the Google Drive persistent storage path that we created earlier to store the training and test images. The second argument is the transformer that we created in the previous step, and finally, there is the dictionary with the labels and IDs of the images.

After this pre-processing, we are now ready to call instances of the `DataLoader` module, which we have used extensively in the majority of chapters:

```
batch_size = 128

cancer_train_dataloader = DataLoader(cancer_train_set,
batch_size, num_workers=2, pin_memory=True, shuffle=True)
cancer_test_dataloader = DataLoader(cancer_test_set,
batch_size, num_workers=2, pin_memory=True)
```

As shown in the preceding code, we are setting the batch size to be 128 and then creating train and test data loaders called `cancer_train_dataloader` and `cancer_test_dataloader`, respectively, using the `DataLoader` module, which takes the output of our custom `LoadCancerDataset` class as the input here along with the batch size (128), the number of workers (2), and with automatic memory pinning (`pin_memory`) set to `True`, which enables rapid data transfer to CUDA-enabled GPUs.

At this point, we are ready with our `cancer_train_dataloader` loader, with around 8,000 images, and our `cancer_test_dataloader` loader, with around 2,000 images. All the images are 224 x 224 in size, converted to a tensor form, and served in batches of 128 images. We will use `cancer_train_dataloader` to train our model, and `cancer_test_dataloader` to measure our model's accuracy.

To summarize, we are first carrying out data engineering steps to download, downsample, and store the data. Then, we are pre-processing the data to make it ready for the `DataLoader` module, and then using the `DataLoader` module to create a training and test dataloader for the PCam dataset.

Building the model

As seen in the previous chapter, any model we build in PyTorch Lightning must be inherited from the `Lightning Module` class. Let's start by creating a class named `CancerImageClassifier`:

```
class CancerImageClassifier(pl.LightningModule):
```

The ResNet-50 model is trained on a different dataset. To make the model work on the PCam dataset, we need to make some configurations and adjustments to the ResNet-50 model, which is done in the model initialization method.

As mentioned earlier, in the ResNet-50 model architecture, there are 48 convolution layers, and after the convolution layers, there is a MaxPool layer and an AvgPool layer. In the previous chapter, we worked with only 2 or 3 convolution layers, so with this architecture having 50 convolution layers, it makes it much denser.

You can read the full implementation of the architecture for ResNet-50 on the GitHub page for the book under the name `ResNet50.txt`, as well as on PyTorch.

In the preceding ResNet-50 architecture, there are several convolution layers, followed by a MaxPool layer and an AvgPool layer. The final classifier layer gives an output of `1000` since this model was built to classify 1,000 classes, but for our use case of training a model using the PCam dataset, we only need 2 classes.

Changes to the ResNet-50 model so that it can handle the dataset can be made in the initialization method.

The `init` method takes the learning rate as input with a default value of `0.001`, and we are using the `CrossEntropyloss` function to compute the cross-entropy loss between the input and target, as shown here:

```
    def __init__(self, learning_rate = 0.001):
        super().__init__()

        self.learning_rate = learning_rate
        self.loss = nn.CrossEntropyLoss()
```

While doing transfer learning, it is important to freeze the weights for the existing layers to avoid backpropagation and re-training since we are going to leverage the existing trained model. The ResNet-50 model has already been trained on millions of images and we can leverage the existing weights for our dataset, so we are freezing the weights, as shown here:

```
self.pretrain_model = resnet50(pretrained=True)
        self.pretrain_model.eval()
        for param in self.pretrain_model.parameters():
            param.requires_grad = False
```

In the preceding code, we are first loading the ResNet-50 model as `pretrain_model`, which was imported from the `torchvision.models` library. Then we are changing the mode to evaluation mode, using the eval method to set the dropout and batch normalization layers to evaluation mode. Then, we are iterating through each model's parameters and setting the `required_grad` value to `False` to ensure that the current weights for the ResNet-50 model will not be changed.

Now we need to change the final layer of the ResNet-50 model so that we can classify the two categories in the PCam dataset, while the ResNet-50 model was built to effect classification into 1000 different categories:

```
self.pretrain_model.fc = nn.Linear(2048, 2)
```

Here, we are changing the output of the last linear, which will take 2,048 input features and return 2 probabilities for the 2 different classes of the PCam dataset.

> **Important Note**
>
> The ResNet-50 model, after all of the convolution layers, outputs 2,048 features. The last `Linear` layer gives an output of 2 because our PCam dataset only consists of 2 classes.

Since the model is now ready to accept the PCam dataset, we will pass the data to the model using the `forward` method, as shown here:

```
def forward(self, input):
        output=self.pretrain_model(input)
        return output
```

The `forward` method is a simple function that takes data as the input, passes it to the pre-trained model (ResNet-50 in this case), and returns the output.

We need to configure the optimizer for our `CancerImageClassifier` for which we will override the `configure_optimizer` life cycle method, as shown here:

```
    def configure_optimizers(self):
        params = self.parameters()
        optimizer = optim.Adam(params=params, lr = self.learning_
rate)
        return optimizer
```

The `configure_optimizer` method is setting Adam as the optimizer with the learning rate, as defined in the `__init__` method. This optimizer is then returned by the `configure_optimizers` method as output.

The next step is to define the training step by overriding the life cycle method, as shown here:

```
    def training_step(self, batch, batch_idx):
        inputs, targets = batch
        outputs = self(inputs)
        preds = torch.argmax(outputs, dim=1)
        train_accuracy = accuracy(preds, targets)
        loss = self.loss(outputs, targets)
        self.log('train_accuracy', train_accuracy, prog_bar=True)
        self.log('train_loss', loss)
        return {"loss":loss, "train_accuracy": train_accuracy}
```

The `training_step` method takes the batch and batch index as inputs. Then it stores the predictions for those inputs using the `torch.argmax` method, which returns the indices of the maximum value of all elements in the input tensor. The training accuracy is calculated using the accuracy method from the `torchmetrics.functional` module by passing the predictions and actual targets as the input. Loss is also calculated using the outputs and the actual targets, and then both loss and accuracy are logged. Finally, the `training_step` method returns the training loss and training accuracy, which is helpful in observing the performance of the model during the training step.

This method is repeated for the test dataset, as shown here:

```
    def test_step(self, batch, batch_idx):
        inputs, targets = batch
```

```
        outputs = self.forward(inputs)
        preds = torch.argmax(outputs, dim=1)
        test_accuracy = accuracy(preds, targets)
        loss = self.loss(outputs, targets)
        return {"test_loss":loss, "test_accuracy":test_accuracy}
```

The preceding code block repeats all the processes explained here for the test dataset. The PyTorch Lightning framework takes care of passing the correct data between the `DataLoader` instances defined in `DataModule`; that is, data is passed from `train_DataLoader` in batches to `training_step`, and test data from `test_DataLoader` is passed to `test_step`. Inside the `training_step` method, we are passing input data to the model to calculate and return the `loss` value. The PyTorch Lightning framework takes care of backpropagation. In the test step, we are calculating the `loss` and `accuracy` values using a prebuilt accuracy method from the `torchmetrics.functional` module.

> **Important Note**
>
> The method for calculating accuracy has changed significantly from the previous versions of PyTorch Lightning in the newer versions (1.5+). The `pl.metrics.Accuracy()` function has been deprecated, so we will now use the accuracy method from the `torchmetrics.functional` module to calculate the accuracy. Since this method requires two arguments – predictions and targets, it can no longer be defined in the `__init__` method. This accuracy method is now called inside the `train_step` and `test_step` methods.

The data for both the training and test life cycle methods is passed in batches of 128. So, the model is trained for every 128 batches of data in `train_step`, and accuracy and loss are also calculated for every 128 batches of data in both `train_step` and `test_step`.

Therefore, to calculate the overall accuracy of the entire dataset, we are going to leverage a life cycle method called `test_epoch_end`. The `test_epoch_end` life cycle method is called at the end of a test epoch with the output of all the test steps, as shown here:

```
    def test_epoch_end(self, outputs):
        test_outs = []
        for test_out in outputs:
            out = test_out['test_accuracy']
            test_outs.append(out)
        total_test_accuracy = torch.stack(test_outs).mean()
```

```
        self.log('total_test_accuracy', total_test_accuracy, on_
step=False, on_epoch=True)
        return total_test_accuracy
```

In the `test_epoch_end` method, we are first looping over the output of all the batches and storing them in the `test_outs` list. Then we are concatenating all the tensor outputs of accuracy for individual batches using the `torch.stack()` function, and using the mean method to calculate the total accuracy. This is the recommended way to calculate the test accuracy of the entire test dataset. This approach can also be used to calculate the accuracy of the complete training and validation datasets if required.

Training the model

To train a model, the process is the same as we saw in the previous chapter. The following is the code for training a model using the `trainer` class.

Note that the following code uses a GPU. Please ensure that you have a GPU enabled in your environment to execute it. You can also replace the GPU with a CPU if needed:

```
model = CancerImageClassifier()
trainer = pl.Trainer(max_epochs=10, gpus=-1)
trainer.fit(model, train_dataloaders=cancer_train_dataloader)
```

In the preceding code, we are calling an instance of `CancerImageClassifier` and saving it as the model. Next, we are initializing the trainer class with a maximum of 10 epochs and setting the GPU equal to -1, which is equivalent to using all the available GPUs. Finally, the model and training dataloaders for the PCam dataset are passed into the `fit` method. Pytorch Lightning makes use of the life cycle methods that we defined in the `DataModule` class to access and set up the data and access the `DataLoader` instances for the training and test data.

Figure 3.5 – Training image classifier for the 10 epochs

At this point, our model is being trained for a total of 10 epochs for the PCam dataset.

During the training phase, only the `training_step` life cycle method is being called.

Evaluating the accuracy of the model

Evaluating the accuracy of the model involves measuring how well the model can classify images into two different categories. Accuracy can be measured on the test dataset, as demonstrated by the following code:

```
trainer.test(test_dataloaders=cancer_test_dataloader)
```

This results in the following output:

Figure 3.6 – Model accuracy on the test dataset

Here, our model is being trained for 10 epochs and achieves an accuracy score of 85% on approximately 2,000 test images.

To summarize, first, we started by building the `DataModule` instance with all the required life cycle methods to process and serve the `DataLoader` instances in exactly the same manner as we did in *Chapter 2, Getting off the Ground with the First Deep Learning Model*. Later, we built a model by configuring and adjusting a ResNet-50 pre-trained model to train on the PCam dataset. We trained the model for just 10 epochs on the training dataset and measured the model's performance on the test dataset, where we achieved an accuracy score of 85%, which is much higher than the 500 epochs that we ran in *Chapter 2, Getting off the Ground with the First Deep Learning Model*, and still got lower accuracy. And it is not just that we got a better model; it was much cheaper as well, with less time and compute spent. This should prove the value of transfer learning to you.

Even with just 10 epochs, we could achieve much better results, since transfer learning uses image representations learned from ImageNet. Without those representations, many more epochs and hyperparameter tuning would have been required to attain the accuracy score we did.

Text classification using BERT transformers

Text classification using BERT transformers is a transformer-based machine learning technique for **Natural Language Processing** (**NLP**) developed by Google. BERT was created and published in 2018 by Jacob Devlin. Before BERT, for language tasks, semi-supervised models such as **Recurrent Neural Networks** (**RNNs**) or sequence models were commonly used. BERT was the first unsupervised approach to language models and achieved state-of-the-art performance on NLP tasks. The large BERT model consists of 24 encoders and 16 bi-directional attention heads. It was trained with Book Corpora words and English Wikipedia entries for about 3,000,000,000 words. It later expanded to over 100 languages. Using pre-trained BERT models, we can perform several tasks on text, such as classification, information extraction, question answering, summarization, translation, and text generation.

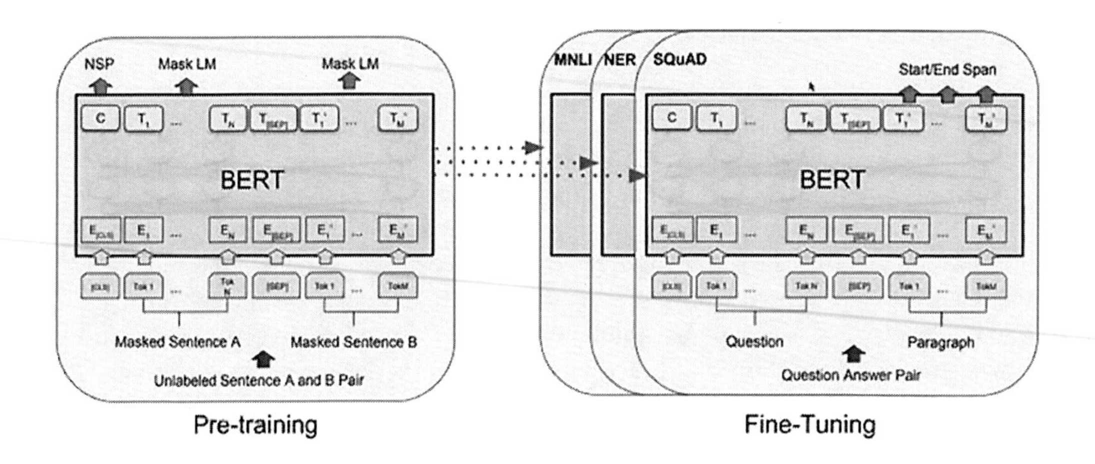

Figure 3.7 – BERT architecture diagram (Image credit: Paper user-generated data: Achilles' heel of BERT)

In this section, we will build our text classification model using a pre-trained BERT model. There are different ways in which to build a model in PyTorch Lightning, and we will cover some different ways and styles of writing models throughout this book. In this section, we will use only the PyTorch Lightning methods to build the model.

Before we get into model building, let's talk about the text data we will be using for our text classifier model. For this exercise, we will use the public health claims dataset. This dataset consists of a collection of 12,288 public health claims from various fact-checking, news review, and news websites. Here is a complete list of the sources from where these public health claims were collected:

URL	Type
http://snopes.com/	fact-checking
http://politifact.com/	fact-checking
http://truthorfiction.com/	fact-checking
https://www.factcheck.org/	fact-checking
https://fullfact.org/	fact-checking
https://apnews.com/	news
https://uk.reuters.com/	news
https://www.healthnewsreview.org/	health news review

Figure 3.8 – List of the sources for public health claims in the dataset

Here is some sample text data from the public health claims dataset regarding an antibody test for coronavirus and its associated label – 2 (true):

main_text (string)	sources (string)	label (class label)	subjects (string)
Antibody tests show whether whether people have been infected with the novel coronavirus and…		2 (true)	Health News
The story did not provide cost estimates for either approach; the story did mention that the…		2 (true)	
As part of President Barack Obama's healthcare reform law, the efforts center around more than…		2 (true)	Health News
The lawsuit brought by Terry Leavitt in Alameda Superior Court in Oakland is the first of over a…	uk.reuters.com/companies/IMTP.PA,uk.reuters.com/companies/JNJ.N	2 (true)	Health News
"The story does not note the cost of a typical statin regimen, Zetia or the combination…		0 (false)	
On 18 March 2016, an image of an opossum was uploaded to Imgur with overlaid text reading as…	http://www.caryinstitute.org/newsroom/opossums-killers-ticks,…	2 (true)	Critter Country, lyme disease, opossum

Figure 3.9 – Sample text data from the public health claims dataset

Our goal here is to use transfer learning techniques and the BERT model to classify text into four different categories – true, false, unproven, and mixture. The following are the steps involved in building our text classification model:

1. Collecting the data
2. Building the model
3. Training the model
4. Evaluating the model

However, before we begin, as we always do; let's get our environment ready.

We will install the following packages:

```
!pip install pytorch-lightning==1.5.2 --quiet
!pip install transformers==3.1.0 --quiet
```

And import them:

```
import torch
from torch import nn, optim
from torch.utils.data import DataLoader
from torch.utils.data import TensorDataset, DataLoader,
RandomSampler, SequentialSampler
import matplotlib.pyplot as plt
%matplotlib inline
import pytorch_lightning as pl
from torchmetrics.functional import accuracy
import transformers
from transformers import BertModel, BertConfig
from transformers import AutoModel, BertTokenizerFast
import pandas as pd
```

Now we are all set.

Collecting the data

We will download the dataset from the Google Drive link, which has been made publicly available:

```
!gdown --id 1eTtRs5cUlBP5dXsx-FTAlmXuB6JQi2qj
!unzip PUBHEALTH.zip
```

This results in the following output:

```
Downloading...
From: https://drive.google.com/uc?id=1eTtRs5cUlBP5dXsx-FTAlmXuB6JQi2qj
To: /content/PUBHEALTH.zip
100% 24.9M/24.9M [00:00<00:00, 60.0MB/s]
Archive:  PUBHEALTH.zip
   creating: PUBHEALTH/
  inflating: PUBHEALTH/train.tsv
  inflating: PUBHEALTH/dev.tsv
  inflating: PUBHEALTH/test.tsv
```

Figure 3.10 – Downloading the dataset

In the preceding code, we are downloading the dataset and then extracting in the Google Colab folder. Now we are going to read the dataset into a pandas dataframe:

```
pub_health_train = pd.read_csv("PUBHEALTH/train.tsv", sep='\t')
pub_health_test = pd.read_csv("PUBHEALTH/test.tsv", sep='\t')
```

Here, we are loading the `train.tsv` and `test.tsv` files into a pandas dataframe named `pub_health_train` and `pub_health_test`.

Preparing the dataset

In the next step, we will validate the labels and check for missing values:

```
pub_health_train = pub_health_train[pub_health_train['label']
!= 'snopes']
pub_health_train = pub_health_train[['main_text','label']]
pub_health_train = pub_health_train.dropna(subset=['main_text',
'label'])
```

We are carrying out the following data processing steps in the preceding code:

- There are only 27 instances where the training data has been classified as `'snopes'` and the test data doesn't contain any such instance, so we have dropped it from the training dataset.
- Then we are selecting only the two columns of interest – 'main text,' which contains the text for the public health claims, and the 'label' column, which represents one of the four classes for the respective public health claim.
- Finally, we will be dropping any row that contains missing values in one of the two columns. We will follow the same steps for the test dataset (the full code is available on GitHub).

	main_text	label
0	"Hillary Clinton is in the political crosshair...	false
1	While the financial costs of screening mammogr...	mixture
2	The news release quotes lead researcher Robert...	mixture
3	The story does discuss costs, but the framing ...	true
4	"Although the story didn't cite the cost of ap...	true

Figure 3.11 – Dataset view after dropping missing values

The classes for the public health claims are false, mixture, true, and unproven. These need to be converted into numbers so that tensors can be created from the list of labels:

```
pub_health_train['label'] = pub_health_train['label'].
map({"true":0, "false":1, "unproven":2, "mixture":3})
pub_health_test['label'] = pub_health_test['label'].
map({"true":0, "false":1, "unproven":2, "mixture":3})
```

Here we are mapping the labels from 0 to 4 to leverage the `prepare_data` life cycle method of PyTorch lightning.

The process of preparing the data may involve loading data, splitting data, transformations, feature engineering, and many other activities to provide better results and, more importantly, to be accepted by the model. So far, we have carried out some data processing steps to extract the relevant data from the raw dataset.

Now, in order to extract features and load the data, we are going to leverage the `prepare_data` life cycle method of the PyTorch Lightning library. This data transformation and any feature engineering can be done outside of our `TextClassifier` class; however, PyTorch Lightning allows us to keep everything in one piece. The `prepare_data` life cycle method is triggered before any training begins; in our case, it's triggered before other life cycle methods, such as `train_dataloader`, `test_dataloader`, `training_step`, and `testing_step`.

In the `prepare_data` method, we begin by initializing `BertTokenizerFast`. The following is the code snippet for this:

```
        tokenizer = BertTokenizerFast.from_pretrained('bert-base-
uncased')

        # tokenize and encode sequences in the training set
        tokens_train = tokenizer.batch_encode_plus(
            pub_health_train["main_text"].tolist(),
            max_length = self.max_seq_len,
            pad_to_max_length=True,
            truncation=True,
            return_token_type_ids=False
        )

        # tokenize and encode sequences in the test set
        tokens_test = tokenizer.batch_encode_plus(
            pub_health_test["main_text"].tolist(),
            max_length = self.max_seq_len,
            pad_to_max_length=True,
            truncation=True,
            return_token_type_ids=False
        )
```

In the preceding code, we started by initializing the tokenizer from the BertTokenizerFast module for our BERT model and storing it as the tokenizer object. Then, we are tokenizing the main_text column in both the pub_health_train and pub_health_test datasets using the tokenizer object. The batch_encode_plus method of the tokenizer returns an object that has input_ids and attention_mask. input_ids and attention_mask will be used as features for our text classification model. max_seq_len is passed to truncate any text data above the established maximum sequence length. The pad_to_max_length argument is set to True, which means anything following the maximum sequence length will be padded. The tokens for training and test data are stored as tokens_train and tokens_test, respectively. Now we need to create features and extract the target variable from the dataset. The following code demonstrates this:

```
        self.train_seq = torch.tensor(tokens_train['input_ids'])
        self.train_mask = torch.tensor(tokens_train['attention_
mask'])
        self.train_y = torch.tensor(train_data["label"].tolist())

        self.test_seq = torch.tensor(tokens_test['input_ids'])
        self.test_mask = torch.tensor(tokens_test['attention_
mask'])
        self.test_y = torch.tensor(test_data["label"].tolist())
```

In the preceding code, we are extracting input_ids and attention_mask and storing them as train_seq and train_mask for the training dataset, and test_seq and test_mask for the test dataset. Also, we are creating a target variable, train_y, for the training dataset, and test_y for the test dataset. Now we have all the features and the target required for the model, which will be used in other life cycle methods, which we will go through shortly.

In the prepare_data life cycle method, we are first loading up our public health claims dataset, tokenizing the data, and creating features and the target variable.

Setting up the DataLoader instances

We have completed the data processing steps by loading the data, preparing the features, and extracting the target in the `prepare_data` life cycle method. So, we can now use the `DataLoader` life cycle method to create an instance of `DataLoader` for the training and test datasets. Here is the code snippet for the life cycle methods for creating test and training `DataLoader` instances:

```
def train_dataloader(self):
  train_dataset = TensorDataset(self.train_seq, self.train_
mask, self.train_y)
  self.train_dataloader_obj = DataLoader(train_dataset, batch_
size=self.batch_size)
  return self.train_dataloader_obj

def test_dataloader(self):
  test_dataset = TensorDataset(self.test_seq, self.test_mask,
self.test_y)
  self.test_dataloader_obj = DataLoader(test_dataset, batch_
size=self.batch_size)
  return self.test_dataloader_obj
```

In the preceding code, we have two life cycle methods, `train_dataloader` and `test_dataloader`. In both methods, we are using the `TensorDataset` method on the features and target created in the last step to create `train_data` and `test_data` datasets. Then, we are passing the `train_dataset` and `test_dataset` datasets to create the `train_dataloader_obj` and `test_dataloader` objects using the `DataLoader` module. Both methods return this data loader object when called.

Building the model

By now, you ought to be familiar with the fact that whenever we build a model in PyTorch Lightning, we always create a class that extends/inherits from a Lightning module so that we can get access to the Lightning life cycle methods.

Let's start by creating a class named `HealthClaimClassifier`, as shown here:

```
class HealthClaimClassifier(pl.LightningModule):
```

We will now initialize `HealthClaimClassifier`, as shown here:

```
def __init__(self, max_seq_len=512, batch_size=128, learning_
rate = 0.001):
```

In the preceding code, `HealthClaimClassifier` accepts three input parameters:

- `max_seq_len`: This parameter controls the maximum length of a sequence that a BERT model can handle, in other words, the maximum length of the words to be considered. The default value is set as `512` in this case.
- `batch_size`: The batch size denotes the subset of our training sample, which is going to be used to train the model for each epoch. The default value is `128`.
- `learning_rate`: The learning rate controls how much we are adjusting the weights of our network with respect to the loss gradient. The default value is `0.001`.

> **Important Note**
>
> Any input text *data* that is less than the `max_seq_len` value will be padded, and anything bigger will be trimmed down.

We will now initialize the required variables and objects in the `__init__` method, as shown here:

```
        super().__init__()
        self.learning_rate = learning_rate
        self.max_seq_len = max_seq_len
        self.batch_size = batch_size
        self.loss = nn.CrossEntropyLoss()
```

In the `__init__` method, we are first setting up the inputs – `learning_rate`, `max_seq_len`, and `batch_size`, received by `HealthClaimClassifier`.

Then we are also creating a loss object using the `CrossEntropyLoss` function from the `torch.nn` module. We will discuss how we make use of the `loss` function in a later part of this chapter.

Now, we will set up our BERT model using the following code snippet:

```
self.pretrain_model = AutoModel.from_pretrained('bert-base-uncased')
self.pretrain_model.eval()
for param in self.pretrain_model.parameters():
    param.requires_grad = False
```

In the preceding code snippet, we are first loading the BERT base uncased model as `pretrain_model` using the transformer's `AutoModel` module. Then we are following the same steps as seen in the previous image classification section. So, we are switching the model to evaluation mode and then setting all the model parameters to `false` in order to freeze the existing weights and prevent re-training of the existing layers.

Customizing the input layers

Now we need to adjust the pre-trained model to accept our own custom inputs similar to what we did in the `CancerImageClassifier` module. This can be done in the `__init__` method, as shown in the following code:

```
self.new_layers = nn.Sequential(
            nn.Linear(768, 512),
            nn.ReLU(),
            nn.Dropout(0.2),
            nn.Linear(512,4),
            nn.LogSoftmax(dim=1)
        )
```

The pre-trained BERT model returns an output of size 768, so we need to adjust the size parameter. To do so, we are creating a sequence layer in the preceding code that consists of two linear layers, the `ReLU` and `LogSoftmax` activation functions, and dropout.

The first linear layer accepts an input of size 768, which is the output size of the pre-trained BERT model, and returns an output of size 512.

Then, the second linear layer takes in the output from the first layer of size 512 and returns an output of 4, which is the total number of classes in the public health claims dataset.

This is the end of the `init` methods for our text classifier. To recap, there are three main aspects:

- We started by setting up the required parameters and the loss object.
- Then, we initialized the pre-trained BERT model in evaluation mode and froze the existing weights.
- Finally, we made some adjustments to the pre-trained model by creating a sequential layer that works with the BERT model to return the output of size 4 for 4 different categories of the public health claims available in the dataset.

Now we need to connect the pre-trained BERT model with our sequential layer so that the model returns an output of size 4. The input data must first go through the pre-trained BERT model and then on to our sequential layer. We can use the `forward` life cycle method to connect these two models. We have already seen the `forward` method in the previous section and the previous chapters, and this is the best way of doing it, so we will continue to use it throughout the book.

The following is the code snippet for the `forward` method:

```
    def forward(self, encode_id, mask):
        _, output= self.pretrain_model(encode_id, attention_
mask=mask)
        output = self.new_layers(output)
        return output
```

In the preceding `forward` method, `encode_id` and `mask`, extracted in the tokenize step of the `prepare_data` life cycle method, are used as input data. They are first passed to the pre-trained BERT model and then to our sequential layers. The `forward` method returns the output from the final sequential layer.

Setting up model training and testing

As you ought to be familiar with by now, we are again going to use the `training_step` life cycle method to train our model, as shown in the following code block:

```
    def training_step(self, batch, batch_idx):
        encode_id, mask, targets = batch
        outputs = self(encode_id, mask)
        preds = torch.argmax(outputs, dim=1)
        train_accuracy = accuracy(preds, targets)
        loss = self.loss(outputs, targets)
        self.log('train_accuracy', train_accuracy, prog_bar=True,
on_step=False, on_epoch=True)
        self.log('train_loss', loss, on_step=False, on_
epoch=True)
        return {"loss":loss, 'train_accuracy': train_accuracy}
```

In the preceding `training_step` method, it takes a batch and batch index as input. Then, the features – `encode_id` and `mask` – as well as targets, are passed to the model and the outputs are stored. Then, the `preds` object is created to get the predictions from the outputs using the `torch.argmax` function. Also, training accuracy is calculated for individual batches using the `accuracy` function from the `torchmetrics.functional` module. Besides accuracy, loss is also calculated by means of the **cross-entropy** `loss` function. Both accuracy and loss are logged in each epoch.

> **Important Note**
> In `training_step`, we are calculating the accuracy for individual batches; this accuracy does not relate to the complete dataset.

Setting up model testing

Similarly, we will again be using the `test_step` life cycle method to evaluate the model. The test data from the `DataLoader` test will be accessed for this method. The accuracy or loss calculated in this step will only relate to the particular batch since the `test_step` method accepts batches of data from the `DataLoader` instances. Therefore, the overall accuracy of the entire test dataset will not be calculated in this step. As shown in the previous section, we will make use of the life cycle method called `test_epoch_end` to calculate the accuracy of the complete test dataset. This method is called at the end of a test epoch with the output of all the test steps:

```
def test_step(self, batch, batch_idx):
    encode_id, mask, targets = batch
    outputs = self.forward(encode_id, mask)
    preds = torch.argmax(outputs, dim=1)
    test_accuracy = accuracy(preds, targets)
    loss = self.loss(outputs, targets)
    return {"test_loss":loss, "test_accuracy":test_accuracy}
```

In the preceding code snippet, the following applies:

- Test data is passed in batches to the model and accuracy is calculated using the `torchmetrics.functional.accuracy` method, while loss is calculated using the cross-entropy `loss` function; the loss and accuracy are returned.
- Here, we have access to the test data in batches, so accuracy and loss are calculated for each batch. To compute the accuracy of the entire test dataset, we may need to wait for the test dataset to be processed. This can be achieved using a life cycle method called `test_epoch_end`.

- The `test_epoch_end` life cycle method is triggered after all the data is processed in the `test_step` life cycle method. The following is the code for the `test_epoch_end` method:

```
    def test_epoch_end(self, outputs):
        test_outs = []
        for test_out in outputs:
            out = test_out['test_accuracy']
            test_outs.append(out)
        total_test_accuracy = torch.stack(test_outs).mean()
        self.log('total_test_accuracy', total_test_
accuracy, on_step=False, on_epoch=True)
        return total_test_accuracy
```

As explained in the previous image classification section of this chapter, we are using the `test_epoch_end` life cycle method to calculate total accuracy.

Training the model

We will again use the same process to train the model as we have used in the previous section and the previous chapter. Here is the code snippet for training the model:

```
model = HealthClaimClassifier()
trainer = pl.Trainer(max_epochs=10, gpus=-1)
trainer.fit(model)
```

Here, we are calling an instance of `HealthClaimClassifier` as the model and then initializing the trainer from PyTorch Lightning. The maximum number of epochs is restricted to 10 and we are setting `gpu` equal to `-1` to use all the GPUs available on the machine. Finally, we are passing the model to the `fit` method to train the model. PyTorch Lightning internally makes use of life cycle methods, including the `DataModule` instance we created earlier. The series of life cycle methods triggered in the `fit` method are as follows: `prepare_data`, `train_dataloader`, and `training_step`.

```
LOCAL_RANK: 0 - CUDA_VISIBLE_DEVICES: [0]

  | Name           | Type             | Params
------------------------------------------------------
0 | loss           | CrossEntropyLoss | 0
1 | pretrain_model | BertModel        | 109 M
2 | new_layers     | Sequential       | 395 K
------------------------------------------------------
395 K     Trainable params
109 M     Non-trainable params
109 M     Total params
439.512   Total estimated model params size (MB)
Epoch 9: 100% 77/77 [06:19<00:00, 4.92s/it, loss=0.854, v_num=0, train_accuracy=0.636]
```

Figure 3.12 – Training a text classifier for 10 epochs

We have now trained our `HealthClaimClassifier` built using the pre-trained BERT model for 10 epochs. The next step is to evaluate the model on the test dataset.

Evaluating the model

We will invoke the `test_step` life cycle method to measure the accuracy of the model on the test dataset using the following code:

```
trainer.test()
```

The following sequence of life cycle methods is triggered when the test method from the trainer class is invoked: `prepare_data`, `test_dataloader`, `test_step`, and then `test_epoch_end`. In the last step, `test_epoch_end` calculates the total accuracy of the test dataset, which is shown here:

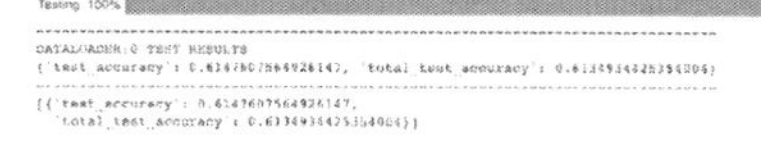

Figure 3.13 – Text classifier accuracy of the complete test dataset

We can observe that we have been able to achieve 61% accuracy on the testing dataset with just 10 epochs and without any hyperparameter tuning. A model improvement exercise on `HealthClaimClassifier` might even help us in getting much better accuracy with the pre-trained BERT model.

To recap, we have built a text classifier model from the BERT transformers model using transfer learning. Also, we have used PyTorch Lightning life cycle methods for loading data, processing data, setting up data loaders, and setting up training and test steps. Everything has been achieved within the `HealthClaimClassifier` class using PyTorch Lightning methods, without much data processing outside of the `HealthClaimClassifier` class.

Summary

Transfer learning is one of the most common ways used to cut compute costs, save time, and get the best results. In this chapter, we learned how to build models with ResNet-50 and pre-trained BERT architectures using PyTorch Lightning.

We have built an image classifier and a text classifier, and along the way, we have covered some useful PyTorch Lightning life cycle methods. We have learned how to make use of pre-trained models to work on our customized datasets with less effort and a smaller number of training epochs. Even with very little model tuning, we were able to achieve decent accuracy.

While transfer learning methods work great, their limitations should also be borne in mind. They work incredibly well for language models because the given dataset's text is usually made up of the same English words as in your core training set. When the core training set is very different from your given dataset, performance suffers. For example, if you want to build an image classifier to identify honeybees and the ImageNet dataset does not have honeybees in it, the accuracy of your transfer learning model will be weaker. You may need to go for a full training option.

We will continue our journey in PyTorch Lightning in the next chapter by looking at another cool framework feature, **PyTorch Lightning Flash**, where we will make use of out-of-the-box model architecture for specific tasks. The majority of such complex tasks, such as text or image classification, are pre-coded and available with zero coding effort required. These out-of-the-box models constitute another important tool that is available to data scientists so that they can reuse other Deep Learning algorithms as a black box and avoid unnecessary coding complexities.

4
Ready-to-Cook Models from Lightning Flash

Building a **Deep Learning** (**DL**) model often involves recreating existing architectures or experiments from top-notch research papers in the field. For example, **AlexNet** was the winning **Convolutional Neural Network** (**CNN**) architecture in 2012 for the **ImageNet** computer vision challenge. Many data scientists have recreated that architecture for their business applications or built newer and better algorithms based on it. It is a common practice to reuse existing experiments on your data before conducting your own experiments. Doing so typically involves either reading the original research paper to code it or tapping into the author's GitHub page to gain an understanding of what's what, which are both time-consuming options. What if the most popular architectures and experiments in DL were easily available for executing various common DL tasks as part of a framework? Meet PyTorch Lightning Flash!

Flash provides out-of-the-box capabilities to recreate popular DL architectures such as image classification, speech recognition, and forecasting on tabular data for quick experimentation, prototyping, and bootstrapping your model baseline. The pre-defined collection of out-of-the-box tasks is quite rich and spans various domains. Within image problems, it provides boilerplate code for multiple image tasks such as segmentation, object detection, style transfer, and video classification. Within NLP, Flash also offers rich out-of-the-box capabilities for doing summarization, classification, question answering, and translation. Data scientists can also easily use standard datasets for training models (such as MNIST and ImageNet) and can further retrain their models using existing architectures with easy-to-use GPU, CPU, and TPU options. Flash also enables an easier approach for carrying out new research by giving the output of one model as the input to another. Flash is not limited to only DL models but also works on traditional **Machine Learning** (**ML**) tasks on tabular/CSV datasets, such as time-series forecasting problems or multi-class classification.

In this chapter, we will see how quick and easy it is to build your own DL models using Flash. It provides the highest level of abstraction to create baseline models for common DL tasks with minimalist coding. It is a great tool for beginners in the field as well as practitioners to do quick experimentation with popular architectures.

We will take in a brief introduction to some of the most commonly used tasks, such as speech recognition and video classification, as well as the latest DL architectures, such as wav2vec. We will see how to get results using some popular experimentation datasets as well as our own ones. This chapter should help you become acquainted with Flash and show you how to use complex DL architectures without bothering about understanding the underlying algorithmic complexity. This should prepare you for solving more advanced problems (such as GAN or semi-supervised learning) that we will see in subsequent chapters.

In this chapter, we will cover the following use cases:

- Video classification using Bolts
- Automatic speech recognition using Bolts

Technical requirements

The code for this chapter has been developed and tested on a macOS with Anaconda or in Google Colab and with Python 3.6. If you are using another environment, please make appropriate changes to your environment variables.

In this chapter, we will primarily be using the following Python modules, mentioned with their versions:

- PyTorch Lightning (version 1.5.10)
- Flash (version 0.7.1)
- Seaborn (version 0.11.2)
- NumPy (version 1.21.5)
- Torch (version 1.10.0)
- pandas (version 1.3.5)

Working examples for this chapter can be found at this GitHub link: `https://github.com/PacktPublishing/Deep-Learning-with-PyTorch-Lightning/tree/main/Chapter04`.

The source datasets can be found at the **Kinetics 400 dataset source**: `https://deepmind.com/research/open-source/kinetics`.

This is the video classification dataset that has been created by DeepMind by scraping YouTube videos. The kinetics dataset was made available by Google Inc. and is one of the most commonly used datasets for benchmarking.

Getting started with Lightning Flash

Imagine you are in the mood to eat Indian food. There are various ways you can go about cooking it. You can get all the veggies, the flour to make dough, and the all-important spices, which you then crush in the right quantities one by one. Once ready, you can cook it by following the proper process. Needless to say, doing so requires immense knowledge of spices and which one goes into which curry, in what quantity, in what sequence, and how long it needs to be cooked.

If you think you are not so much of an expert, the second option is to use ready-to-use spices (such as chicken tikka masala or biryani masala) and just add them to your raw ingredients and cook them. While this definitely simplifies cooking than the first step, this still requires a bit of cooking, but without worrying too much about the nitty-gritty, you can still get good results.

But even the second option is a bit time-consuming, and if you want to get it quickly, then you can try a "ready-to-cook" meal and heat it up by mixing it with rice or onions and adjusting the spice level as needed. Unsurprisingly, the quickest result comes from the third option, which is a bit like Lightning Flash.

Lightning Flash, as the name indicates, is the quickest way to get your DL model ready. It's the highest level of abstraction in terms of coding on PyTorch. If coding in PyTorch is like making your meal from scratch, then PyTorch Lightning itself is an abstraction layer akin to using ready-made spices to quickly make your meal. Lightning Flash is an even higher abstraction than PyTorch Lightning. It's like a bunch of meals ready on the shelf, which you can pick and choose and then quickly eat.

Lightning Flash comes with a variety of tasks that span the majority of popular DL applications. It comes with simple hooks for loading data along with access to most of the popular datasets and proven network architectures. It's an especially attractive option for industry practitioners who want to rely on the best architectures from academia to get started. It serves as the baseline model for rapid prototyping and generating a baseline model.

Lightning Flash is community-built, and the list of tasks supported out of the box keeps growing. At the moment, it supports the following:

- Image and video tasks for segmentation, classification, object detection, keypoint detection, instance segmentation, style transfer, and so on
- Audio tasks for speech recognition and classification
- Tabular data classification and time-series forecasting
- NLP tasks for classification, question answering, summarization, and translation
- Graph learning tasks for classification

In this chapter, we will see how to use Flash for some of the tasks.

Flash is as simple as 1-2-3

We started the book by creating the first DL model in the form of CNN. We then used transfer learning to see that we can get higher accuracy by using representations learned on popular datasets and train models even quicker. Lightning Flash takes it to another level by providing a standardized framework for you to quickly access all the pre-trained model architectures as well as some popular datasets.

Using Flash means writing some of the most minimal forms of code to train a DL model. In fact, a simple Flash model can be as lightweight as five lines of code.

Once the libraries are imported, we only have to perform three basic steps:

1. **Supply your data**: Create a data module to provide data to the framework:

```
datamodule = yourData.from_json(
    "yourFile",
    "text",
```

2. **Define your task and backbone**: Now, it's time to define what you want to do with the data. You can select from the various tasks listed previously (classification, segmentation, and so on). For each task, there is a list of backbones – that is, some predefined network architectures that are available to choose from. Such a backbone provides your convolution layers out of the box:

```
model = SomeRecogntion(backbone="somemodelarchitecture/
ResNET50")
```

3. **Fine-tune the model**: Now, you are all set to train the model using the `trainer` class and fine-tuning on your dataset. As we saw in previous chapter, all the nice goodies to control training (epochs and GPU options) are available for you to manage training:

```
trainer = flash.Trainer(max_epochs=1, gpus=torch.cuda.
device_count())
trainer.finetune(model, datamodule=datamodule,
strategy="no_freeze")
```

Voila! You are done! The next step is to do the predictions.

Instead of looking at what coding in Flash includes, it is important to note what it excludes. It excludes the complications of defining convolution layers, fully connected layers and softmax layers, an optimizer, learning rate, and so on. All these are hidden away behind the wall of abstraction when we select the backbone. This is why Flash makes it so easy and fast to build DL models.

Now, it is possible to switch the dataset and pass your data to the data module. It is also possible to select from a wide list of architecture. We will try doing both one by one. We will first train a video classification model by swapping it for a different architecture. Later, we will train an audio speech recognition model by swapping the dataset.

Before we begin, it is also important to understand that there is no such thing as a free lunch; while Flash provides the highest and easiest level of abstraction, the same characteristic limits its flexibility. It is best suited for pre-defined tasks and may not be the ideal option if you want to perform other tasks, create a new architecture, or train the model from scratch.

To come back to our cooking analogy, there is little control over the taste that you get from ready-to-cook meals. However, since it is built on PyTorch Lightning, there is complete backward compatibility to it as well as to PyTorch. In terms of ease and control, perhaps PyTorch Lightning is the golden means to perform new modeling and is the recommended option for advanced use cases, whereas if you want to be a master chef for DL, then you can always go further with PyTorch. Nevertheless, Flash is an excellent way to get started, so let's get going with our first model!

Video classification using Flash

Video classification is one of the most interesting yet challenging problems in DL. Simply speaking, it tries to classify an action in a video clip and recognize it (such as walking, bowling, or golfing):

Figure 4.1 – The Kinetics human action video dataset released by DeepMind is comprised of annotated ~10-second video clips sourced from YouTube

Training such a DL model is a challenging problem because of the sheer amount of compute power it takes to train the model, given the large size of video files compared to tabular or image data. Using a pre-trained model and architecture is a great way to start your experiments for video classification.

PyTorch Lightning Flash relies internally on the `PyTorchVideo` library for its backbone. `PyTorchVideo` caters to the ecosystem of video understanding. Lightning Flash makes it easy by creating the predefined and configurable hooks into the underlying framework. There are hooks for tasks of video classification, which you can use without being overwhelmed by the nitty-gritty of defining the network layers, optimizers, or loss functions. Additionally, there is a large number of SOTA architectures available to choose from Model Zoo, released by Facebook AI. Model Zoo contains benchmarks for video tasks for various SOTA model architectures.

In this section, we will be using the Kinetics 400 dataset and will then try different video classification architectures out of the box to fine-tune the model.

> **Important Note – Model Zoo**
>
> The complete Model Zoo for PyTorch video can be accessed here along with its benchmark: `https://github.com/facebookresearch/pytorchvideo/blob/main/docs/source/model_zoo.md`. Model Zoo is provided by the Facebook AI Research team and contains links to the pre-trained model in case you need to override hooks provided by Lightning Flash.

Slow and SlowFast architecture

SlowFast is a widely used model architecture for video classification. It basically consists of two pathways, slow and fast, for video classification. It was first proposed by Facebook AI Research in the paper *SlowFast Networks for Video Recognition* by Christoph Feichtenhofer et al:

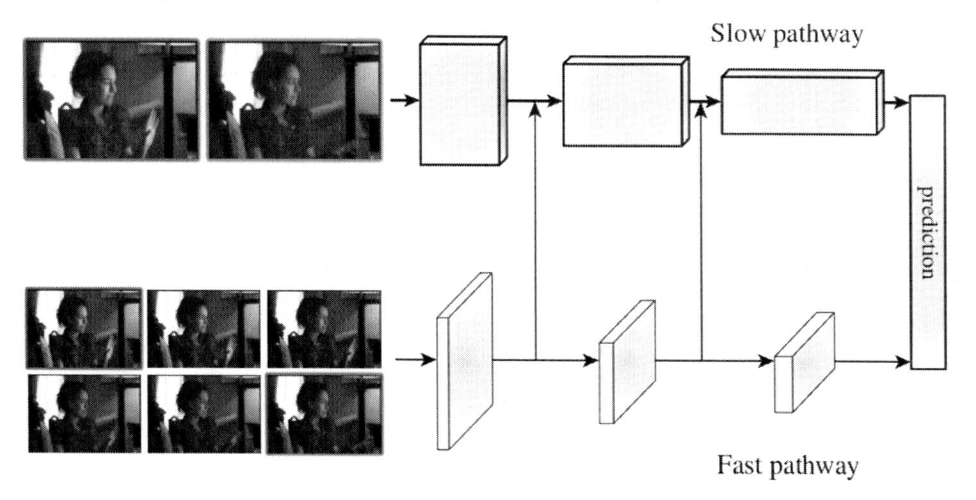

Figure 4.2 – A high-level illustration of the SlowFast network (source – SlowFast)

The model architecture is based on the concept of slow and fast temporal frequencies to recognize moving objects, as inspired by the retinas in our eyes. It consists of a high-definition slow pathway to analyze static content along with a low definition fast pathway to analyze dynamic content. Both pathways internally use ResNet convolution architecture for CNN but use different temporal strides. The fast pathway uses smaller temporal strides but a high frequency (15 frames per second), while the slow pathway uses large temporal strides but a low frequency (2 frames per second). For this reason, a slow pathway is more compute-heavy than a fast pathway.

While the results of SlowFast architecture are impressive and considered some of the best (at about 94%), the results of just using slow or fast architecture were also published. The results of slow architecture are also good (about 91%). Both these model architectures (and many others) are available out of the box in Flash. In this example, we will be fine-tuning the video classification model using the slow architecture.

The video classification model using Flash will consist of the following five steps:

1. Importing libraries
2. Loading the dataset
3. Configuring the backbone
4. Training and fine-tuning the model
5. Predicting actions based on the model

Now, we will start the model-building process.

Importing libraries

We will get started with the following steps:

We will start by importing the necessary libraries:

```
!pip install torch==1.10.0 torchvision==0.11.1
torchtext==0.11.0 torchaudio==0.10.0 --quiet
!pip install pytorch-lightning==1.5.10 --quiet
!pip install lightning-flash==0.7.1 --quiet
!pip install 'lightning-flash[audio,image, video, text]'
--quiet
!pip install Pillow==9.0.0
```

Once installed, you can import the libraries:

```
import pytorch_lightning as pl
import torch
import pandas as pd
import numpy as np
import seaborn as sns

import flash
from flash.core.data.utils import download_data
from flash.video import VideoClassificationData,
VideoClassifier
```

Once the libraries are imported in the previous steps, you can check the version:

```
print("pandas version:",pd.__version__)
print("numpy version:",np.__version__)
print("seaborn version:",sns.__version__)
print("torch version:",torch.__version__)
print("flash version:",flash.__version__)
print("pytorch ligthening version:",pl.__version__)
```

This code snippet should show the following output:

```
pandas version: 1.3.5
numpy version: 1.21.5
seaborn version: 0.11.2
torch version: 1.10.0+cu111
flash version: 0.7.1
pytorch ligthening version: 1.5.10
```

Figure 4.3 – The versions of packages used for video classification

Now, we are ready to load the dataset.

Loading the dataset

The dataset we are going to use in this section is the Kinetics 400 dataset. This dataset was originally curated by DeepMind and consists of 400 human actions for the task of video classification. The video clips actions include an array of activities such as playing sports or group interactions such as dancing. The dataset is also available as part of the Lightning Flash (and PyTorch Video) dataset collection. This makes it very easy to load the dataset directly.

As a first step, we download the data:

```
download_data("https://pl-flash-data.s3.amazonaws.com/kinetics.
zip", "./data")
```

Once the dataset is downloaded from the Flash server, we can load the data into `DataModule`. It will also create a train and test validation dataset folder. We are making use of the `from_folders` hook in order to do so:

```
kinetics_videodatamodule = VideoClassificationData.from_
folders(
    train_folder="data/kinetics/train",
    val_folder="data/kinetics/val",
    clip_sampler="uniform",
    clip_duration=2,
    decode_audio=False,
    batch_size=4
)
```

In the preceding code snippet, we have used the `from_folders` hook to load the data as well as specify the key characteristics:

- `train_folder` and `val_folder` define the location of the training and validation folders respectively in the dataset.
- `clip_sampler` is used to determine how the frames will be sampled from the underlying video file, and `clip_duration` defines the duration in seconds. In this case, we are uniformly sampling 2 seconds of a clip from the video at each iteration.
- `decode_audio` defines whether we wish to load the audio along with the video. In this case, we have chosen not to use audio. If you set it as true, the video clip is then selectively read or decoded into the canonical video tensor with shape (C, T, H, and W) and the audio tensor with shape (S).
- Finally, `batch_size` determines the number of videos in a single batch. In this case, we have set it as four. The higher the batch size, the higher the need for the memory in the environment.

Once the data is loaded, we are ready to select the pre-trained model architecture.

> **Important Note**
>
> `DataModule` is a predefined hook to load the dataset, which is in the following structure: `dir_path/<class_name>/<video_name>.{mp4, avi}`. If you wish to try the model on your custom dataset, you will need to organize it in this format. Alternatively, you can use a custom data loader.

Configuring the backbone

In this section, we will be doing the following:

- Selecting the backbone
- Configuring the task

The next step for us is now to select the pre-trained model architecture, also called the "backbone," in Flash. You can list the available model architecture options by printing it:

```
print(VideoClassifier.available_backbones())
```

This should show all the available architectures, such as the following:

```
['c2d_r50', 'csn_r101', 'efficient_x3d_s', 'efficient_x3d_xs', 'i3d_r50', 'r2plus1d_r50', 'slow_r50', 'slow_r50_detection', 'slowfast_16x8_r101_50_50', 'slowfast_r101', 'slowf
```

For this example, we will choose the `slowfast_r50` model architecture. In Model Zoo, this has nearly a 91% top 5 accuracy.

We can print the details of the model arguments using the following statement:

```
print(VideoClassifier.get_backbone_details("slowfast_r50"))
```

This should show an argument that we can define while building a task on top of this model:

```
[('pretrained', <Parameter "pretrained: bool = False">), ('progress', <Parameter "progress: bool = True">), ('kwargs', <Parameter "**kwargs: Any">)]
```

Now, it's time for us to create a task using a SlowFast architecture:

```
# 2. Build the task
slowfastr50_model = VideoClassifier(backbone="slowfast_r50",
labels=kinetics_videodatamodule.labels, pretrained=True)
```

We define `VideoClassfier` and pass `slowfast_r50` as our backbone, along with the kinetics data labels that we loaded earlier.

We will be using the pre-trained option; hence, we selected that as **True**. Otherwise, the model will be trained from scratch.

This should show the following output:

```
Using 'slow_r50' provided by Facebook Research/PyTorchVideo (https://github.com/facebookresearch/pytorchvideo).
```

Now that our task is defined, we are all set to fine-tune our model for the Kinetics dataset.

Fine-tuning the model

Now, we can train the model (or fine-tune it, to be specific):

```
trainer = flash.Trainer(max_epochs=25, gpus=torch.cuda.device_
count(), precision=16)
```

```
trainer.finetune(slowr50_model, datamodule=kinetics_
videodatamodule, strategy="freeze")
```

We first create a `Trainer` class using (`flash.Trainer`) and define the hyperparamaters. In this case, we will be using all the available GPU and run it for 25 epochs using 16-bit precision. A 16-bit precision model makes the training faster by reducing computational dimensionality.

We will define a `trainer.finetune` class, which takes arguments of the model task and dataset we defined earlier.

This should show the following output:

```
trainer = flash.Trainer(max_epochs=25, gpus=torch.cuda.device_count(), precision=16)
trainer.finetune(slowr50_model, datamodule=kinetics_videodatamodule, strategy="freeze")

Using 16bit native Automatic Mixed Precision (AMP)
GPU available: True, used: True
TPU available: False, using: 0 TPU cores
IPU available: False, using: 0 IPUs
LOCAL_RANK: 0 - CUDA_VISIBLE_DEVICES: [0]

  | Name          | Type       | Params
---------------------------------------------
0 | train_metrics | ModuleDict | 0
1 | val_metrics   | ModuleDict | 0
2 | test_metrics  | ModuleDict | 0
3 | backbone      | Net        | 32.5 M
4 | head          | Sequential | 2.0 K
---------------------------------------------
55.1 K    Trainable params
32.4 M    Non-trainable params
32.5 M    Total params
64.912    Total estimated model params size (MB)
/usr/local/lib/python3.7/dist-packages/pytorch_lightning/utilities/data.py:60: UserWarning: Trying to infer the `batch_size` from an ambiguous collection. The
  "Trying to infer the `batch_size` from an ambiguous collection. The batch size we"
Epoch 24:
120/? [07:30<00:00, 3.76s/it, loss=0.0506, v_num=0, train_accuracy_step=1.000, train_cross_entropy_step=0.0545, val_accuracy=0.868, val_cross_entropy=0.594, train_accuracy_epoch=0.991, train_cross_entropy_epoch=0.0474]
```

Figure 4.4 – Fine-tuning the model output

As you can see, we are getting a pretty decent accuracy of over 87% on the validation set. This model seems to be ready to make the predictions now.

Making predictions using the model

Now that model is fine-tuned, we can use it to make the predictions.

You can save the model checkpoint and use `predict` method to make the predictions later as well. This model is optimized for video, so if you are creating a mobile application, deployment will be easy:

```
trainer.save_checkpoint("finetuned_kinetics_slowr50_video_
classification.pt")

datamodule = VideoClassificationData.from_folders(predict_
folder="data/kinetics/predict", batch_size=1)
predictions = trainer.predict(slowr50_model,
datamodule=datamodule, output="labels")
print(predictions)
```

This should show the top five predictions for that video clip:

```
LOCAL_RANK: 0 - CUDA_VISIBLE_DEVICES: [0]
Predicting:                                              58/? [00:04<?, ?it/s
[['archery', 'marching', 'bowling', 'flying_kite'], ['high_jump']]
```

Figure 4.5 – Predictions of the model

As you can see, we got the top five predicted actions for the video in the clip.

And that's it. That's how easy it was to fine-tune a model using Flash – just five steps, all with barely a single line of code.

> **Important Note**
>
> In order to see the predictions for your own video clip, you would need to deploy this model. We will cover deployment in *Chapter 9*, *Deploying and Scoring Models*. Additionally, Flash also offers some features for easy-to-deploy options as well as Flash Zero as the CLI. These features are currently in their beta, so please use them with caution.

Next steps for additional learning

As you can see, it's as simple as picking right hooks and specifying a couple of arguments to train your Flash model. This is a quick way to benchmark and prototype specific video tasks for your applications. You can continue to do more, such as the following:

- There are more video datasets available in the PyTorch Video dataset collection, such as Charades, Domsev, EpicKitchen, HMDB51, SSV2, and UCF101. You can try them as additional learning.
- Another thing to change and then compare the results is the model architecture. SlowFast is another widely used architecture for video classification. You can try it directly from Model Zoo. The arguments for that architecture are found here: `https://pytorchvideo.readthedocs.io/en/latest/api/models/slowfast.html`.
- The next step would be to change the video dataset to your own custom dataset with the help of some data preprocessing if needed and train the video classification model. One very good dataset to try is the YouTube video dataset, which can be found here: `https://research.google.com/youtube8m/download.html`.

In the next section, we will use Flash for a custom dataset, which can come in handy for these exercises.

Automatic speech recognition using Flash

Recognizing speech from an audio file is perhaps one of the most widely used applications of AI. It's part of smartphone speakers such as Alexa, as well as automatically generated captions for video streaming platforms such as YouTube, and also many music platforms. It can detect speech in an audio file and convert it into text. Detection of speech involves various challenges such as speaker modalities, pitch, and pronunciation, as well as dialect and language itself:

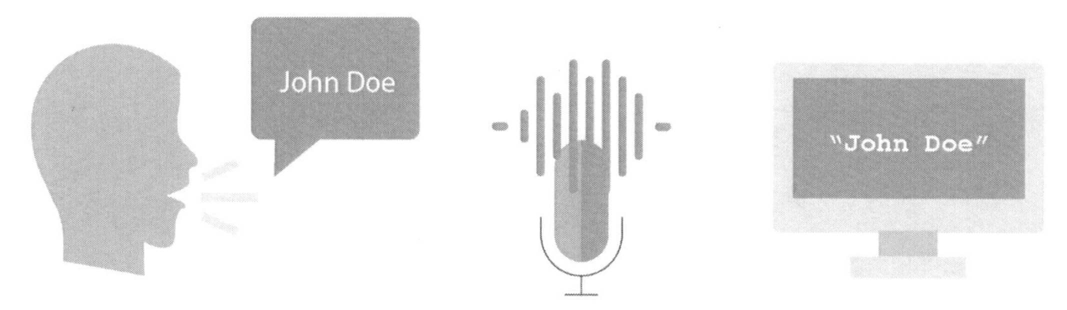

Figure 4.6 – A concept of automatic speech recognition

To train a model for **Automatic Speech Recognition** (**ASR**), we need a training dataset that is a collection of audio files along with the corresponding text transcription that describes that audio. The more diverse the set of audio files with people from different age groups, ethnicities, dialects, and so on is, the more robust the ASR model will be for the unseen audio files.

In the previous section, we created a model using an on-the-shelf dataset; in this section, we will use a custom dataset and train it using a ready-to-cook model architecture such as wav2vec for ASR.

While there are many architectures available for ASR, wav2vec is a really good cross-lingual architecture developed by Facebook AI. It can arguably work on any language and is extremely scalable. It has recently outperformed the LibriSpeech benchmark. It was first published in the paper *wav2sec: Unsupervised Pre-training for Speech Recognition* by Steffen Schneider, Alexei Baevski, Ronan Collobert, and Michael Auli:

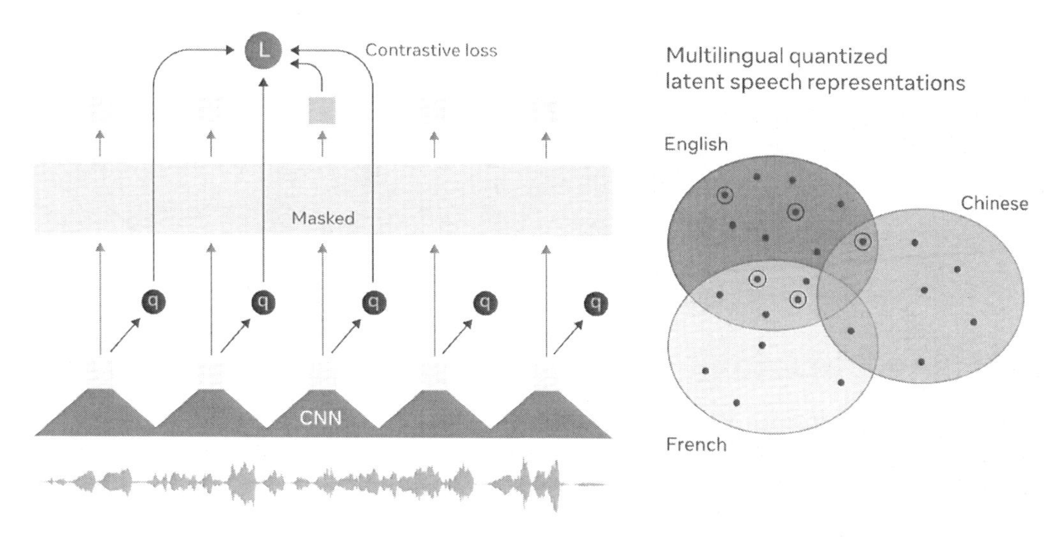

Figure 4.7 – wav2vec architecture – Image source – https://ai.facebook.com/blog/wav2vec-20-learning-the-structure-of-speech-from-raw-audio/

The wav2vec model is an improvement over the BERT Transformer model, which we saw in *Chapter 3, Using Pre-Trained Models*. This model uses much less labeled data than other models since it relies on "self-supervised learning." It learns the latent representation of audio files in a set of small speech units (25 ms), which are shorter than the phenomes. These small latent representations are fed into the transformer in masked form along with knowledge from the entire sequence. A contrastive loss function is used to find the converge of masked positions and speech units. It uses the concepts of self-supervision and contrastive loss, which we will cover in more depth in *Chapter 8, Self-Supervised Learning*.

The pre-trained model is trained on nearly 960 hours of audio. The most interesting part of the architecture is that it is cross-lingual and has been tried in various languages. We will try this model for a Scottish language dataset.

The ASR model using Flash consists of the following five steps similar to the video classification task:

1. Importing libraries
2. Loading the dataset
3. Configuring the backbone
4. Training and fine-tuning the model
5. Predicting speech based on the model

Now, we will start the model-building process.

Installing Libraries

We will run following block to install required packages into our env.

```
!pip install torch==1.10.0 torchvision==0.11.1
torchtext==0.11.0 torchaudio==0.10.0 --quiet
!pip install pytorch-lightning==1.5.10 --quiet
!pip install lightning-flash==0.7.1 --quiet
!pip install 'lightning-flash[audio,image, video, text]'
--quiet
!pip install Pillow==9.0.0
```

Importing libraries

We will start by importing the necessary libraries:

```
import pandas as pd
import random
```

```
import torch
import flash

from sklearn.model_selection import train_test_split
from flash import Trainer
from flash.audio import SpeechRecognitionData,
SpeechRecognition
```

Once the libraries are imported in the preceding steps, you can check the version:

```
print("pandas version:",pd.__version__)
print("torch version:",torch.__version__)
print("flash version:",flash.__version__)
```

This code snippet should show the following output:

```
pandas version: 1.3.5
torch version: 1.10.0+cu111
flash version: 0.7.1
```

Figure 4.8 – Versions of the packages used for ASR

Now, we are ready to load the dataset.

Loading the dataset

We will be using the Scottish language dataset. You can download the dataset to your Google drive or your local drive as per your working environment.

In this example, we are downloading audio files for `Scottish_english_female`, which contains speech files for 894 people from this location: `https://www.openslr.org/83/`. The audio files are in the `.wav` format, while the text files are in the `.csv` format.

As a first step, we will download the data and add it to our drive. We have shared the steps to mount a drive in previous chapters; please refer to them if needed:

```
from google.colab import drive
drive.mount('/content/gdrive')
!unzip '/content/gdrive/My Drive/Colab Notebooks/scottish_
english_female.zip'
```

```
random.seed(10)
df_scottish = pd.read_csv("line_index.csv", header=None,
names=['not_required', 'speech_files', 'targets'])
df_scottish = df_scottish.sample(frac=0.06)
print(df_scottish.shape)
df_scottish.head()
```

In the preceding code snippet, we are collecting the dataset and down-sampling it to use only 6% of the dataset. This is done because of compute resource limitation. If you have more compute available, you can try a higher number or the entire dataset. Then we are printing the head of the dataframe as shown below:

(54, 3)

	not_required	speech_files	targets
802	EN0007	scf_05223_01592871455	Throughout the centuries people have explaine...
807	EN0003	scf_05223_00004260276	These take the shape of a long round arch wit...

Figure 4.9 – An output of the file view

As you can see, we have audio speech files in the WAV format along with text transcriptions.

Now, we will create a train-test split for the dataset:

```
df_scottish = df_scottish[['speech_files', 'targets']]
df_scottish['speech_files'] = df_scottish['speech_files'].str.
lstrip()

df_scottish['speech_files'] = df_scottish['speech_files'].
astype(str) + '.wav'
df_scottish.head()

random.seed(10)
train_scottish, test_scottish_raw = train_test_split(df_
scottish, test_size=0.2)
test_scottish = test_scottish_raw['speech_files']
test_scottish.head()

train_scottish.to_csv('train_scottish.csv')
test_scottish.to_csv('test_scottish.csv')
```

In the preceding code snippet, we have done the following:

1. Created the DataFrame for our dataset
2. Created a train test split of 80–20% with 80% training data and 20% testing data

This should show the following output for printing some test files.

```
310    scf_03397_01072622319.wav
223    scf_07049_01133867565.wav
868    scf_04310_00395537459.wav
835    scf_04310_02050219481.wav
620    scf_07049_00239785467.wav
Name: speech_files, dtype: object
```

Figure 4.10 – The output of the test audio files view after the split

Now, we are ready to create a data module for this dataset:

```
datamodule = SpeechRecognitionData.from_csv(
        "speech_files",
        "targets",
        train_file="train_scottish.csv",
        predict_file="test_scottish.csv",
        batch_size=10)
```

In the preceding code snippet, we have used the `datamodule` hook from Flash and passed the train and test files, as well as speech.

We are using a batch size of 10 files in this use case.

You should see the following output after the execution of this snippet:

```
Using custom data configuration default-15b9ea74ae447d33
Downloading and preparing dataset csv/default to /root/.cache/huggingface/datasets/csv/default-15b9ea74ae447d33/0.0.0/433e0ccc46f9880962cc2b12065189
100%  1/1 [00:00<00:00, 34.15it/s]
100%  1/1 [00:00<00:00, 29.72it/s]
Dataset csv downloaded and prepared to /root/.cache/huggingface/datasets/csv/default-15b9ea74ae447d33/0.0.0/433e0ccc46f9880962cc2b12065189766fbb2bee
100%  1/1 [00:00<00:00, 35.79it/s]
Using custom data configuration default-bfc3565a6d97d227
Downloading and preparing dataset csv/default to /root/.cache/huggingface/datasets/csv/default-bfc3565a6d97d227/0.0.0/433e0ccc46f9880962cc2b12065189
100%  1/1 [00:00<00:00, 43.19it/s]
100%  1/1 [00:00<00:00, 31.51it/s]
Dataset csv downloaded and prepared to /root/.cache/huggingface/datasets/csv/default-bfc3565a6d97d227/0.0.0/433e0ccc46f9880962cc2b12065189766fbb2bee
100%  1/1 [00:00<00:00, 35.89it/s]
```

Figure 4.11 – The output of the audio data module

Now, we are ready to choose our backbone for this model.

Important Note

The batch size is a key parameter in terms of memory requirements for fine-tuning your model. Typically, the higher the batch size, the higher the GPU and memory that is needed, although you can adjust it by the number of epochs. A very low batch size on a new language may not yield any learning either, so choose wisely.

One key aspect to compare in batch size is the size of the average WAV/audio file. In the examples given in Flash documentation, WAV files are smaller; however, in the Scottish dataset, the average speech file is larger. The larger the file, the more there is a need for memory and compute.

Configuring the backbone

In this section, we will be doing the following:

1. Selecting the backbone
2. Configuring the task

The next step for us is to select the pre-trained model architecture, also called the "backbone," in Flash. You can list the available model architecture options by printing it:

```
SpeechRecognition.available_backbones()
```

This should show all the available architectures, such as the following:

```
['Anything available from: Hugging Face/transformers (https://github.com/huggingface/transformers)',
 'facebook/wav2vec2-base-960h',
 'facebook/wav2vec2-large-960h-lv60']
```

Figure 4.12 – The output of the available backbones for ASR

For this use case, we will be using `'facebook/wav2vec2-base-960h'`, provided by Hugging Face/transformers (`https://github.com/huggingface/transformers`).

Now, it's time for us to create a task using a wav2vec2-base-960h architecture:

```
model = SpeechRecogntion(backbone="facebook/wav2vec2-base-
960h")
```

In this code snippet, we have defined the model architecture.

Now that our task is defined, we are all set to fine-tune our model for the Scottish language dataset.

Fine-tuning the model

Now, we can train the model (or fine-tune, to be specific):

```
trainer = Trainer(max_epochs=4, gpus=-1, precision=16)
trainer.finetune(model, datamodule=datamodule, strategy="no_
freeze")
```

We first create a `Trainer` class using (`flash.Trainer`) and define the hyperparamaters. In this case, we will be using all the available GPU and run it for 4 epochs using 16-bit precision, with no freeze strategy. A 16-bit precision model makes the training faster by reducing computational dimensionality. In the "no-freeze" strategy, we have kept our backbone and its head unfrozen from the beginning. This means that all layers will be trained for fine-tuning; however, it means longer computational resources will be used. We will define a `trainer.fintune` class, which takes arguments of the model task and dataset we defined earlier.

This should show the following output:

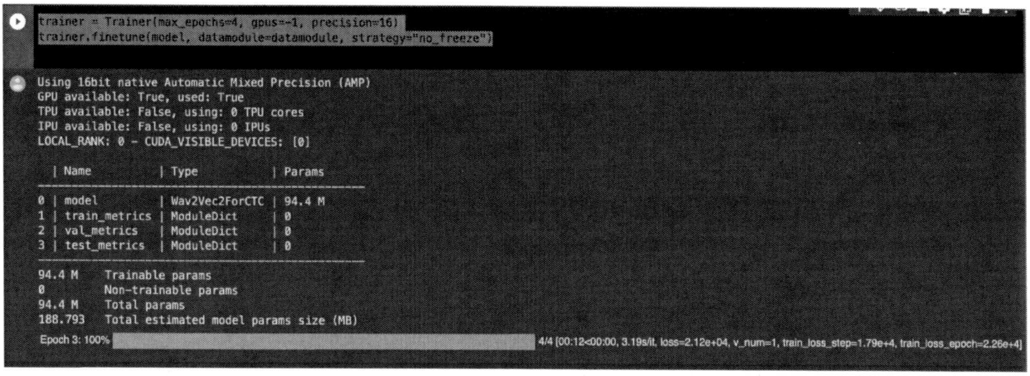

```
trainer = Trainer(max_epochs=4, gpus=-1, precision=16)
trainer.finetune(model, datamodule=datamodule, strategy="no_freeze")

Using 16bit native Automatic Mixed Precision (AMP)
GPU available: True, used: True
TPU available: False, using: 0 TPU cores
IPU available: False, using: 0 IPUs
LOCAL_RANK: 0 - CUDA_VISIBLE_DEVICES: [0]

  | Name          | Type            | Params
----------------------------------------------
0 | model         | Wav2Vec2ForCTC  | 94.4 M
1 | train_metrics | ModuleDict      | 0
2 | val_metrics   | ModuleDict      | 0
3 | test_metrics  | ModuleDict      | 0
----------------------------------------------
94.4 M    Trainable params
0         Non-trainable params
94.4 M    Total params
188.793   Total estimated model params size (MB)
Epoch 3: 100% 4/4 [00:12<00:00, 3.19s/it, loss=2.12e+04, v_num=1, train_loss_step=1.79e+4, train_loss_epoch=2.26e+4]
```

Figure 4.13 – Fine-tuning the model output

Since this was an unfrozen model, we have trained for only 3 epochs; however, we will see that it still gives very good results on predictions.

Speech prediction using the model

Now that the model is fine-tuned, we can use it to make the predictions.

You can save the model checkpoint and use `predict` method to make the predictions later as well. We will first try getting some predictions:

```
trainer.predict(model, datamodule=datamodule)
```

Here, we are making use of the `predict` class method to get the model predictions:

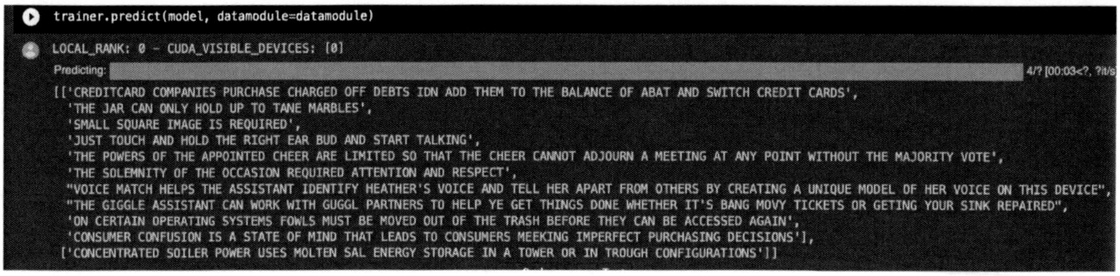

```
trainer.predict(model, datamodule=datamodule)

LOCAL_RANK: 0 - CUDA_VISIBLE_DEVICES: [0]
Predicting:                                                            4/? [00:03<?, ?it/s]
[['CREDITCARD COMPANIES PURCHASE CHARGED OFF DEBTS IDN ADD THEM TO THE BALANCE OF ABAT AND SWITCH CREDIT CARDS',
  'THE JAR CAN ONLY HOLD UP TO TANE MARBLES',
  'SMALL SQUARE IMAGE IS REQUIRED',
  'JUST TOUCH AND HOLD THE RIGHT EAR BUD AND START TALKING',
  'THE POWERS OF THE APPOINTED CHEER ARE LIMITED SO THAT THE CHEER CANNOT ADJOURN A MEETING AT ANY POINT WITHOUT THE MAJORITY VOTE',
  'THE SOLEMNITY OF THE OCCASION REQUIRED ATTENTION AND RESPECT',
  "VOICE MATCH HELPS THE ASSISTANT IDENTIFY HEATHER'S VOICE AND TELL HER APART FROM OTHERS BY CREATING A UNIQUE MODEL OF HER VOICE ON THIS DEVICE",
  "THE GIGGLE ASSISTANT CAN WORK WITH GUGGL PARTNERS TO HELP YE GET THINGS DONE WHETHER IT'S BANG MOVY TICKETS OR GETING YOUR SINK REPAIRED",
  'ON CERTAIN OPERATING SYSTEMS FOWLS MUST BE MOVED OUT OF THE TRASH BEFORE THEY CAN BE ACCESSED AGAIN',
  'CONSUMER CONFUSION IS A STATE OF MIND THAT LEADS TO CONSUMERS MEEKING IMPERFECT PURCHASING DECISIONS'],
 ['CONCENTRATED SOILER POWER USES MOLTEN SAL ENERGY STORAGE IN A TOWER OR IN TROUGH CONFIGURATIONS']]
```

Figure 4.14 – Predictions of the model

As you can see, are able to predict speech from audio files..

Now, we can try it on our test dataset and pick some of the unseen audio files to predict the result of the ASR model built using Flash:

```
test_scottish_raw.head()
datamodule = SpeechRecognitionData.from_files(predict_
files='scf_02484_01925002707.wav', batch_size=10) # Scottish

predictions = trainer.predict(model, datamodule=datamodule)
print(predictions)
```

This should show the following prediction for this audio file (you can try listening in on your computer to the particular audio file to see for yourself the accuracy of the result). For reference, here is the original transcript:

scf_02484_01925002707	Ask her to carefully bring these things with her from the store

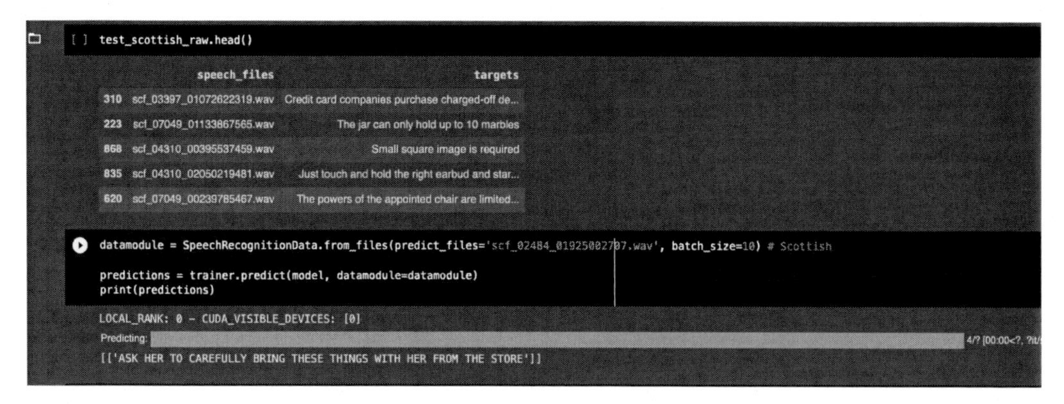

Figure 4.15 – The output on the test dataset

Comparing this to the original transcript, you can see that it's a total match. This means that our model is working great. You can also serve the model to get the model output and integrate it with your application, using the `model.serve` method.

That's it. That's how smooth it was to train your model for highly complex tasks such as audio recognition and video classification.

Further learning

- **Other languages**: The ASR dataset from which we used the Scottish language dataset also contains many other languages, such as Sinhala, and many Indian languages, such as Hindi, Marathi, and Bengali. The next logical step would be to try this ASR model for another language and compare the results. It is also a great way to learn how to manage training requirements as some of the audio files in these datasets are bigger; hence, they will need more compute power.

  Many non-English languages don't have apps widely available on mobiles (for example, the Marathi language spoken in India) and a lack of technical tools in native languages limits the adoption of many tools in remote parts of the world. Creating an ASR in your local language can add great value to the technical ecosystem as well.

- **Audio and video together**: Another interesting task is to combine the audio speech recognition and video classification tasks that we have seen today and use machine learning to classify video actions, as well as show the subtitles.

- **Endangered languages**: One of the rarely discussed challenges is the demise of rare languages around the world. There are thousands of languages that are classified as endangered languages, which are dying due to the lack of resources available in those languages. Take an example from *The Jungle Book*, which was set in central India; tribes there speak the Gond-Madia language, which, like many endangered languages, doesn't have script. Having ASR can be not just a lifesaver for such languages but also a great tool of social empowerment. Please consider creating an app from scratch for one such unserved language using ASR.

Summary

Lightning Flash is still in the early stages of development and will continue to evolve rapidly. Flash is also a community project where model code can be contributed by data science practitioners, and so the quality of code may vary from architecture to architecture. We advise you to follow due diligence when it comes to the source of any model code, as it may not always be from the PyTorch Lightning team; try to avoid bugs.

However, Flash is extremely useful, whether you are a beginner in DL or an advanced practitioner looking to establish a baseline for a new project. The first point of order is to start with the latest and greatest architecture in the field. It helps get you off the ground easily with your dataset and sets the baseline for the different algorithms of your use case. Flash, with its out-of-the-box capability for state-of-the-art DL architectures, is not just a timesaver but a big productivity booster.

Vision neural networks are widely used and are also growing very fast. In this chapter, we saw how we can use out-of-the-box models from PyTorch Lightning Flash without defining any convolutional layers, performing extensive preprocessing, or training the model from scratch. Flash models enable us to configure, train, and build models with ease. However, Flash models may not always yield perfect results, and for some complex applications, they will need tuning or coding, which is when we go back to PyTorch Lightning.

We saw how quickly Flash can help us build models for audio and video tasks. There are more ready-to-cook models available for graph, tabular forecasting, or NLP tasks.

So far in this book, we have seen the basic types of DL models. In the next section of the book, we will turn our focus to how PyTorch Lightning can be used to solve some real-world use cases with complex FE and large-scale training. We will start with a time-series forecasting use case and will take a look at how PyTorch Lightning helps us create industrial-scale solutions.

Section 2: Solving using PyTorch Lightning

This section will cover more details on how to build various Deep Learning applications using the Lightning framework. It will include practical examples aimed at solving key industrial applications.

This section comprises the following chapters:

- *Chapter 5, Time Series Models*
- *Chapter 6, Deep Generative Models*
- *Chapter 7, Semi-Supervised Learning*
- *Chapter 8, Self-Supervised Learning*

5
Time Series Models

There are many datasets that are generated naturally in a sequence that is separated by a quantum of time, such as ocean waves that come to the shore every few minutes or transactions in the stock market that happen every few microseconds. Models that forecast when the next wave will hit the shore or what the price of the next stock transactions could be, by analyzing the history of previous occurrences, are a type of data science algorithm known as **Time Series models**. While traditional time series methods have long been used for forecasting, using Deep Learning, we can use advanced approaches for better results. In this chapter, we will focus on how to build commonly used Deep Learning-based time series models such as **Recurrent Neural Networks** (**RNNs**) and **Long Short-Term Memory** (**LSTM**), using PyTorch Lightning to perform time series forecasting.

In this chapter, we will start with a brief introduction to time series problems and then see a use case in PyTorch Lightning. Ever wondered how the weather app on your mobile shows you how warm or cold the next day is going to be? It is done with the help of a time series forecasting model using history of weather data.

We will see how time series forecasting can be useful for a business to forecast upcoming traffic volume, using which they can estimate how much time will it take to reach destination in the next hour or how it will vary throughout the day.

Different PyTorch Lightning approaches and features will be covered during the phases of build, train, load, and forecast. We will also be using different features available in PyTorch Lightning for your benefit, such as identifying the learning rate in an automated fashion to get a more advanced understanding of the framework.

This chapter should help you to prepare for advanced types of time series models using PyTorch Lightning, along with giving you familiarity with the hidden functionalities and the features.

In this chapter, we will cover the following topics:

- Introduction to time series
- Getting started with time series models
- Traffic volume forecasting using the LSTM time series model

Technical requirements

The code for this chapter has been developed and tested on a macOS with Anaconda or in Google Colab with Python 3.6. If you are using another environment, please make the appropriate changes to your environment variables.

In this chapter, we will primarily be using the following Python modules, mentioned with their versions:

- PyTorch Lightning (version 1.5.2)
- Seaborn (version 0.11.2)
- NumPy (version 1.21.5)
- Torch (version 1.10.0)
- pandas (version 1.3.5)

Working examples for this chapter can be found at this GitHub link: `https://github.com/PacktPublishing/Deep-Learning-with-PyTorch-Lightning/tree/main/Chapter05`.

n order to make sure that these modules work together and not go out of sync, we have used the specific version of torch, torchvision, torchtext, torchaudio with PyTorch Lightning 1.5.2. You can also use the latest version of PyTorch Lightning and torch compatible with each other. More details can be found on the GitHub link: `https://github.com/PacktPublishing/Deep-Learning-with-PyTorch-Lightning`

```
!pip install torch==1.10.0 torchvision==0.11.1
torchtext==0.11.0 torchaudio==0.10.0 --quiet
!pip install pytorch-lightning==1.5.2 --quiet
```

The source datasets can be found in the Metro Interstate Traffic Volume dataset: `https://archive.ics.uci.edu/ml/datasets/Metro+Interstate+Traffic+Volume`.

This is the donated dataset that has been obtained from the UCI Machine Learning Repository. The dataset is made available by Dua, D. and Graff, C. (2019), UCI Machine Learning Repository (`http://archive.ics.uci.edu/ml`), Irvine, CA: University of California, School of Information and Computer Science.

Introduction to time series

In a typical machine learning use case, a dataset is a collection of features (x) and target variables (y). The model uses features to learn and predict the target variable.

Take the following example. To predict house prices, the features could be the number of bedrooms, the number of baths, and square footage, and the target variable is the price of the house. Here, the goal can be to use all the features (x) to train the model and predict the price (y) of the house. One thing we observe in such a use case is that all the records in the dataset are treated equally when predicting target variables, which is the price of the house in our example, and the order of the data doesn't matter much. The outcome (y) depends only on the values of x.

On the other hand, in time series prediction, the order of the data plays an important role in capturing some of the features, such as trends and seasons. Time series datasets are typically datasets where a time measure is involved – for example, a climate dataset where the temperature is being recorded on an hourly basis. The prediction in time series is not always divided nicely between features (x) and variables (y), but we predict the *next* values of x depending on the previous values of x (such as predicting tomorrow's temperature based on today's temperature).

Time series datasets can have one or more features. If there is a single feature, it is called a **univariate time series**, and if there are multiple features, it is called a **multivariate time series**. This can be time in any quantum, be it microseconds, hours, days, or even years.

While there are multiple methods for solving time series problems using traditional machine learning methods (such as ARIMA), Deep Learning methods offer much easier and better ways. We will look at how time series problems are handled using Deep Learning methods and how PyTorch Lightning helps in its implementation with the help of examples.

Time series forecasting using Deep Learning

Technically speaking, time series forecasting is a form of building a regression model to predict the desired outcome by using historical time series data. In simple terms, time series forecasting uses historical data to train the model and predict future values.

While traditional methods for time series are useful, Deep Learning in time series forecasting overcomes the disadvantages of traditional machine learning, such as the following:

- Identifying complex patterns, trends, and seasons
- Forecasting for long terms
- Handling missing values

There are various Deep Learning algorithms to perform time series forecasting, such as the following:

- RNN
- LSTM
- Gated recurrent units
- Encoder-decoder models

In the following section, we will see LSTMs in action using use cases.

Getting started with time series models

In the next sections of this chapter, we will go through real-world examples of time series forecasting, explained in detail. Every time series model typically follows the following structure:

1. Load and apply feature engineering on the dataset.
2. Build the model.
3. Train the model.
4. Perform time series forecasting.

Let's get started in the following section.

Traffic volume forecasting using the LSTM time series model

Time series models also have various other business applications, such as predicting stock prices, forecasting the demand for products, or predicting the number of passengers per hour at an airport.

One of the most commonly used applications of such a model (which you must have used unknowingly while driving) is traffic predictions. In this section, we will try to predict the traffic volume for Interstate 94, which can be used by ride share companies such as Uber, Lyft, and/or Google Maps for predicting traffic and the time required to reach a destination for both the drivers and ride share customers. The traffic volume varies notoriously by hour (depending on the time of day, office hours, commute hours, and so on), and a time series model is helpful in making such predictions.

In this use case, we will use the Metro Interstate Traffic Volume dataset to build a multi-layer stacked LSTM model and forecast the traffic volume. We will also focus on some of the PyTorch Lightning techniques for handling a validation dataset inside the model, as well as using one of the PyTorch Lightning automated techniques to identify the model learning rate value.

In this section, we're going to cover the following main topics:

- Dataset analysis
- Feature engineering
- Creating a custom dataset
- Configuring the LSTM model using PyTorch Lightning
- Training the model
- Measuring the training loss
- Loading the model
- A prediction on the test dataset

Dataset analysis

The dataset we are going to use in this chapter is called the *Metro Interstate Traffic Volume* dataset, which has historical data for traffic volume made available on the UCI Machine Learning Repository. It has hourly recordings of the traffic volume of westbound I-94 between Minneapolis and Saint Paul, Minnesota, from October 2, 2012 to September 30, 2018. This dataset is available on the UCI Machine Learning Repository and can be downloaded from this URL: `https://archive.ics.uci.edu/ml/machine-learning-databases/00492/`.

The ZIP folder contains a CSV file that has 8 columns and 48,204 rows of data from October 2, 2012 to September 30, 2018.

Here is a screenshot of the top five rows of our training dataset:

	holiday	temp	rain_1h	snow_1h	clouds_all	weather_main	weather_description	traffic_volume
date_time								
2012-10-02 09:00:00	None	288.28	0.0	0.0	40	Clouds	scattered clouds	5545
2012-10-02 10:00:00	None	289.36	0.0	0.0	75	Clouds	broken clouds	4516
2012-10-02 11:00:00	None	289.58	0.0	0.0	90	Clouds	overcast clouds	4767
2012-10-02 12:00:00	None	290.13	0.0	0.0	90	Clouds	overcast clouds	5026
2012-10-02 13:00:00	None	291.14	0.0	0.0	75	Clouds	broken clouds	4918

Figure 5.1 – Displaying the top five rows of data

The columns are as follows:

- `holiday`: Categorical US national holidays, plus regional holidays and the Minnesota State Fair
- `temp`: Numeric average temperature in kelvin
- `rain_1h`: Numeric amount in mm of rain that occurred in the hour
- `snow_1h`: Numeric amount in mm of snow that occurred in the hour
- `clouds_all`: Numeric percentage of cloud cover
- `weather_main`: Categorical short textual description of the current weather
- `weather_description`: Categorical longer textual description of the current weather
- `date_time`: `DateTime` hour of the data collected in local CST time
- `traffic_volume`: Numeric hourly I-94 ATR 301 reported westbound traffic volume

We will be loading the CSV file into the pandas DataFrame first in order to carry out **Exploratory Data Analysis** (**EDA**) and data processing before feeding it into our custom data module.

Loading the dataset

After installing and importing the required libraries, the first step is to load the dataset in the Google Colab workspace. Firstly, we will download the dataset from the UCI Machine Learning Repository using this URL: `https://archive.ics.uci.edu/ml/machine-learning-databases/00492/`.

Then, we will extract the compressed file to find the `Metro_Interstate_Traffic_Volume.csv` file in the extracted folder. We have seen several methods of downloading the dataset from Kaggle, Google Drive, and so on into the Colab notebook directly. In this section, we will use the manual method of uploading the data directly into the Colab session storage. Click on the **Files** icon on the left, as shown here:

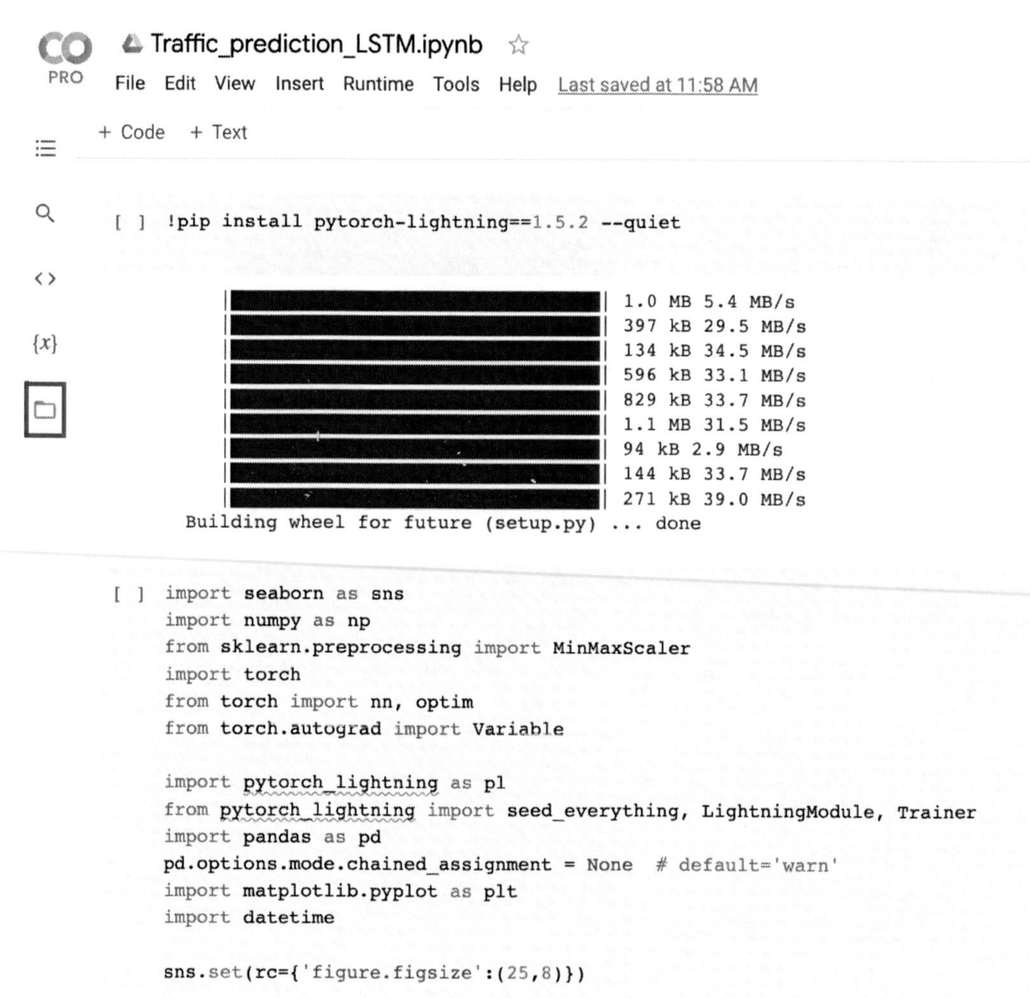

Figure 5.2 – Opening the Files menu on Google Colab

After opening the **Files** menu, select the **Upload to session storage** option by clicking on the icon, as shown here:

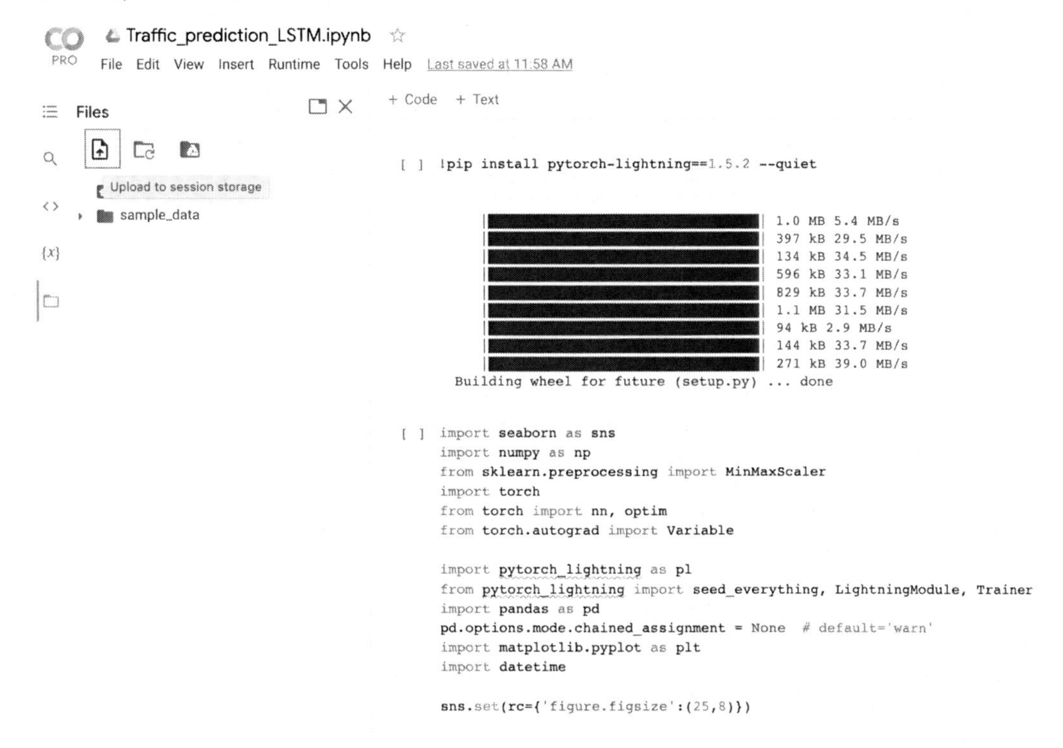

Figure 5.3 – Uploading local data to the Google Colab environment

As shown previously, finally select the `Metro_Interstate_Traffic_Volume.csv` file that you downloaded earlier from the UCI Machine Learning Repository.

Now, it's time to load our dataset into the pandas DataFrame. Since we know that our dataset has a column named `date_time`, we will use this column to parse dates and also set it as the index column, as shown in the following code snippet:

```
df_traffic = pd.read_csv('Metro_Interstate_Traffic_Volume.csv',
parse_dates=['date_time'], index_col="date_time")
```

After loading the CSV file into the pandas DataFrame, as shown previously, we can display the first five rows using the `head` method on the DataFrame, as shown here:

```
df_traffic.head()
```

The following output is displayed:

date_time	holiday	temp	rain_1h	snow_1h	clouds_all	weather_main	weather_description	traffic_volume
2012-10-02 09:00:00	None	288.28	0.0	0.0	40	Clouds	scattered clouds	5545
2012-10-02 10:00:00	None	289.36	0.0	0.0	75	Clouds	broken clouds	4516
2012-10-02 11:00:00	None	289.58	0.0	0.0	90	Clouds	overcast clouds	4767
2012-10-02 12:00:00	None	290.13	0.0	0.0	90	Clouds	overcast clouds	5026
2012-10-02 13:00:00	None	291.14	0.0	0.0	75	Clouds	broken clouds	4918

Figure 5.4 – The indexed timestamp

We will now check the total number of rows and columns in our dataset using the `shape` method on the `df_traffic` DataFrame, as shown here:

```
print("Total number of row in dataset:", df_traffic.shape[0])
print("Total number of columns in dataset:", df_traffic.
shape[1])
```

The following output is displayed:

```
print("Total number of row in dataset:", df_traffic.shape[0])
print("Total number of columns in dataset:", df_traffic.shape[1])

Total number of row in dataset: 48204
Total number of columns in dataset: 8
```

Figure 5.5 – The dataset size

This shows that we have 48,204 rows in the raw data.

Exploratory Data Analysis

Now, it's time to carry out exploratory data analysis to get a better understanding of the data and to check for data quality issues. We will start by analyzing the categorical columns first. Let's begin with the frequency distribution of the `weather_main` column, as shown here:

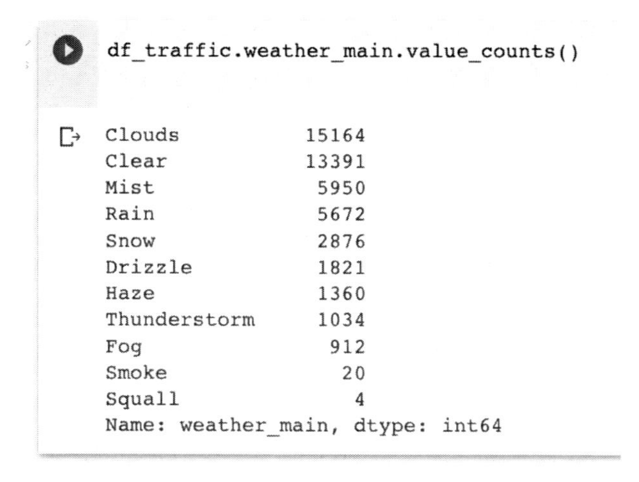

Figure 5.6 – The row counts of the weather data file

In the preceding figure, we are using the `value_counts` method on the `weather_main` column of the `df_traffic` DataFrame to get a count of the unique values. It can be seen that there are 11 different types of weather, with Clouds being the most frequent one.

We will now get the frequency distribution of the `holiday` column, as shown here:

```
df_traffic.holiday.value_counts()
```

```
None                         48143
Labor Day                        7
Thanksgiving Day                 6
Christmas Day                    6
New Years Day                    6
Martin Luther King Jr Day        6
Columbus Day                     5
Veterans Day                     5
Washingtons Birthday             5
Memorial Day                     5
Independence Day                 5
State Fair                       5
Name: holiday, dtype: int64
```

Figure 5.7 – The basic stats about the holiday file

There are 12 different types of holidays recorded in the dataset along with a None value, which implies 11 holidays only, and most of them have a very small frequency.

It is always important to check for duplicate timestamps in the time series; we will be using pandas' `duplicated()` method to identify the duplicate timestamps, as shown here:

```
df_traffic[df_traffic.index.duplicated()]
```

date_time	holiday	temp	rain_1h	snow_1h	clouds_all	weather_main	weather_description	traffic_volume
2012-10-10 07:00:00	None	281.25	0.0	0.0	99	Drizzle	light intensity drizzle	6793
2012-10-10 08:00:00	None	280.10	0.0	0.0	99	Drizzle	light intensity drizzle	6283
2012-10-10 09:00:00	None	279.61	0.0	0.0	99	Drizzle	light intensity drizzle	5680
2012-10-14 09:00:00	None	282.43	0.0	0.0	57	Mist	mist	2685
2012-10-14 09:00:00	None	282.43	0.0	0.0	57	Haze	haze	2685
...	...	...	...	...	...	...	...	...
2018-09-25 16:00:00	None	284.25	0.0	0.0	90	Drizzle	light intensity drizzle	6597
2018-09-27 07:00:00	None	285.17	0.0	0.0	90	Drizzle	light intensity drizzle	6589
2018-09-29 19:00:00	None	280.68	0.0	0.0	90	Clouds	overcast clouds	3818
2018-09-30 14:00:00	None	283.48	0.0	0.0	90	Drizzle	light intensity drizzle	4380
2018-09-30 15:00:00	None	283.84	0.0	0.0	75	Drizzle	light intensity drizzle	4302

7629 rows × 8 columns

Figure 5.8 – Checking the dataset for duplicates

We can see from the previous screenshot that there are 7,629 rows with duplicate timestamps. We need to drop all the duplicate timestamps, which can be easily done using the `duplicated` method combined with pandas slicing, as shown here:

```
df_traffic = df_traffic[~df_traffic.index.
duplicated(keep='last')]
```

In the preceding code, we are using the duplicated method to keep the last record and dropping all the other duplicate records from the `df_traffic` DataFrame. After deduplication, we can check the number of rows remaining in the DataFrame using the `shape` method:

```
df_traffic = df_traffic[~df_traffic.index.duplicated(keep='last')]
df_traffic.shape

(40575, 8)
```

Figure 5.9 – The output for the number of rows

We can see that the DataFrame now contains 40,575 rows after removing the duplicated timestamps instead of 48,204.

Now, let's plot the time series for the traffic volume using the Matplotlib and Seaborn libraries, as shown here:

```
plt.xticks(
    rotation=90,
    horizontalalignment='right',
    fontweight='light',
    fontsize='x-small'
)
sns.lineplot(df_traffic.index, df_traffic["traffic_volume"]).
set_title('Traffic volume time series')
```

In the preceding code, we are using the timestamp (which has already been converted to the index of the `df_traffic` DataFrame) as the *x* axis and plotting the values of `traffic_volume` on the *y* axis to get the following plot:

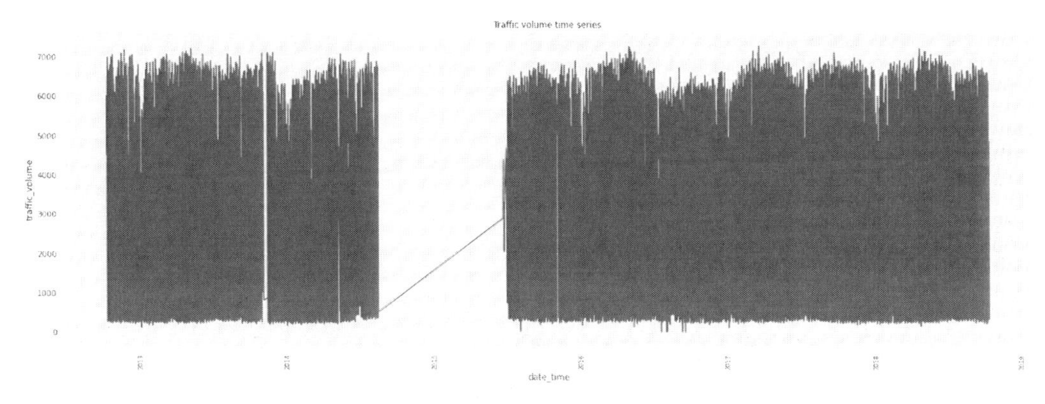

Figure 5.10 – The traffic volume time series plot

It can be observed from the preceding time series that there are missing values throughout the dataset, but almost all the values starting from the end of 2014 until the end of 2015 are missing. Most of the data imputation techniques work if the missing values are intermittent, as is the case in 2013 to 2014 or 2016 to 2018, but they would fail for the traffic volume from 2014 to 2015. Therefore, we will only consider the last 3 years of data, as it seems to be consistent enough due to the rare presence of missing values, which can be imputed using simple interpolations.

It is always a good idea to visualize the time series in order to get an overview of the missing values, but in order to get the exact number of missing values, we will be creating dummy data and comparing the timestamp in our dataset with it, as shown here:

```
date_range = pd.date_range('2012-10-02 09:00:00', '2018-09-30 23:00:00', freq='1H')
df_dummy = pd.DataFrame(np.random.randint(1, 20, (date_range.shape[0], 1)))
df_dummy.index = date_range  # set index
df_missing = df_traffic

#check for missing datetimeindex values based on reference index (with all values)
missing_hours = df_dummy.index[~df_dummy.index.isin(df_missing.index)]

print(missing_hours)
```

In the preceding code, we are creating a date range variable called `date_range` with the start time and end time equal to the start and end time for the records in our dataset. We are setting the index of the dummy data called `df_dummy` as `date_range`, which has a frequency of 1 hour. Then, we are comparing the two indices to find out all the timestamps, which should have been there in our dataset but are missing. The output of the preceding code snippet is shown here:

```
DatetimeIndex(['2012-10-03 07:00:00', '2012-10-03 10:00:00',
               '2012-10-03 11:00:00', '2012-10-03 17:00:00',
               '2012-10-05 02:00:00', '2012-10-05 04:00:00',
               '2012-10-06 03:00:00', '2012-10-07 01:00:00',
               '2012-10-07 02:00:00', '2012-10-09 03:00:00',
               ...
               '2018-03-24 05:00:00', '2018-03-24 06:00:00',
               '2018-03-24 07:00:00', '2018-03-29 02:00:00',
               '2018-05-05 02:00:00', '2018-06-02 02:00:00',
               '2018-08-07 07:00:00', '2018-08-07 08:00:00',
               '2018-08-07 09:00:00', '2018-08-23 02:00:00'],
              dtype='datetime64[ns]', length=11976, freq=None)
```

Figure 5.11 – The output of the missing data analysis

It can be observed from the preceding output that there are 11,976 missing timestamps in our dataset.

Now, we will explore the interval variable temperature using pandas' `describe` method, as shown here:

```
df_traffic['temp'].describe()

count    40575.000000
mean       281.315009
std         13.818404
min          0.000000
25%        271.840000
50%        282.860000
75%        292.280000
max        310.070000
Name: temp, dtype: float64
```

Figure 5.12 – Exploring the temperature variable

We can observe in the statistics for the temperature that the minimum temperature in our dataset is 0 kelvin, which is not possible, so we need to handle these outliers. Since this is time series data, instead of removing the outliers, we need to replace them in order to maintain continuity, as shown here:

```
df_traffic['temp']=df_traffic['temp'].replace(0,df_
traffic['temp'].median())
```

In the preceding code snippet, we are replacing 0 kelvin temperature values with the `median` of the temperatures recorded in the dataset. (Alternatively, you can use `mean` as well for replacing.)

In the next step, we will select the last 3 years of data, as discussed previously, since that is more consistent with a few intermittent missing values:

```
df_traffic = df_traffic[df_traffic.index.year.
isin([2016,2017,2018])].copy()

# Filling missing values using backfill and interpolation
methods
df_traffic = pd.concat([df_traffic.select_
dtypes(include=['object']).fillna(method='backfill'),
                df_traffic.select_dtypes(include=['float']).
```

```
interpolate()], axis=1)
df_traffic.shape
```

In the preceding code, we are first selecting the data for the years 2016, 2017, and 2018. Then, we are filling the missing values using the backfill and interpolation methods. Finally, we have a dataset with 24,096 rows for the last 3 years with no missing values, which can be checked, as shown here:

```
df_traffic.isna().sum()

holiday                0
temp                   0
rain_1h                0
snow_1h                0
clouds_all             0
weather_main           0
weather_description    0
traffic_volume         0
dtype: int64
```

Figure 5.13 – Checking the dataset again for missing values

We do not have any more missing values in the dataset, as shown in the preceding output.

Now, it's time to convert our categorical variables into dummy/indicator variables. We will be using pandas' `get_dummies()` method for this purpose, as shown here:

```
df_traffic = pd.get_dummies(df_traffic, columns = ['holiday', 'weather_main'], drop_first=True)
df_traffic.drop('weather_description', axis=1, inplace=True)
```

In the preceding code, we are first creating dummy variables for the `holiday` and `weather_main` categorical variables, and then we are dropping the original categorical variable from the dataset. We are also dropping the `weather_description` column, which is an extension of the `weather_main` column, and it doesn't contain any additional information that can be useful for our forecasting model:

	temp	rain_1h	snow_1h	clouds_all	traffic_volume	holiday_Columbus Day	holiday_Independence Day	holiday_Labor Day	holiday_Martin Luther King Jr Day	holiday_Memorial Day	holiday_New Years Day	holiday_No
2016-01-01 00:00:00	265.940	0.0	0.0	90.0	1513.0	0	0	0	0	0	1	
2016-01-01 01:00:00	266.000	0.0	0.0	90.0	1550.0	0	0	0	0	0	0	
2016-01-01 02:00:00	266.005	0.0	0.0	90.0	1134.5	0	0	0	0	0	0	
2016-01-01 03:00:00	266.010	0.0	0.0	90.0	719.0	0	0	0	0	0	0	
2016-01-01 04:00:00	264.800	0.0	0.0	90.0	533.0	0	0	0	0	0	0	

Figure 5.14 – A sample view of the dataset

A sample output after converting categorical data is shown previously.

Splitting the dataset into training, test, and validation sets

The dataset will be split into training, testing, and validation for training the model, evaluating the model, and estimating the model performance during the training phase.

Since this is a time series dataset, we are not going to use the standard 70–30/80–20 split; instead, we will be splitting the dataset based on the time period. In order to do so, we need to check the start and end time of our down-sampled data, which can be achieved using the following code snippet:

```
print("Date starting from :",df_traffic.index.min())
print("Date end :",df_traffic.index.max())

Date starting from : 2016-01-01 00:00:00
Date end : 2018-09-30 23:00:00
```

Figure 5.15 – The results for the down-sampled data

Training dataset

We will consider the data for 2 years, starting from 1 January, 2016 to 31 December, 2017, for the training dataset. The following code snippet divides the dataset within our required date range. This training dataset will be used to train our model:

```
df_traffic_train = df_traffic.loc[:datetime.
datetime(year=2017,month=12,day=31,hour=23)]

print("Total number of row in train dataset:", df_traffic_
train.shape[0])
print("Train dataset start date :",df_traffic_train.index.
```

```
min())
print("Train dataset end date:",df_traffic_train.index.max())
```

The following output is displayed:

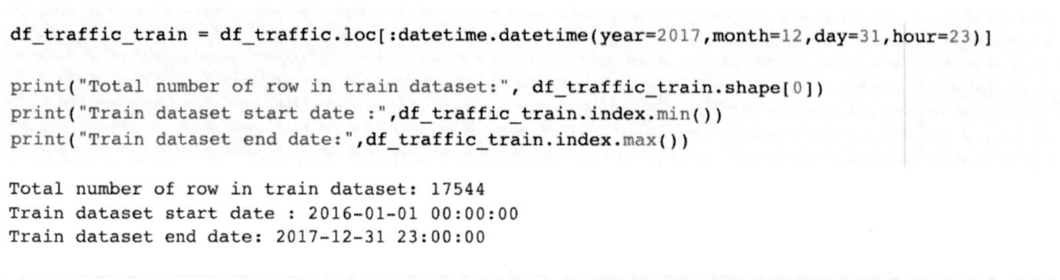

```
df_traffic_train = df_traffic.loc[:datetime.datetime(year=2017,month=12,day=31,hour=23)]

print("Total number of row in train dataset:", df_traffic_train.shape[0])
print("Train dataset start date :",df_traffic_train.index.min())
print("Train dataset end date:",df_traffic_train.index.max())

Total number of row in train dataset: 17544
Train dataset start date : 2016-01-01 00:00:00
Train dataset end date: 2017-12-31 23:00:00
```

Figure 5.16 – The training dataset

The size of the training dataset along with its start and end date is displayed.

Validation dataset

Now, we will consider the next 6 months of data for the purpose of validation. The following code snippet divides the dataset within our required date range:

```
df_traffic_val = df_traffic.loc[datetime.
datetime(year=2018,month=1,day=1,hour=0):datetime.
datetime(year=2018,month=6,day=30,hour=23)]

print("Total number of row in validate dataset:", df_traffic_
val.shape[0])
print("Validate dataset start date :",df_traffic_val.index.
min())
print("Validate dataset end date:",df_traffic_val.index.max())
```

This results in the following output:

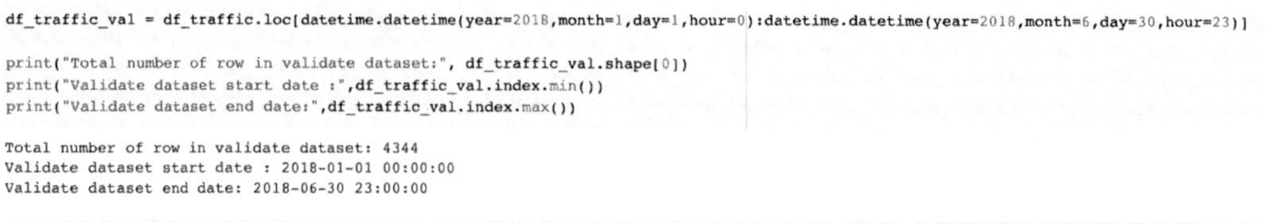

```
df_traffic_val = df_traffic.loc[datetime.datetime(year=2018,month=1,day=1,hour=0):datetime.datetime(year=2018,month=6,day=30,hour=23)]

print("Total number of row in validate dataset:", df_traffic_val.shape[0])
print("Validate dataset start date :",df_traffic_val.index.min())
print("Validate dataset end date:",df_traffic_val.index.max())

Total number of row in validate dataset: 4344
Validate dataset start date : 2018-01-01 00:00:00
Validate dataset end date: 2018-06-30 23:00:00
```

Figure 5.17 – The validation dataset

The validation dataset is now ready.

The test dataset

Finally, for the test dataset, we will consider the remaining time period from July 2018 to September 2018, which is the end period in the dataset. The following code snippet divides the dataset within our required date range. This test dataset is used to forecast our results after the model is trained:

```
df_traffic_test = df_traffic.loc[datetime.
datetime(year=2018,month=7,day=1,hour=0):]

print("Total number of row in test dataset:", df_traffic_test.
shape[0])
print("Validate dataset start date :",df_traffic_test.index.
min())
print("Validate dataset end date:",df_traffic_test.index.max())
```

So far, we have read the data, carried out EDA and data preprocessing, and split it into three different pandas DataFrames for training, testing, and validation:

- `df_traffic_train`: This is the training dataset, which is used to train our model.
- `df_traffic_val`: This is the validation dataset, which is used to validate our model after every epoch.
- `df_traffic_test`: This is the test dataset for when our model is trained and ready. We will use this data to perform forecasting and compare results.

Feature engineering

One of the key feature engineering steps was converting a categorical variable into a dummy/indicator variable, which was done before the data was split into training, testing, and validation.

The next and the most important feature engineering step is the process of normalizing the interval variables. It is always recommended to perform normalization to obtain better results and train the model faster. There are many normalization techniques available, and we are going to use the min-max scaler from the `sklearn preprocessing` module. We will apply the scaler to all the interval variables in the training, validation, and test datasets – `temp`, `rain_1h`, `snow_1h`, `clouds_all`, and `traffic_volume`:

```
#create scalers
temp_scaler = MinMaxScaler()
```

```
rain_scaler = MinMaxScaler()
snow_scaler = MinMaxScaler()
cloud_scaler = MinMaxScaler()
volume_scaler = MinMaxScaler()

#Create transformers
temp_scaler_transformer = temp_scaler.fit(df_traffic_
train[['temp']])
rain_scaler_transformer = rain_scaler.fit(df_traffic_
train[['rain_1h']])
snow_scaler_transformer = snow_scaler.fit(df_traffic_
train[['snow_1h']])
cloud_scaler_transformer = cloud_scaler.fit(df_traffic_
train[['clouds_all']])
volume_scaler_transformer = volume_scaler.fit(df_traffic_
train[['traffic_volume']])
```

In the preceding code block, we are primarily performing these steps:

1. **Creating scalers**: We are creating five different min-max scalers for each of the interval columns, since we have five interval columns (`temp`, `rain_1h`, `snow_1h`, `clouds_all`, and `traffic_volume`).
2. **Creating transformers**: The next step is creating transformers using the scalers defined in the previous steps. This can be done by invoking the `fit` method for five individual scalers on the training dataset. Here, we are creating five different transformers for each interval column (`temp`, `rain_1h`, `snow_1h`, `clouds_all`, and `traffic_volume`) for our Metro Interstate Traffic Volume dataset.
3. Now, we will apply scaling, as defined and fitted previously, to the training datasets, as shown here:

```
df_traffic_train["temp"] = temp_scaler_transformer.
transform(df_traffic_train[['temp']])
df_traffic_train["rain_1h"] = rain_scaler_transformer.
transform(df_traffic_train[['rain_1h']])
df_traffic_train["snow_1h"] = snow_scaler_transformer.
transform(df_traffic_train[['snow_1h']])
df_traffic_train["clouds_all"] = cloud_scaler_
transformer.transform(df_traffic_train[['clouds_all']])
df_traffic_train["traffic_volume"] = volume_scaler_
transformer.transform(df_traffic_train[['traffic_
```

```
volume']])
```

As shown in the preceding code, the scalers are applied on the training dataset using the `transform` method on the defined scaler.

4. We will use the same scaler fitted on the training dataset to apply the scaling on the testing and validation dataset, as shown here:

```
df_traffic_val["temp"] = temp_scaler_transformer.
transform(df_traffic_val[['temp']])
df_traffic_val["rain_1h"] = rain_scaler_transformer.
transform(df_traffic_val[['rain_1h']])
df_traffic_val["snow_1h"] = snow_scaler_transformer.
transform(df_traffic_val[['snow_1h']])
df_traffic_val["clouds_all"] = cloud_scaler_transformer.
transform(df_traffic_val[['clouds_all']])
df_traffic_val["traffic_volume"] = volume_scaler_
transformer.transform(df_traffic_val[['traffic_volume']])

df_traffic_test["temp"] = temp_scaler_transformer.
transform(df_traffic_test[['temp']])
df_traffic_test["rain_1h"] = rain_scaler_transformer.
transform(df_traffic_test[['rain_1h']])
df_traffic_test["snow_1h"] = snow_scaler_transformer.
transform(df_traffic_test[['snow_1h']])
df_traffic_test["clouds_all"] = cloud_scaler_transformer.
transform(df_traffic_test[['clouds_all']])
df_traffic_test["traffic_volume"] = volume_scaler_
transformer.transform(df_traffic_test[['traffic_
volume']])
```

In the preceding code, we are again using the transform method on the scaler fitted on the training dataset to scale the interval columns in the testing and the validation dataset.

Creating a custom dataset

In this section, we will create a utility class to extract features and targets from the dataset. So, we will be loading the training, validation, and testing DataFrames that we split earlier and creating features from these DataFrames to be used in the model. The output of this custom dataset class will be used to create a data loader in a later part of this section.

Loading data

Let's start with loading the DataFrames. At the end of the feature engineering section, we were ready with three different pandas DataFrames for training, validation, and testing:

```
#STEP1: Load the data
self.df_traffic_train = df_traffic_train
self.df_traffic_val = df_traffic_val
self.df_traffic_test = df_traffic_test
```

In the preceding code, we are making copies of the three training, validation, and testing DataFrames.

Creating features

Now, we will create features and target variables:

```
#STEP2: Creating Features
if train: #process train dataset
  features = self.df_traffic_train
  target = self.df_traffic_train.traffic_volume
elif validate: #process validate dataset
  features = self.df_traffic_val
  target = self.df_traffic_val.traffic_volume
else: #process test dataset
  features = self.df_traffic_test
  target = self.df_traffic_test.traffic_volume
```

In this code block, we are creating two variables – one is the feature that consists of `DataFrame` with our `features` column, which is the DataFrame with `temp`, `rain_1h`, `snow_1h`, `clouds_all`, `traffic_volume`, and all the columns created from the categorical variables. The second variable is the target, which is a pandas Series of `traffic_volume`.

The condition for selecting the DataFrame is also defined in this step. If the `train` parameter is `True`, `features` and the `target` variable are set up for our training dataset – that is, with the `df_traffic_train` dataset; if the validation parameter is `True`, the features and the target variable are set up for the validation dataset – that is, with the `df_traffic_val` DataFrame; and similarly, if the test parameter is `True`, the features and the target variable are set up for our test dataset – that is, with the `df_traffic_test` DataFrame.

Creating windows/sequencing

Before we perform the windowing step, let's briefly discuss what it is and why we need to do it.

In time series forecasting, it is important to give the model the most complete information possible at a given time, and historical data in time series plays an important role in making future predictions.

It, therefore, expects data that is generated in the specific intervals of the periods with rolling outputs. If the dataset is not in this format, we would need to reshape the dataset before it can be passed to the time series model algorithms. The most commonly used process to do so is called "windowing" or "sequencing." The fixed windows give the model the span to work with rolling targets (as explained in the previous section).

Let's consider a univariant time series dataset with nine rows:

Date	Target
1/1/20	1.00
1/2/20	2.00
1/3/20	3.00
1/4/20	4.00
1/5/20	5.00
1/6/20	6.00
1/7/20	7.00
1/8/20	8.00
1/9/20	9.00

Figure 5.18 – A dataset with the Date and Target columns

The preceding table has the **Date** column represented in the `<mm/dd/YY>` format and a column called **Target**. Let's apply windowing to the preceding dataset with the window size as `3`. The following figure shows the results of windowing with a window size of `3`:

	Features			Target
Window 1	1/1/20	1/2/20	1/3/20	4.00
Window 2	1/2/20	1/3/20	1/4/20	5.00
Window 3	1/3/20	1/4/20	1/5/20	6.00
Window 4	1/4/20	1/5/20	1/6/20	7.00
Window 5	1/5/20	1/6/20	1/7/20	8.00
Window 6	1/6/20	1/7/20	1/8/20	9.00

Figure 5.19 – Windowing with a window size of 3

After applying windowing with a window size of `3`, we can see that there are six rows of data being generated; the features for **Window 1** will be the collection of all the features of **1/1/20**, **1/2/20**, and **1/3/20**, and the target variable will be the target value of **1/4/20**.

For example, if we are predicting the temperature for a day by using the humidity recorded, then for **Window 1**, the features will be a collection of the humidity recorded for the days **1/1/20**, **1/2/20**, and **1/3/20**, and the target variable will be the temperature value of **1/4/20**.

Windowing/sequencing is one of the most commonly used techniques in time series forecasting, and it helps us to provide complete information to our model for better forecasting.

Now, so far, we have learned how to get data prepared for time series forecasting to work. In the next section, we will use LSTM models to perform forecasting using PyTorch Lightning.

Now, we will perform the data preparation step of windowing:

```
#STEP3: Create windows/sequencing
self.x, self.y = [], []
for i in range(len(features) - window_size):
    v = features.iloc[i:(i + window_size)].values
    self.x.append(v)
    self.y.append(target.iloc[i + window_size])
```

In this step, we are converting our dataset into windows with a default size of `480` – that is, 20 days' worth of data. We will be training our LSTM model with 20 days of historical data to make a prediction for the next day.

In the preceding code, we have two Python class variables; `x` will have a sequence of the past 20 days of features (`temp`, `rain_1h`, `snow_1h`, `clouds_all`, `traffic_volume`, and all the columns created from the categorical variables), and the `y` class variable will have the target variable (`traffic_volume`) for the next consecutive day.

Calculating the length of the dataset

In this custom data class, we are also calculating the total number of records for our data after performing windowing, which will later be used for the `__len__(self)` method:

```
#STEP4: Calculate length of dataset
self.num_sample = len(self.x)
```

To summarize our `__init__()` method, it takes three Boolean parameters as input, and depending on the flag that is set, it picks up either a training, validation, or test dataset. Then, the features and target are extracted from the dataset, and it performs windowing on the features and target data with a default window size of `480`. After windowing, this sequence data is stored in class variables called `x` and `y`, which represent the features and target variable.

Returning the number of rows

We will also define a utility function to return the number of rows in the dataset, which is stored as a `num_sample` class variable. This is calculated and initialized in `__init__()`:

```
  def __len__(self):
    #returns the total number of records for data set
    return self.num_sample

```

Finally, we define the `__getitem__` method to get the value of `x` and `y` at the index, as shown here:

```
  def __getitem__(self, index):
    x = self.x[index].astype(np.float32)
    y = self.y[index].astype(np.float32)
    return x, y
```

In the preceding code, the `__getitem__` method takes `index` as a parameter and returns the record for both our features and target variable – that is, it returns the value at `index` from both class variables, `x` and `y`. This is done after performing windowing on our dataset in the `__init__` method.

Now, we are ready to test `TrafficVolumeDataset` before moving on to the next section of building the LSTM model. One quick way to test it is by using a `for` loop and, after a single iteration, stopping the loop by calling a `break` statement:

```
traffic_volume =  TrafficVolumeDataset(test=True)

#let's loop it over single iteration and print the shape and
also data
for i, (features,targets) in enumerate(traffic_volume):
  print("Size of the features",features.shape)
  print("Printing features:\n", features)
```

```
    print("Printing targets:\n", targets)
    break
```

In the preceding code, we are creating `TrafficVolumeDataset` for the testing data, looping it over a single iteration, and printing the size of the features, the content of the features, and the targets.

The following output is displayed:

```
Size of the features (480, 26)
Printing features:
 [[0.84078825 0.          0.          ... 0.          0.          0.          ]
 [0.8329684  0.          0.          ... 0.          0.          0.          ]
 [0.8251486  0.          0.          ... 0.          0.          0.          ]
 ...
 [0.78026277 0.          0.          ... 0.          0.          0.          ]
 [0.7715045  0.          0.          ... 0.          0.          0.          ]
 [0.7636847  0.          0.          ... 0.          0.          0.          ]]
Printing targets:
 0.16964285
```

Figure 5.20 – The shape of the features for our dataset

Our feature size is multi-dimensional with **480** rows and **26** columns – that is, we have **480** rows of historical data because our default window size is `480`, and **26** columns because we have 5 interval columns and 21 indicator variables created from 2 categorical variables. Finally, there is a single future target value.

> **Important Note**
>
> If you overwrite the `window_size` parameter with a new value, then you may not produce the same output – that is, have the size of features as (480, 26).

Configuring the LSTM model using PyTorch Lightning

We have loaded the dataset into pandas, carried out exploratory data analysis, performed feature engineering, and created a custom dataset to access data. Now, we are ready for our processed data and the engineered features with windows to be fed into the time series forecasting model.

Let's start building our Deep Learning-based forecasting model. We'll build a multi-layer double-stacked LSTM model to forecast Metro Interstate Traffic Volume.

To build our LSTM model using PyTorch Lightning, let's divide the process into the following steps:

1. Define the model.
2. Set up the optimizer.
3. Set up data.
4. Configure the training loop.
5. Configure the validation loop.

Defining the model

In defining the model, we will do the following:

1. Initialize and build the LSTM model using the `torch nn` module with the input size, the total required hidden dimensions, and the number of layers. Also, we're setting the `batch_first` parameter as `True`, since the LSTM layer is our first layer here.
2. Create a linear layer with the `torch nn` module, where the input size is the total number of hidden dimensions times the window size, and the second parameter is the size of the output. In our case, we are predicting the `traffic_volume` column, so our output size is `1`.

Initialize the loss function

We are using the MSE loss function to calculate losses. The MSE loss function creates a criterion that measures the mean squared error between each element in the *xx* input and the *yy* target .

Also, we set the learning rate as `0.0001`. However, in a later part of this section, we will also try PyTorch Lightning's learning rate finder to ascertain the learning rate and reduce the amount of guesswork when choosing a good learning rate.

Let's create a class called `TrafficVolumePrediction` that is inherited from the `LightningModule` class from PyTorch Lightning:

```
  def __init__(self, input_size=26, output_size=1, hidden_
dim=10, n_layers=2, window_size=480):
    """
    input_size: Number of features in the input
    hidden_dim: number of hidden layers
    n_layers: number of RNN to stack over each other
```

```
        output_size: number of items to be outputted
        """
        super(TrafficVolumePrediction, self).__init__()

        self.hidden_dim = hidden_dim
        self.n_layers = n_layers
        self.lstm = nn.LSTM(input_size, hidden_dim, n_layers,
bidirectional=False, batch_first=True)
        self.fc = nn.Linear(hidden_dim * window_size, output_size)

        self.loss = nn.MSELoss()

        self.learning_rate = 0.0001
```

This config code block takes the following input or parameters in the constructor:

- `input_size`: This represents the number of expected features in the *x* input. In our case, the total number of features in our Metro Interstate Traffic Volume dataset is 26, so the default value for this parameter is `26`.
- `hidden_dim`: This parameter represents the total number of hidden LSTMs – that is, the replicas of LSTM – required. The default value is set to 10 – that is, we have 10 hidden layers.
- `n_layers`: This parameter represents the number of LSTM layers stacked on top of each other. In this chapter, we are going to use a two-LSTM-layer neural network, so the default value is set to 2 here.
- `output_size`: The number of outputs expected from the model. Since we are forecasting `traffic_volume`, which is a regression problem, the output size is `1`.
- `window_size`: The size of the window the data is to be divided into. The default size is `480` – that is, we are considering 20 days' worth of data.

> **Important Note**
>
> During the automated process for identifying the learning rate, by default, PyTorch Lightning looks for variables with the `learning_rate` name or the `lr` inside our init method. It's always a good practice to set learning with variable names as `learning_rate` or `lr`.

Defining hidden layers

Now, we can define the hidden layers:

```
    def get_hidden(self, batch_size):
        # hidden = torch.zeros(self.n_layers, batch_size, self.
hidden_dim)

        hidden_state = torch.zeros(self.n_layers, batch_size, self.
hidden_dim)
        cell_state = torch.zeros(self.n_layers, batch_size, self.
hidden_dim)
        hidden = (hidden_state, cell_state)
        return hidden
```

The `get_hidden` method takes the batch size and input and returns a tuple containing two tensors for the hidden state and a cell state for our LSTM hidden layer. The two tensors are initialized with zeros.

Defining the forward pass

By now, we are familiar with the `forward` method, which acts like a mapper where data is passed through layers to generate a model's output. We will now use the `forward` method to connect all the layers by configuring the input and output, as shown here:

```
    def forward(self, x):
        batch_size = x.size(0)
        hidden = self.get_hidden(batch_size)
        out, hidden = self.lstm(x, hidden)
        out =out.reshape(out.shape[0], -1)
        out = self.fc(out)
        return out
```

In the `forward` method, we do the following:

1. Firstly, we extract the batch size from `x` using the `size` method.
2. Then, we call the `get_hidden` utility function defined previously to initialize the hidden layer, which will return the multi-dimensional tensor filled with zeros.
3. In the next step, we pass the `x` input along with the hidden layer to our LSTM model, which returns the output and the hidden layer.

4. The output is then flattened to a single dimension before being sent to our fully connected layer. Finally, the `forward` method returns the output from the fully connected layer.

Setting up the optimizer

As we have learned in previous chapters, optimizers in PyTorch Lightning can be configured in a life cycle method called `configure_optimizers`. The code for the `configure_optimizers` life cycle method is as follows:

```
    def configure_optimizers(self):
      params = self.parameters()
      optimizer = optim.Adam(params=params, lr = self.learning_
rate)
      return optimizer
```

In the `configure_optimizer` method, we are primarily doing two operations:

- Getting the model parameters: Since this method is written inside our model class, parameters for the model can be accessed by calling the `self.parameters()` method.
- Then, we use the `Adam` optimizer (accessed from the `torch.optim` module) with a learning rate that has been initialized in the `__init__` method.

  `configure_optimizer` finally returns the Adam optimizer once the parameters and the learning rate are set up.

> **Important Note**
> For this use case, we have used Adam as our optimizer and the learning rate as `0.0001`. This can always be tried with different optimizers, and we can try it out with different learning rates for improved model performance. The model has also been tried with the `RMSprop` optimizer, which is another good option for the LSTM type of model.

Setting up data

In the previous section, we created a training, validation, and testing dataset. We will now use the training data to train the model and validation data to estimate it during the training period. Since PyTorch Lightning needs data loaders to access the data, we will be now defining the `train_dataloader` and `val_dataloader` life cycle methods in the following code block. Let's overwrite the `train_dataloader` method of `pl.LightningModule` as follows:

```
    def train_dataloader(self):
        traffic_volume_train =  TrafficVolumeDataset(train=True)
        train_dataloader = torch.utils.data.DataLoader(traffic_
volume_train, batch_size=50)
        return train_dataloader
```

In the `train_dataloader` method, we first initialize an instance of `TrafficVolumeDataset`, the class that we defined earlier, with the training data. Then, we pass the output of `TrafficVolumeDataset` stored as `traffic_volume_train` to the `torch.utils.data.DataLoader` module with a batch size of 50 to create the `train` data loader. Finally, the `train` data loader with a batch size of 50 is returned by this method.

Similar to the preceding step, to train our LSTM model on our validation dataset, let's set up our `validate` data loader by overwriting the method of `pl.LightningModule` called `val_dataloader`:

```
    def val_dataloader(self):
        traffic_volume_val = TrafficVolumeDataset(validate=True)
        val_dataloader = torch.utils.data.DataLoader(traffic_
volume_val, batch_size=50)
        return val_dataloader
```

In the preceding code, we call an instance of TrafficVolumeDataset that we defined in the previous section to create a validation dataset called traffic_volume_val. Then, we pass traffic_volume_val to the torch.utils.data.DataLoader class to create our validation data loader. This method returns the validation data loader with a batch size of 50.

> **Important Note**
> When creating the dataset from our TrafficVolumeDataset class, for the train_dataloader method, we set the train flag to true, and for the val_dataloader method, we set the val flag to true.

In the preceding code, we set the batch size to 50. Depending on the hardware requirements and performance, this batch size can be increased or decreased.

Configuring the training loop

Now, we can define the training_step life cycle method to train the model while calculating the loss, as shown here:

```
def training_step(self, train_batch, batch_idx):
    features, targets = train_batch
    output = self(features)
    output = output.view(-1)
    loss = self.loss(output, targets)
    self.log('train_loss', loss, prog_bar=True)
    return {"loss": loss}
```

In the preceding code block, the training_step method takes two inputs:

- batch_idx: The index of the batch.
- train_batch: This is the data batch from the data loader returned from the train_dataloader method.

The following is a step-by-step explanation of the training_step method:

1. The first step is to extract the features and targets from the train_batch parameter, which is a tuple type. The first element of the tuple is the features, and the second element of the tuple is the targets.
2. In the next step, we pass the features of x to our LSTM model using the self method. The self method takes in the features as input, passes it to our LSTM model, and returns the output.

3. Then, the output from the LSTM model is converted into a single-dimensional array with the help of the PyTorch `view` method. After converting the output, the loss is calculated using the `loss` object defined in the `__init__` method.
4. As we have seen in previous chapters, it's a good idea to log the training loss before the `return` statement. This will be plotted on TensorBoard later on. Logging the training loss is achieved by calling the `log` method, with the first input as the name of the log. Here, we are calling it `train_log`. The second input is the log itself, and we set the `prog_bar` flag to `True`. By setting `prog_bar` to `True`, the `train_loss` value will be shown on the progress bar during the Trainer process.
5. Finally, the `training_step` method returns the loss, which is stored as loss inside a dictionary.

> **Important Note**
> Any data that is being logged will be logged inside the PyTorch Lightning logging directory and can also be shown inside TensorBoard.

Configuring the validation loop

Now, we will define our `validation_step` life cycle method to estimate the validation loss during the training period, as shown here:

```
def validation_step(self, val_batch, batch_idx):
    features, targets = val_batch
    output = self(features)
    output = output.view(-1)
    loss = self.loss(output, targets)
    self.log('val_loss', loss, prog_bar=True)
```

In the preceding code block, the `training_step` method takes two inputs:

- `batch_idx`: The index of the batch.
- `val_batch`: This is the data batch from the data loader returned from the `val_dataloader` method.

This method works in exactly the same manner as `training_step`, described previously. So, it will train the model and calculate the loss on the validation data, which can be later plotted using TensorBoard to evaluate the performance of the model.

> **Important Note**
>
> Any data that is being logged will be logged inside the PyTorch Lightning logging directory and can also be shown inside TensorBoard.

Training the model

Now that we have completed the configuration for the model, we can kick-start model training:

```
seed_everything(10)
model = TrafficVolumePrediction()
trainer = pl.Trainer( max_epochs=40, progress_bar_refresh_
rate=25)
# Run learning rate finder
lr_finder = trainer.tuner.lr_find(model, min_lr=1e-04, max_
lr=1, num_training=30)
# Pick point based on plot, or get suggestion
new_lr = lr_finder.suggestion()
print("Suggested Learning Rate is :", new_lr)
# update hparams of the model
model.hparams.lr = new_lr
```

The following is a step-by-step explanation of training the model:

1. We first set the seed to `10` in order to make the experiment results reproducible. Then, we call an instance of `TrafficVolumePrediction`, which we created in the previous section.
2. Next, we create a `Trainer` object with the maximum number of epochs as `40`, and by refreshing the progress bar every 25 units. We can try training for more epochs and compare the accuracy.
3. We also call the `lr_find` method in the `Trainer` object. This is the method that helps us to identify the optimal learning rate, as discussed in the previous section. The `lr_find` method takes in the input of the model, the minimum learning rate (which is `0.0001`, in this case), the maximum learning rate (which is `1`), and the total number of trainings.
4. Then, we call the `suggestion` method to get the optimal learning rate suggested by `lr_method`. This effectively overwrites the earlier learning rate.
5. In the final step, we overwrite our learning rate hyperparameter with a new learning rate.

The easiest way to check the learning rate is shown in the following code snippet:

```
print("model learning rate:",model.hparams)
```

The output is as follows:

```
print("model learning rate:",model.hparams)


model learning rate: "lr": 0.5411695265464638
```

Figure 5.21 – The model learning rate

Now, since we have identified the optimal learning rate, it's time to train our model:

```
trainer.fit(model)
```

We are passing the model, which is an instance of `TrafficVolumePrediction`, using the `fit` method on the trainer to train the model.

The following output is displayed:

Figure 5.22 – The training result

> **Important Note**
>
> When we pass the `auto_lr_find` input as `True`, PyTorch Lightning searches for the variable with the `learning_rate` name or `lr` within our LSTM class. Make sure you have created a variable with the `learning_rate` name or `lr` within the `LSTM` class.

The learning rate is one of the most important hyperparameters, and it's not easy to determine the best learning rate. PyTorch Lightning helps us to determine the optimal learning rate, but it may not be the best learning rate. However, it's a good way to start identifying the best learning rate. We will also train the model here without the suggested learning rate from PyTorch Lightning and compare the results.

Measuring the training loss

In the preceding steps, at the training step, we logged `train_loss`. Now, let's use TensorBoard to plot and monitor our training loss throughout each epoch. Let's start TensorBoard by running the following code:

```
%load_ext tensorboard
%tensorboard --logdir Lightning_logs/
```

The output is as follows:

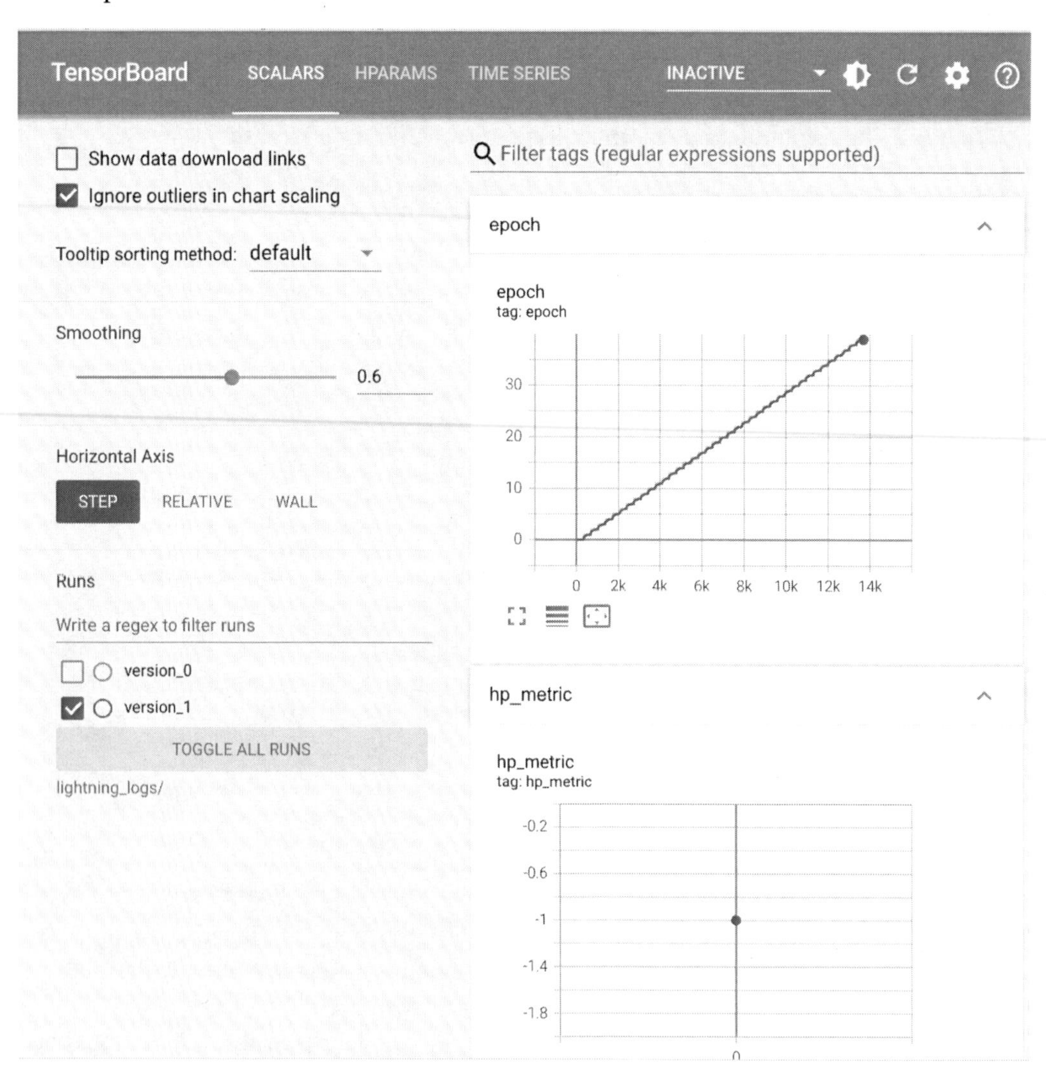

Figure 5.23 – A screenshot of the TensorBoard dashboard

The two values, `train_loss` and `val_loss`, that we logged in our LSTM model can now be accessed from TensorBoard. These charts help us to monitor our model's performance.

The training loss is as follows:

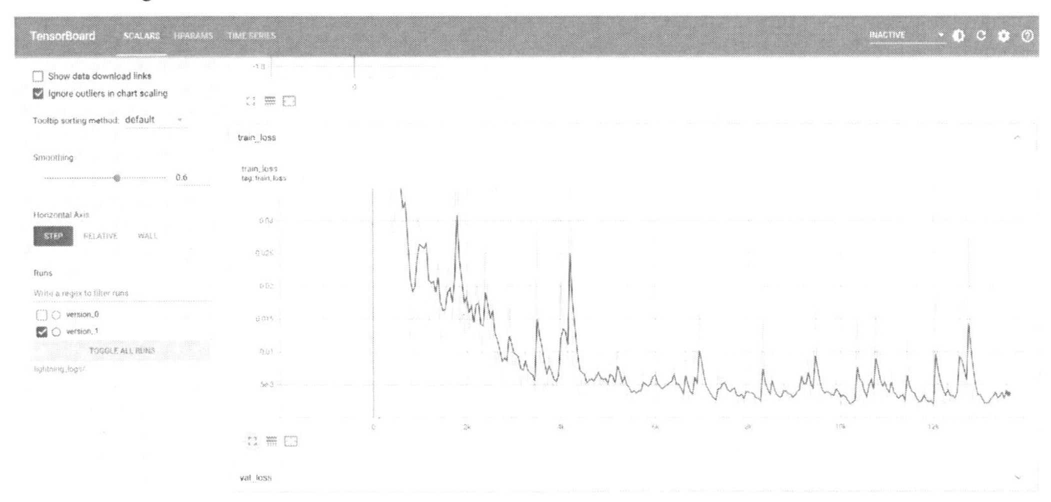

Figure 5.24 – The training loss plot on TensorBoard

As we can see, the training loss is reducing.

The validation loss is as follows:

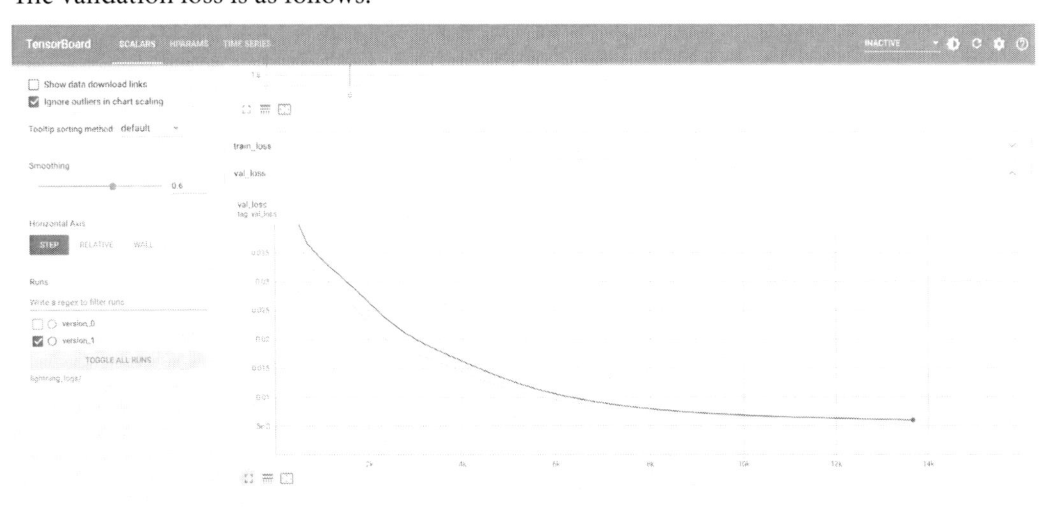

Figure 5.25 – The validation loss plot on TensorBoard

As you can see, the validation loss is also reducing, which means the model is converging and is stable.

Loading the model

Before we predict on the test data and compare results, which we will do in the next section of this chapter, we need to first load the model, which can be done with the following steps.

List the files at the PyTorch Lightning default path (`lightning_logs`). Once we know the model's filename, we can make use of the following code, which uses the `load_from_checkpoint` method to load the model and change the mode to `eval`. Now, the model is being loaded from the file and is ready to perform predictions:

```
PATH = 'lightning_logs/version_0/checkpoints/epoch=39-step=13679.ckpt'
trained_traffic_volume_TrafficVolumePrediction = model.load_from_checkpoint(PATH)
trained_traffic_volume_TrafficVolumePrediction.eval()
```

The following output is displayed:

```
TrafficVolumePrediction(
  (lstm): LSTM(26, 10, num_layers=2, batch_first=True)
  (fc): Linear(in_features=4800, out_features=1, bias=True)
  (loss): MSELoss()
)
```

Figure 5.26 – The loaded model

A prediction on the test dataset

This is the final step in this section, where we use the model to make a prediction on the test dataset that we created and plot the chart of actual values versus predicted values. The steps involved in the following code to perform predictions on the test dataset are as follows:

1. First, create the `TrafficVolumeDataset` object by passing the `test` parameter as `True` and use the dataset to create a loader with a batch size of `20`.
2. Iterate over the data loader and collect the features; these features are used to make predictions over the trained model.

3. All the predicted and actual target values are stored in local variables called `predicted_result` and `actual_result` respectively:

```
#Initialize Dataset
traffic_volume_test_dataset =
TrafficVolumeDataset(test=True)
traffic_volume_test_dataloader = torch.utils.data.
DataLoader(traffic_volume_test_dataset, batch_size=20)
predicted_result, actual_result = [], []
#let's loop it over single iteration and print the shape
and also data
for i, (features,targets) in enumerate(traffic_volume_
test_dataloader):
  result = trained_traffic_volume_
TrafficVolumePrediction(features)
  predicted_result.extend(result.view(-1).tolist())
  actual_result.extend(targets.view(-1).tolist())
```

4. Before we plot the chart, let's use `volume_scaler_transformer`, which was created in the feature engineering phase, to perform an inverse transform on the dataset:

```
actual_predicted_df = pd.DataFrame(data={"actual":actual_
result, "predicted": predicted_result})
inverse_transformed_values = volume_scaler_transformer.
inverse_transform(actual_predicted_df)
actual_predicted_df["actual"] = inverse_transformed_
values[:,[0]]
actual_predicted_df["predicted"] = inverse_transformed_
values[:,[1]]
actual_predicted_df
```

The following output is displayed:

	actual	predicted
0	1234.999954	1165.939453
1	780.999981	839.036589
2	648.000016	534.142674
3	418.000002	52.269110
4	478.000026	-116.379431
...	...	...
1723	3543.000033	2719.729722
1724	2780.999916	2391.758597
1725	2158.999898	2000.535991
1726	1449.999968	1326.937029
1727	953.999997	566.273879

1728 rows × 2 columns

Figure 5.27 – Actual versus predicted results

5. Now, let's plot the line chart for the actual versus predicted values:

```
plt.plot(actual_predicted_df["actual"],'b')
plt.plot(actual_predicted_df["predicted"],'r')
plt.show()
```

Here, we are plotting the values for traffic volume forecast actual values versus predicted values. The blue line represents the actual traffic volume, and the red line represents predicted values from our LSTM model:

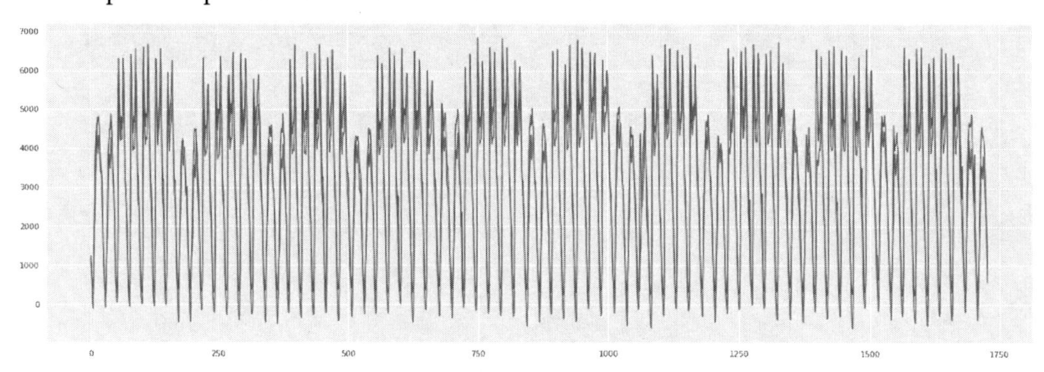

Figure 5.28 – Chart plotting actual versus predicted traffic volume

As we can see, the model is predicting very well and in line with expected results. LSTM is one of the strongest algorithms for time series and is widely used due to its good predictive capabilities.

Additional training and testing results

You can also train the model by disabling the auto-learning rate option. We have trained the model with a learning rate of 0.001 and the Adam optimizer with 140 epochs (you can comment out the `auto_lr` portion to achieve this in the preceding code):

```
trainer.fit(model)

  | Name                     | Type    | Params
------------------------------------------------
0 | TrafficVolumePrediction | LSTM    | 2.4 K
1 | fc                       | Linear  | 4.8 K
2 | loss                     | MSELoss | 0
------------------------------------------------
7.2 K     Trainable params
0         Non-trainable params
7.2 K     Total params
0.029     Total estimated model params size (MB)
Validation sanity check: 0%                                                    0/2 [00:00<?, ?it/s]
Global seed set to 10
Epoch 139: 100% 420/420 [01:30<00:00, 4.62it/s, loss=0.000991, v_num=0, train_loss=0.000199, val_loss=0.0023]
```

Figure 5.29 – The training results after 140 epochs

Compared to the previous results, you can see that loss is much lower and accuracy is a lot better. We have improved the model by a factor of 10. This can be a combination of not relying on the recommended learning rate as well as more training epochs.

The actual versus predicted plot also looks a lot better than the previous one:

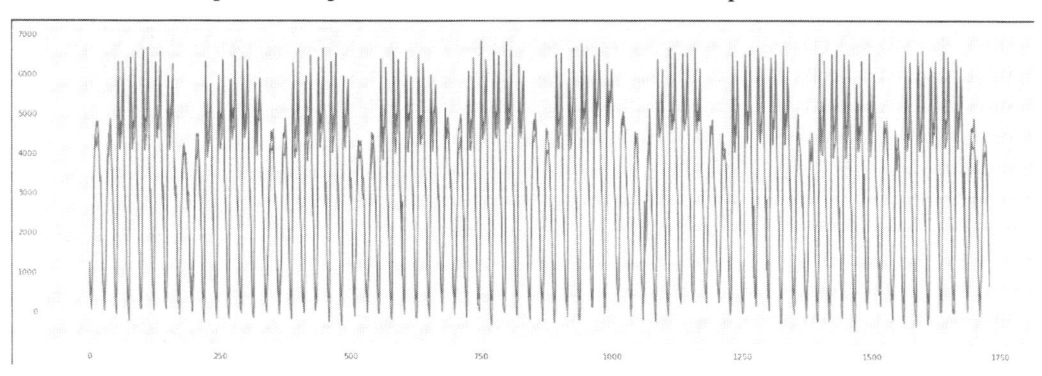

Figure 5.30 – The revised actual versus predicted plot

The next steps

- Try training a model with the RMSProp optimizer with both preset and automatic learning rate options.
- Change the source dataset and rerun the code. Some recommended options are the London bike sharing dataset or weather prediction datasets.
- We have used the LSTM model for time series forecasting in this chapter. There are also other RNN architectures available, such as **Gated Recurrent Units** (**GRUs**). Try another network architecture to improve your forecasting skills.

Summary

Time series modeling is one of the oldest and most ubiquitous applications of machine learning in industry and academia alike. In this chapter, we saw how PyTorch Lightning facilitates time series modeling using Deep Learning algorithms such as RNN and LSTM. This also provides data scientists with various tools to define RNN and LSTM configurations, with capabilities for easily monitoring learning and loss rates. We learned how we can quickly build complex Deep Learning models for time series forecasting using PyTorch Lightning.

We will continue our journey with PyTorch Lightning in the next chapter with one of the most fascinating and newest algorithms in machine learning – **Generative Adversarial Networks** (**GANs**). It can generate realistic faces of humans and objects that do not exist, and they look so real that no one can say for certain that they are artificial entities. Using PyTorch Lightning, you will see that it is much easier to carry out **Generative Modeling**.

6
Deep Generative Models

It has always been the dream of mankind to build a machine that can match human ingenuity. While the word *intelligence* comes with various dimensions, such as calculations, recognition of objects, speech, understanding context, and reasoning; no aspects of human intelligence make us *more human* than our creativity. The ability to create a piece of art, be it a piece of music, a poem, a painting, or a movie, has always been the epitome of human intelligence, and people who are good at such creativity are often treated as "*geniuses*." The question that remains fully unanswered is, can a machine learn creativity?

We have seen machines learn to predict images using a variety of information and sometimes even with little information. A machine learning model can learn from a set of training images and labels to recognize various objects in an image; however, the success of vision models depends on their capability for vast generalizations – that is, recognizing objects in images that were not part of the training set. This is achieved when a Deep Learning model learns the *representation* of an image. The logical question that you may ask is, if a machine can learn the representation of an existing image, can we extend the same concept to teach a machine to generate images that do not exist?

As you may imagine, the answer is *yes*! The family of Deep Learning algorithms that is particularly good at doing so is **Generative Adversarial Networks** (**GANs**). Various models of GANs have been widely used to create images of humans who do not exist or even new paintings. Some of these paintings have even been sold in auctions held by Sotheby's!

GANs are a popular modeling method. In this chapter, we will build generative models to see how they can create cool new images. We will see the advanced use of GANs to create fictional species of butterfly from a known image set, and similarly images of fake food from real food. Then, we will also use another architecture, namely a **Deep Convolutional Generative Adversarial Network** (**DCGAN**), for better results.

In this chapter, we will cover the following topics:

- Getting started with GAN models
- Creating new fake food items using GANs
- Creating new butterfly species using GANs
- Creating new images using DCGANs

Technical requirements

In this chapter, we will primarily be using the following Python modules, mentioned with their versions:

- `pytorch lightning` (version 1.5.2)
- `torch` (version 1.10.0)
- `matplotlib` (version 3.2.2)

Working examples for this chapter can be found at this GitHub link: `https://github.com/PacktPublishing/Deep-Learning-with-PyTorch-Lightning/tree/main/Chapter06`.

In order to make sure that these modules work together and not go out of sync, we have used the specific version of `torch`, `torchvision`, `torchtext`, `torchaudio` with PyTorch Lightning 1.5.2. You can also use the latest version of PyTorch Lightning and torch compatible with each other. More details can be found on the GitHub link: `https://github.com/PacktPublishing/Deep-Learning-with-PyTorch-Lightning`

```
!pip install torch==1.10.0 torchvision==0.11.1
torchtext==0.11.0 torchaudio==0.10.0 --quiet
```

```
!pip install pytorch-lightning==1.5.2 --quiet
```

We will be using the Food dataset, which contains a collection of 16,643 food images, grouped in 11 major food categories, and can be found here: `https://www.kaggle.com/trolukovich/food11-image-dataset`.

We will also use a similar model with the Butterfly dataset which contains 9,285 images for 75 butterfly species. The Butterfly dataset can be found here: `https://www.kaggle.com/gpiosenka/butterfly-images40-species`.

Both these datasets are available in the public domain under CC0.

Getting started with GAN models

One of the most amazing applications of GANs is generation. Just look at the following picture of a girl; can you guess whether she is real or simply generated by a machine?

Figure 6.1 – Fake face generation using StyleGAN (image credit – https://thispersondoesnotexist.com)

Creating such incredibly realistic faces is one of the most successful use cases of GANs. However, GANs are not limited to just generating pretty faces or deepfake videos; they also have key commercial applications as well, such as generating images of houses or creating new models of cars or paintings.

While generative models have been used in the past in statistics, deep generative models such as GANs are relatively new. Deep generative models also include **Variational Autoencoders** (**VAEs**) and auto-regressive models. However, with GAN being the most popular method, we will focus on them here.

What is a GAN?

Interestingly, GAN originated not as a method of generating new things but as a way to improve the accuracy of vision models for recognizing objects. Small amounts of noise in the dataset can make image recognition models give wildly different results. While researching methods on how to thwart adversarial attacks on **Convolutional Neural Network** (**CNN**) models for image recognition, *Ian Goodfellow* and his team at Google came up with a rather simple idea. (There is a funny story about Ian and his team discovering GANs, involving a lot of beer and ping-pong, which every data scientist who also loves to party may be able to relate to!)

Every CNN type of model takes an image and converts it into a lower-dimensional matrix that is a mathematical representation of that image (which is a bunch of numbers to capture the essence of the image). What if we do the reverse? What if we start with a mathematical number and try to reconstruct the image? Well, it may be hard to do so directly, but by using a neural network, we can teach machines to generate fake images by feeding them with lots of real images, their representations in numbers, and then create some variation of those numbers to get a new fake image. That is precisely the idea behind a GAN!

A typical GAN architecture consists of three parts – the **generator**, **discriminator**, and **comparison** modules:

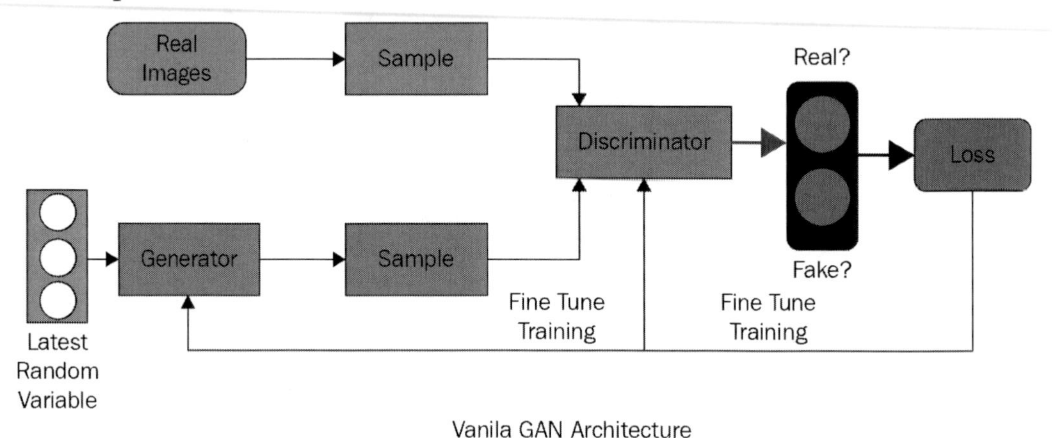

Figure 6.2 – Vanilla GAN architecture

Both the generator and the discriminator are neural networks. We start with real images and, using an **encoder**, convert them into a lower-dimensional entity. Both the generator and the discriminator participate in a play-off, trying to beat each other. The job of the generator is to generate a fake image using random mathematical values (which is a combination of real values plus some random noise) and the job of the discriminator is to determine whether it's real or fake. A loss function acts as a measure of who is winning the play-off. As loss is reduced by running through various epochs, the overall architecture is getting better at generating *realistic* images.

The success of GANs relies mostly on the fact that they use a very small number of parameters and thereby can give amazing results, even with a small amount of data. There are many variants of a GAN, such as a **StyleGAN** and a **BigGAN**, each with different neural network layers; however, they all follow the same architecture. The preceding image of a fake girl uses the StyleGAN variant.

Creating new food items using a GAN

GANs are one of the most common and powerful algorithms used in generative modeling. GANs are used widely to generate fake faces, pictures, anime/cartoon characters, image style translations, semantic image translation, and so on.

We will start by creating an architecture for our GAN model:

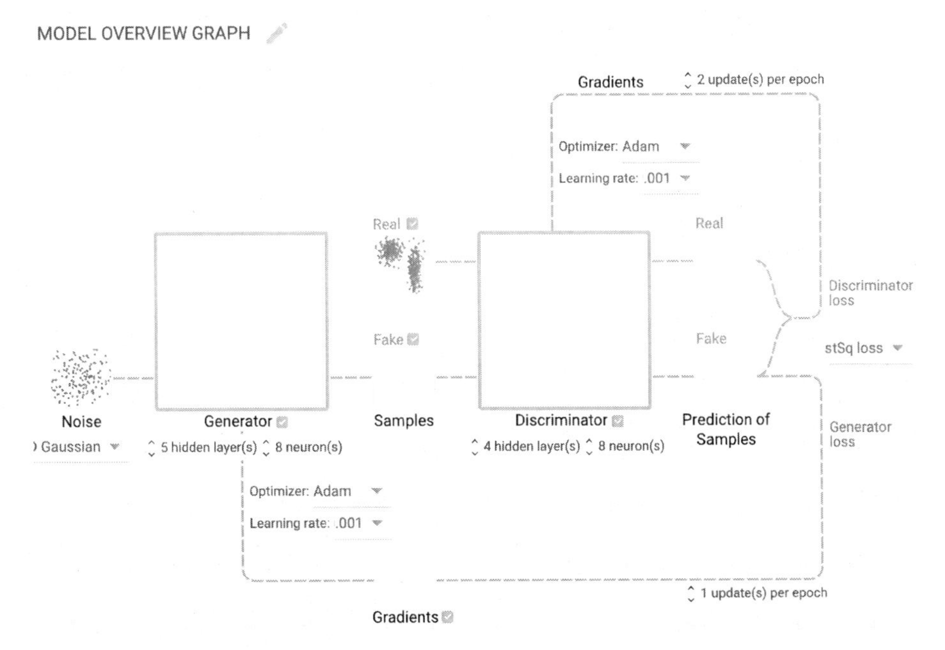

Figure 6.3 – GAN architecture for creating a new food

Firstly, we will define the neural networks for the generator and the discriminator with multiple layers of convolution and fully connected layers. In the architecture that we will be building, we will have **four convolutional and one fully connected layer** for the discriminator, and we will be utilizing **five transposed convolution layers** for the generator. We will attempt to generate fake images by adding Gaussian noise and use the discriminator to detect these fake images. Then, we will use the **Adam** optimizer to optimize the neural network. For this use, we will use **cross-entropy** loss to minimize the loss function.

There are several other hyperparameters such as image size, batch size, latent size, learning rate, channel, kernel size, stride, and padding that are also optimized to get output from the GAN model. These parameters can be fine-tuned as per the model configuration. The goal here is to train a GAN model architecture with the food dataset and generate fake food images and, similarly, use the same GAN model architecture with the butterfly dataset to generate fake butterfly images. We will save the generated images at the end of every epoch to compare new food or butterfly images at every epoch.

In this section, we're going to cover the following main steps to generate fake food images:

1. Load the dataset.
2. Feature-engineer the utility functions.
3. Configure the discriminator model.
4. Configure the generator model.
5. Configure the generative adaptive model.
6. Train the GAN model.
7. Get output for the fake food images.

Loading the dataset

The dataset contains 16,643 food images, grouped in 11 major food categories. This dataset can be downloaded from Kaggle with this URL: `https://www.kaggle.com/trolukovich/food11-image-dataset`.

The code for downloading the dataset is shown here:

```
dataset_url = 'https://www.kaggle.com/trolukovich/food11-image-dataset'

od.download(dataset_url)
```

In the preceding code, we are using the download method from the `opendatasets` package to download the dataset into our Colab environment.

The total size of the food dataset is 1.19 GB and the dataset has three subfolders – `training`, `validation`, and `evaluation`. Each subfolder has food images stored in the nested subfolder under the 11 major food categories. For this chapter, to build our GAN model, we shall be training our model on the training images, so we will use only the `training` subfolder. All the images are colored and stored in the nested subfolders with respect to their food category.

Here are some of the sample images of food from the dataset:

Figure 6.4 – Original random images of food from the dataset

Data processing is always the most important step for any model. So, we will carry out some transformations on the input image data for our GAN model to perform better and faster. In this use case, we will focus primarily on the four major transformations, as shown in the following steps:

1. **Resize**: First, we shall resize the images to 64 pixels.
2. **Center crop**: Then, we will crop the resized image in the center. This converts our images to squares. Center crop is a critical transformation for our GAN model to perform better.
3. **Convert to tensors**: Once the image has been resized and center-cropped, we shall convert the image data to tensor so that it can be processed in the GAN model.
4. **Normalize**: Finally, we shall normalize the tensors in the range of -1 to 1 with a mean of 0 and a standard deviation of 0.5.
5. All of the preceding transformations will not only help our GAN model to perform better but also reduce the training time significantly.

> **Important Note**
> There are many other transformations you can try to improve the model performance, but for this use case, the preceding transformations are good enough to start with.

The following code snippet shows some of the key configurations for our GAN model:

```
image_size = 64
batch_size = 128
normalize = [(0.5, 0.5, 0.5), (0.5, 0.5, 0.5)]
latent_size = 256

food_data_directory = "/content/food11-image-dataset/training"
```

In the preceding code, we are first initializing the variables to be used in the next step. The image size is set to 64 pixels, the batch size is 128, and the mean and standard deviation for normalizing the tensors are both 0.5. The latent size is set to 256, and the path to the food training images is saved as `food_data_directory`. In the next step, we will use these variables to transform our input images to prepare it for our GAN model:

```
food_train_dataset = ImageFolder(food_data_directory,
transform=T.Compose([
    T.Resize(image_size),
```

```
    T.CenterCrop(image_size),
    T.ToTensor(),
    T.Normalize(*normalize)]))

food_train_dataloader = DataLoader(food_train_dataset, batch_
size, num_workers=4, pin_memory=True, shuffle=True)
```

In the preceding code, we are using the `ImageFolder` class from the `torchvision.datasets` library to load the images dataset. We are using the `Compose` method from the `torchvision.transforms` library to compose several transformations together. Inside the `compose` method, the first step is the `Resize` method to set the image size to 64 pixels. In the next transform, we are using the `CenterCrop` method to convert the image into a square. Then, we are converting the resized and cropped image to tensors and, finally, normalizing them between -1 and 1 with a mean and standard deviation of 0.5. We are saving these transformed images in `food_train_dataset`. In the final step, we are using the `DataLoader` class from `torch.utils.data` library to create `food_train_dataloader` with a batch size of 128 and 4 workers, and setting up some of the parameters to make the data loader work better.

So far, in the preceding code, we have loaded our dataset and performed some of the transformations, and `food_train_dataloader` is ready with images in batches of `128`.

In the data processing step, we are transforming and normalizing our images, so it is important for us to bring them back to their original form by denormalizing them. We also need to compare the images generated by our GAN model for each epoch, so we need to save the images at the end of every epoch. Therefore, we will write some utility functions to make these happen in the following section of this chapter.

Feature engineering utility functions

Let's go through the two main functions that are important to understand.

The first utility function that we need is to denormalize the images back to the original form. The `denormalize` utility function is shown here:

```
def denormalize(input_image_tensors):
    input_image_tensors = input_image_tensors * normalize[1][0]
    input_image_tensors = input_image_tensors + normalize[0][0]
    return input_image_tensors
```

The denormalize utility function takes in the tensors and denormalizes them by multiplying by 0.5 and then adding 0.5. These normalization values (mean and standard deviation) are defined at the beginning of this section.

The second utility function required is for saving the images at the end of every epoch. The following is the code snippet for the second utility function:

```
def save_samples(index, sample_images):
    fake_fname = 'generated-images-{}.png'.format(index)
    save_image(denormalize(sample_images[-64:]), os.path.
join(".", fake_fname), nrow=8)
```

The save_samples utility function takes the index, which is the epoch number, and sample_images, which is the image returned by the GAN model at the end of every epoch, as input. Then, it saves the last 64 images in a grid of 8 x 8.

> **Important Note**
> In this function, there is a total of 128 images in the same batch input passed, but we are saving only the last 64 images. You can easily change this to save fewer or more images. More images typically require more compute (GPU) power and memory.

We also have other utility functions used in the chapter, which can be found in the full notebook of the GitHub page for our book.

The discriminator model

As mentioned previously, the discriminator in a GAN is a classifier that tries to distinguish real data from the data created by the generator. In this use case, the discriminator acts as a binary classification for the images classifying the images between real and fake classes.

Defining parameters

Let's start by creating a class called FoodDiscriminator that is inheriting from the PyTorch nn module. Some of the important features/attributes for the Discriminator class are shown in the following code snippet:

```
class FoodDiscriminator(nn.Module):
    def __init__(self, input_size):
        super().__init__()

        self.input_size = input_size
```

```
        self.channel = 3
        self.kernel_size = 4
        self.stride = 2
        self.padding = 1
        self.bias = False
        self.negative_slope = 0.2

```

The input for `FoodDiscriminator` is the output generated from the generator, which is sized 3 x 64 x 64. We are also setting some of the variables, such as a channel size of 3, a kernel size of `4`, a stride of `2`, padding of `1`, a bias of `False`, and a negative slope value of `0.2`.

The input channel is set to 3, since we have color images, and the 3 channel represents red, green, and blue. The kernel size is 4, which represents the height and width of the 2D convolution window. The stride with the `2` value moves the kernel two steps when performing convolutions. The padding adds a `1`-pixel layer to all the boundaries of the images. Setting the bias to `False` means that it is not allowing the convolution network to add any learnable bias to the network.

The `negative_slope` is set to 0.2, which controls the angle of the negative slope for the `LeakyReLU` activation function. We will be using **Leaky ReLU** for the activation function here. There are multiple activation functions available, such as ReLU, *tan-h*, and sigmoid, but discriminators perform better with the Leaky ReLU activation function. The difference between a ReLU activation function and the Leaky ReLU activation function is that the ReLU function allows only positive values as output, whereas Leaky ReLU allows negative values as output. We are allowing `0.2` times the negative value as the output of the Leaky ReLU activation function by setting the value in `negative_slope`.

Building convolutional layers

Now, we will define the layers of the discriminator to build our binary classification model.

The following is the code snippet for the layers of the discriminator model:

```
        #input size: (3,64,64)
        self.conv1 = nn.Conv2d(self.channel, 128, kernel_
size=self.kernel_size, stride=self.stride, padding=self.
padding, bias=self.bias)
        self.bn1 = nn.BatchNorm2d(128)
        self.relu = nn.LeakyReLU(self.negative_slope,
```

```
inplace=True)

        #input size: (64,32,32)
        self.conv2 =  nn.Conv2d(128, 256, kernel_size=self.
kernel_size, stride=self.stride, padding=self.padding,
bias=self.bias)
        self.bn2 = nn.BatchNorm2d(256)

        #input size: (128,16,16)
        self.conv3 =  nn.Conv2d(256, 512, kernel_size=self.
kernel_size, stride=self.stride, padding=self.padding,
bias=self.bias)
        self.bn3 = nn.BatchNorm2d(512)

        #input size: (256,8,8)
        self.conv4 =  nn.Conv2d(512, 1024, kernel_size=self.
kernel_size, stride=self.stride, padding=self.padding,
bias=self.bias)
        self.bn4 = nn.BatchNorm2d(1024)
        # nn.LeakyReLU(self.negative_slope, inplace=True)

        self.fc = nn.Sequential(
            nn.Linear(in_features=16384,out_features=1),
            # nn.Flatten(),
            nn.Sigmoid()
        )
```

In the preceding code, we are defining the layers of the discriminator model to build a binary classification model that takes in output from the generator model, which is an image with a size of 3 x 64 x 64 and generates output of either `0` or `1`. Thus, the discriminator is able to identify whether an image is fake or real.

The discriminator model shown previously consists of four convolutional layers and a fully connected layer, where the first layer takes in an image generated from the generator model, and each consecutive layer takes in input from the previous layer and passes output to the next layer.

We will split this code block into sections to understand it better. Let's talk more about each layer in detail.

The first convolutional layer

The following is the code snippet for our first convolution layer:

```
        #input size: (3,64,64)
        self.conv1 = nn.Conv2d(self.channel, 128, kernel_
size=self.kernel_size, stride=self.stride, padding=self.
padding, bias=self.bias)
        self.bn1 = nn.BatchNorm2d(128)
        self.relu = nn.LeakyReLU(self.negative_slope,
inplace=True)
```

The first layer, `conv1`, takes the image generated by the generator as input, which is of the size 3 x 64 x 64, with a kernel size of `4`, the stride as `1`, a padding of `1` pixel, and bias = `False`. The `conv1` layer then generates an output of 128 channels, each with a size of `32` – that is, 128 x 32 x 32. Then, the convolution output is normalized using batch normalization, which helps convolutional networks to perform better. Finally, we are using Leaky ReLU as our activation function in the final step of the first layer.

The second convolutional layer

The following is the code snippet for our second convolution layer:

```
        #input size: (128,32,32)
        self.conv2 =  nn.Conv2d(128, 256, kernel_size=self.
kernel_size, stride=self.stride, padding=self.padding,
bias=self.bias)
        self.bn2 = nn.BatchNorm2d(256)
  self.relu = nn.LeakyReLU(self.negative_slope, inplace=True)
```

In the preceding code, we have defined the second convolution layer, `conv2`, which takes in output of the first convolution layer, which is of the size 128 x 32 x 32 with the same kernel size, stride, padding, and bias as the first layer. Now, this layer generates output with 256 channels, each with a size of 16 – that is, 256 x 16 x 16 – and passes it to batch normalization. Again, we are using Leaky ReLU as our activation function in the final step of the second layer.

The third convolutional layer

The following is the code snippet for our third convolution layer:

```
        #input size: (256,16,16)
        self.conv3 =  nn.Conv2d(256, 512, kernel_size=self.
```

```
kernel_size, stride=self.stride, padding=self.padding,
bias=self.bias)
        self.bn3 = nn.BatchNorm2d(512)
  self.relu = nn.LeakyReLU(self.negative_slope, inplace=True)
```

The third convolution layer, `self.conv3`, takes in the output from the second layer as input, which is of the size 256 x 16 x 16 with the same kernel size, stride, padding, and bias as the first two convolution layers. This layer applies convolution to generate output with 512 channels, each with a size of 8 – that is, 512 x 8 x 8 – and passes it to batch normalization. Again, we are using Leaky ReLU as our activation function in the final step of the third layer.

The fourth convolutional layer

The following is the code snippet for our fourth convolution layer:

```
        #input size: (512,8,8)
        self.conv4 =  nn.Conv2d(512, 1024, kernel_size=self.
kernel_size, stride=self.stride, padding=self.padding,
bias=self.bias)
        self.bn4 = nn.BatchNorm2d(1024)
        self.relu = nn.LeakyReLU(self.negative_slope,
inplace=True)
```

The fourth convolution layer, `self.conv4`, takes in output from the third layer as input, which is of the size 512 x 8 x 8 with the same kernel size, stride, padding, and bias as the first three convolution layers. This layer applies convolution to generate output with 1,024 channels, each with a size of 4 – that is, 1,024 x 4 x 4 – and passes it to batch normalization. Again, we are using Leaky ReLU as our activation function in the final step of the fourth layer.

The fifth fully connected layer (final layer)

The following is the code snippet for our final fully connected layer:

```
        self.fc = nn.Sequential(
            nn.Linear(in_features=16384,out_features=1),
            nn.Sigmoid()
        )
# output size: 1 x 1 x 1
```

The final layer of the discriminator model as shown previously is built using the sequential function. There is a fully connected layer in this final layer that takes in the output from the fourth layer, which is of the size 1,024 x 4 x 4. So, the total number of features for a fully connected linear layer is 16,384. Since this is a binary classification task, the final fully connected layer will generate output with 1 channel each of size 1 – that is, of size 1 x 1 x 1. This output is then passed to the **sigmoid** activation function, which generates output between `0` and `1`, and helps the discriminator to work as a binary classification model.

To summarize, we have defined the layers of our discriminator model as a combination of convolutional layers and fully connected linear networks. These layers will take an image generated from the generator as input to classify them between fake or real. Now, it's time to pass in data from the different layers and activation functions. This can be achieved by overwriting the `forward` method. The code for the `forward` method of the `FoodDiscriminator` class is shown here:

```
    def forward(self, input_img):
        validity = self.conv1(input_img)
        validity = self.bn1(validity)
        validity = self.relu(validity)
        validity = self.conv2(validity)
        validity = self.bn2(validity)
        validity = self.relu(validity)
        validity = self.conv3(validity)
        validity = self.bn3(validity)
        validity = self.relu(validity)
        validity = self.conv4(validity)
        validity = self.bn4(validity)
        validity = self.relu(validity)
        validity=validity.view(-1, 1024*4*4)
        validity=self.fc(validity)
        return validity
```

In the preceding code, we have the following:

1. We pass the data (the image output from the generator model) in our first convolution layer (`self.conv1`). The output from `self.conv1` is passed to the batch normalization function, `self.bn1`, and the output from the batch normalization function is passed to the Leaky ReLU activation function, `self.relu`.

2. Then, the output is passed to the second convolution layer (`self.conv2`). Again, the output from the second convolution layers is passed to the batch normalization function, `self.bn2`, and then to the Leaky ReLU activation function, `self.relu`.
3. Similarly, the output is now passed to the third convolution layer (`self.conv3`). And, as with the first two convolution layers, this output is passed to the batch normalization function, `self.bn3`, and then to the leaky ReLU activation function, `self.relu`.
4. The same pass is repeated for the fourth convolution layer (`self.conv4`), batch normalization function (`self.bn4`), and leaky ReLU activation (`self.relu`).
5. Data is passed through the convolution layer, and the output from these layers is multidimensional. To pass the output to our linear layer, it is converted to single-dimensional form. This can be achieved using the tensor `view` method.
6. Once the data is ready in single-dimensional form, it is passed over the fully connected layer, and the final output is returned, which is binary 1 or 0.

To reiterate, in the `forward` method, the image data which is the output from the generator is first passed over the four convolution layers, and then output from the convolution layers is passed over one fully connected layer. Finally, the output is returned.

> **Important Note**
>
> The activation function that we have used in our discriminator model is Leaky ReLU, which tends to perform better and helps the GAN to perform better.

Now that we have completed the discriminator part of the architecture, we will move toward building the generator.

The generator model

As mentioned in the introduction, the role of the generator part of a GAN is to create fake data (images in this case) by incorporating feedback from the discriminator. The goal of the generator is to generate fake images that are very close to real images so that the discriminator fails to recognize them as fake images.

Let's start by creating a class called `FoodGenerator` that is inheriting from the PyTorch `nn` module. Some of the important features/attributes for the `FoodGenerator` class are shown in the following code snippet:

```
class FoodGenerator(nn.Module):
    def __init__(self, latent_size = 256):
        super().__init__()
        self.latent_size = latent_size
        self.kernel_size = 4
        self.stride = 2
        self.padding = 1
        self.bias = False

```

The latent size is one of the most important features in the generator model. It represents the compressed low-dimensional representation of the input (food images, in this case) and is set to 256 by default here. Then, we set the kernel size to be 4 with a stride of 2, which moves the kernel by two steps when performing convolutions. We are also setting the padding to 1, which adds one additional pixel to all boundaries of the food images. Finally, the bias is set to `False`, which means it does not allow the convolution network to add any learnable bias to the network.

We will use the Sequential function from the neural network module of the torch library (`torch.nn`) to build the layers of our generator model. The following is the code snippet for building the generator model:

```
        self.model = nn.Sequential(
                #input size: (latent_size,1,1)
                nn.ConvTranspose2d(latent_size, 512, kernel_
size=self.kernel_size, stride=1, padding=0, bias=self.bias),
                nn.BatchNorm2d(512),
                nn.ReLU(True),

                #input size: (512,4,4)
                nn.ConvTranspose2d(512, 256, kernel_size=self.
kernel_size, stride=self.stride, padding=self.padding,
bias=self.bias),
                nn.BatchNorm2d(256),
                nn.ReLU(True),

```

```
            #input size: (256,8,8)
            nn.ConvTranspose2d(256, 128, kernel_size=self.
kernel_size, stride=self.stride, padding=self.padding,
bias=self.bias),
            nn.BatchNorm2d(128),
            nn.ReLU(True),

            #input size: (128,16,16)
            nn.ConvTranspose2d(128, 64, kernel_size=self.
kernel_size, stride=self.stride, padding=self.padding,
bias=self.bias),
            nn.BatchNorm2d(64),
            nn.ReLU(True),

            nn.ConvTranspose2d(64, 3, kernel_size=self.
kernel_size, stride=self.stride, padding=self.padding,
bias=self.bias),
            nn.Tanh()
            # output size: 3 x 64 x 64
        )
```

In the preceding code, we are defining the layers of the generator model to generate fake images sized 3 x 64 x 64. The generator model shown previously consists of five deconvolutional layers where each layer takes in input and passes output to the next layer.

The generator model is almost the opposite of the layers of the discriminator model, except for a fully connected linear layer.

> **Comparing Transposed Convolution and Deconvolution**
>
> The two terms are often used interchangeably in the Deep Learning community, and that is the case in this book. Mathematically speaking, deconvolution is a mathematical operation that reverses the effect of convolution. Imagine throwing an input through a convolutional layer and collecting the output. Now, throw the output through the deconvolutional layer, and you get back the exact same input. It is the inverse of the multivariate convolutional function.
>
> What we are doing here is not getting back the exact same input. So, while the operation is similar, it is strictly speaking NOT deconvolution but transposed convolution. A transposed convolution is somewhat similar because it produces the same spatial resolution as a hypothetical deconvolutional layer would. However, the actual mathematical operation that's being performed on the values is different. A transposed convolutional layer carries out a regular convolution but reverses its spatial transformation.
>
> Deconvolution, as discussed, is not very popular, and often, the community refers to transposed convolution as deconvolution, which is what is being referred to here.

We will split this code block into sections to understand it better. Let's talk more about each layer in detail.

The first transposed convolution layer

Here is the code snippet for our first `ConvTranspose2d` layer:

```
                    #input size: (latent_size,1,1)
                    nn.ConvTranspose2d(latent_size, 512, kernel_
size=self.kernel_size, stride=1, padding=0, bias=self.bias),
                    nn.BatchNorm2d(512),
                    nn.ReLU(True),
```

The first `ConvTranspose2d` layer takes `latent_size` as input, which is 256, with a kernel size of `4`, the stride as `1`, a padding of `0` pixels, and bias = `False`. The `ConvTranspose2d` layer then generates an output of 512. Then, the transposed convolution output is normalized using batch normalization, which helps transposed convolutional networks to perform better. Finally, we are using ReLU as our activation function in the final step of the first layer.

The second transposed convolution layer

The following is the code snippet for our second `ConvTranspose2d` layer:

```
            #input size: (512,4,4)
            nn.ConvTranspose2d(512, 256, kernel_size=self.
kernel_size, stride=self.stride, padding=self.padding,
bias=self.bias),
            nn.BatchNorm2d(256),
            nn.ReLU(True),
```

In the preceding code, we have defined the second transposed convolution layer that takes in the output of the first transposed convolution layer, which is sized 512 x 4 x 4, with a kernel size of `4`, the stride as `2`, a padding of `1` pixel, and bias = `False`. Now, this layer generates output with 256 channels and passes it to batch normalization. Again, we are using ReLU as our activation function in the final step of the second layer.

The third transposed convolution layer

The following is the code snippet for our third `ConvTranspose2d` layer:

```
            #input size: (256,8,8)
            nn.ConvTranspose2d(256, 128, kernel_size=self.
kernel_size, stride=self.stride, padding=self.padding,
bias=self.bias),
            nn.BatchNorm2d(128),
            nn.ReLU(True),
```

The third transposed convolution layer takes in the output from the second layer as input, which is sized 256 x 8 x 8, with the same kernel size, stride, padding, and bias as the second transposed convolution layers. This layer applies transposed convolution to generate output with 128 channels and passes it to batch normalization. Again, we are using ReLU as our activation function in the final step of the third layer.

The fourth transposed convolution layer

The following is the code snippet for our fourth `ConvTranspose2d` layer:

```
            #input size: (128,16,16)
            nn.ConvTranspose2d(128, 64, kernel_size=self.
kernel_size, stride=self.stride, padding=self.padding,
bias=self.bias),
```

```
            nn.BatchNorm2d(64),
            nn.ReLU(True),
```

The fourth transposed convolution layer takes in the output from the third layer as input, which is sized 128 x 16 x 16, with the same kernel size, stride, padding, and bias as the last two transposed convolution layers. This layer applies transposed convolution to generate output with 64 channels and passes it to batch normalization. Again, we are using ReLU as our activation function in the final step of the fourth layer.

The fifth transposed convolution layer (final layer)

The following is the code snippet for our fifth and final `ConvTranspose2d` layer:

```
nn.ConvTranspose2d(64, 3, kernel_size=self.kernal_size,
stride=self.stride, padding=self.padding, bias=self.bias),
nn.Tanh()
# output size: 3 x 64 x 64
```

In the final deconvolution neural network layer, we are generating output with `3` channels of `64 x 64` size and with the activation function as `Tanh`. Here, we are using a different activation function because this is a generator model, which works better with `Tanh`.

Note that for the first transposed convolutional layer, we are using a stride of 1 and no padding, while for the rest of the layers, we are using padding sized 1 and with a stride of 2.

To summarize, we have defined the layers of our generator model as five transposed convolutional layers. These layers will take in latent size as input, go through multiple deconvolutional layers, and scale up the channels from `256` to `512`, then down to `256` to `128`, and finally, to `3` channels.

Now, it's time to pass in the data from the different layers and the activation functions. This can be achieved by overwriting the `forward` method. The code for the `forward` method of the `FoodGenerator` class is shown here:

```
def forward(self, input_img):
    input_img = self.model(input_img)
    return input_img
```

In the preceding code, the `forward` method of the `FoodGenerator` class takes in the image as input, passes it to the model, which is a sequence of the transposed convolutional layer, and returns the output, which is the generated fake image.

The generative adversarial model

Now that we have defined our discriminator and generator models, it's time to combine them and build our GAN model. We shall be configuring the loss function and optimizer in the GAN model and passing the data to the generator and the discriminator. In order to get good results (which means generating fake images that are as good-looking as real images), we will try to minimize the loss. Let's look at the PyTorch Lightning implementation for GANs in detail.

Building our GAN model using PyTorch Lightning primarily includes the following steps:

1. Define the model.
2. Configure the optimizer and loss function.
3. Configure the training loop.
4. Save the generated fake images.
5. Train the GAN model.

Let's look at these steps in detail.

Defining the model

Let's create a class called `FoodGAN` that is inherited from a PyTorch `LightningModule`. The `Module` class takes the following parameters in the constructor:

- `latent_size`: This represents the compressed low-dimensional representation of the food images. The default value is 256.
- `lr`: This is the learning rate for the optimizers used for both the discriminator and the generator. The default value is `0.0002`.
- `bias1` and `bias2`: `b1` and `b2` are the bias values used for the optimizers for both the discriminator and the generator. The default value for `b1` is `0.5`, and for `b2`, it is `0.999`.
- `batch_size`: This represents the number of images that will be propagated through the network. The default value for the batch size is `128`.

Now, we will initialize, configure and construct our `FoodGAN` class using the `__init__` method. The following is the code snippet for the `__init__` method:

```
    def __init__(self, latent_size = 256,learning_rate =
0.0002,bias1 = 0.5,bias2 = 0.999,batch_size = 128):
        super().__init__()
```

```
        self.save_hyperparameters()

        # networks
        # data_shape = (channels, width, height)
        self.generator = FoodGenerator()
        self.discriminator = FoodDiscriminator(input_size=64)

        self.batch_size = batch_size
        self.latent_size = latent_size
        self.validation = torch.randn(self.batch_size, self.
latent_size, 1, 1)
```

The `__init__` method defined previously takes in the latent size, learning rate, `bias1`, `bias2`, and the batch size as input. These are all the hyperparameters required for the discriminator and generator models, so these variables are saved inside the `__init__` method. Finally, we are also creating a variable called `validation`, which we will use for the validation of the model.

Configuring the optimizer and loss function

We shall also define a utility function in the `FoodGAN` model to calculate loss, as explained in the previous section, since we want to minimize the loss to get better results. The following is the code snippet for the loss function:

```
    def adversarial_loss(self, preds, targets):
        return F.binary_cross_entropy(preds, targets)
```

In the preceding code snippet, the `adversarial_loss` method takes in two parameters - `preds`, which is the predicted value, and `targets`, which is the real target values. Then, it uses a `binary_cross_entropy` function to calculate the loss from the predicted value and the target value and, finally, returns the entropy value calculated.

> **Important Note**
>
> It is also possible to have different loss functions for the generator and the discriminator. Here, we kept things simple and only used binary cross-entropy loss.

The next important method is for configuring optimizers, since we have two models, the discriminator and the generator, in the FoodGAN model, and each model needs its own optimizers. This can be easily achieved using one of the PyTorch Lightning life cycle methods, called configure_optimizer. The following is the code snippet for the configure_optimizer method:

```
    def configure_optimizers(self):
        learning_rate = self.hparams.learning_rate
        bias1 = self.hparams.bias1
        bias2 = self.hparams.bias2

        opt_g = torch.optim.Adam(self.generator.parameters(),
lr=learning_rate, betas=(bias1, bias2))
        opt_d = torch.optim.Adam(self.discriminator.
parameters(), lr=learning_rate, betas=(bias1, bias2))

        return [opt_g, opt_d], []
```

In the __init__ method, we have invoked a method called self.save_hyperparameters(). This saves all the input sent to the init method to a special variable called hparams. This special variable is leveraged in the configure_optimizer method to access our learning rate and the bias values. Here, we are creating two optimizers – opt_g is the optimizer for the generator and opt_d is the optimizer for the discriminator, as each of them needs its own optimizer. The configure optimizer method returns two lists – the first list contains multiple optimizers and the second list, which is empty in our case, is where we can pass LR schedulers.

To summarize, we are creating two optimizers, one for the generator and one for the discriminator, by accessing hyperparameters from the hparams special variable. This method returns two lists as output, where the first element of the first list is the optimizer for the generator and the second element is the optimizer for the discriminator.

> **Important Note**
>
> The configure_optimizer method returns two values; both are a list, and out of them, the second is an empty list. The *list* has two values – the value at the 0 index has an optimizer for the generator, and the value at the 1 index has an optimizer for the discriminator.

Another important life cycle method is the `forward` method. The following is the code snippet for this method:

```
    def forward(self, z):
        return self.generator(z)
```

In the preceding code, the `forward` method takes in input, passes it to the generator model, and returns the output.

Configuring the training loop

We have overwritten the method to configure optimizers for the discriminator and generator models. Now, it's time to configure the training loop for the discriminator and the generator. It is important to access the correct optimizer for the discriminator and generator during the training of the GAN model, which can be done by using data that is being passed as input by the PyTorch Lightning module during training. Let's try to understand more about the input passed for the training life cycle method and training process in detail.

The following inputs are passed to the `training_step` life cycle methods:

- `batch`: This represents batch data that is being served by `food_train_dataloader`.
- `batch_idx`: This is the index of the batch that is being served for training.
- `optimizer_idx`: This helps us to identify the two different optimizers for the generator and the discriminator. This input parameter has two values, `0` for the generator and `1` for the discriminator.

Training the generator model

Now that we understand how we can identify the optimizers for the discriminator and the generator, it's time to understand how to train our GAN model using both of them. The code snippet for training the generator is as follows:

```
        real_images, _ = batch

        # train generator
        if optimizer_idx == 0:

            # Generate fake images
            fake_random_noise = torch.randn(self.batch_size,
```

```
self.latent_size, 1, 1)
            fake_random_noise = fake_random_noise.type_as(real_
images)
            fake_images = self(fake_random_noise) #self.
generator(latent)

            # Try to fool the discriminator
            preds = self.discriminator(fake_images)
            targets = torch.ones(self.batch_size, 1)
            targets = targets.type_as(real_images)

            loss = self.adversarial_loss(preds, targets)
            self.log('generator_loss', loss, prog_bar=True)

            tqdm_dict = {'g_loss': loss}
            output = OrderedDict({
                'loss': loss,
                'progress_bar': tqdm_dict,
                'log': tqdm_dict
            })
            return output
```

In the preceding code, we are first storing the images received from the batch in a variable called `real_images`. These inputs are in tensor format. It is important to make sure all the tensors are making use of the same device – in our case, the GPU, so that it can run on the GPUs. In order to convert all the tensors to the same type so that they are pointing it to the same device, we are leveraging the PyTorch Lightning-recommended method called `type_as()`. The `type_as` method will convert the tensor to the same type as the others to make sure that all the tensor types are the same and can make use of the GPUs, while also making our code scale to any arbitrary number of GPUs or TPUs. More information about this method can be found in the PyTorch Lightning documentation.

As we discussed in the previous section, it is important to identify the optimizer for the generator to train our generator model. We are identifying the optimizer for the generator by checking optimizer_idx, which has to be 0 for the generator. There are three main steps in training the generator model – creating random noise data, converting the type of the random noise, and generating fake images from random noise. The following is the code snippet demonstrating this:

```
            fake_random_noise = torch.randn(self.batch_size, 
self.latent_size, 1, 1)
            fake_random_noise = fake_random_noise.type_as(real_
images)
            fake_images = self(fake_random_noise)
```

In the preceding code, the following steps are carried out:

1. The first step is to create some random noise data. In order to create random noise data, we are leveraging the randn method from the torch package, which returns a tensor filled with random numbers of size equal to the latent size. This random noise is saved as the fake_random_noise variable.
2. The next step is converting the tensor type of the random noise to the same as our real_images tensor. This is achieved by the type_as method described previously.
3. Finally, the random noise is passed to the self-object, which is passing the random noise data to our generator model to generate fake images. These are saved as fake_images.

Since we have generated our fake image now, the next step is to calculate the loss. However, it is important to identify how close our fake image is to the real image before calculating loss. We have already defined our discriminator and can easily leverage it to identify this by passing our fake image to the discriminator and comparing the output. So, we shall pass the fake image generated in the preceding step to our discriminator and save the predictions, where the values can be either 0 or 1. The following code snippet shows how to pass the fake images to the discriminator:

```
            # Try to fool the discriminator
            preds = self.discriminator(fake_images)
            targets = torch.ones(self.batch_size, 1)
            targets = targets.type_as(real_images)
```

In the preceding code, we are first passing the fake images to the discriminator and saving them in the variable `preds`. Then, we are creating a `target` variable with all but one, assuming that all the images generated by the generator are the real images.
This will start improving after a few epochs as the GAN model is being trained. Finally, we are converting the type of the tensors for the targets to the same type as our `real_images` tensors.

In the next step, we shall calculate the loss. This is achieved by using our `adversarial_loss` utility function, as shown here:

```
            loss = self.adversarial_loss(preds, targets)
            self.log('generator_loss', loss, prog_bar=True)
```

The `adversarial_loss` method takes in the predicted values from the discriminator and the target values, which are all ones as the input and calculates loss. The loss is logged as `generator_loss`, which is important if you want to plot the loss using TensorBoard later.

Finally, we shall return the loss function and other attributes to make use of the loss being logged and shown on the progress bar, as shown here:

```
            tqdm_dict = {'g_loss': loss}
            output = OrderedDict({
                'loss': loss,
                'progress_bar': tqdm_dict,
                'log': tqdm_dict
            })
            return output

```

In the preceding code, the loss and other attributes are stored in the dictionary called `output`, and this is returned in the final step of training the generator. Once this loss value is returned in the training step, PyTorch Lightning will take care of updating weights.

Training the discriminator model

Now, let's try to understand how to train our discriminator model.

Similar to the generator model, we will begin by comparing the optimizer index and train the discriminator only when the index is `1`, as shown here:

```
        # train discriminator
        if optimizer_idx == 1:
```

There are four steps that we will follow to train our discriminator model – train our discriminator to identify the real images, save the output of the discriminator model, convert the type of the tensors for the output of the discriminator, and calculate the loss. These steps are achieved by the code snippet shown here:

```
real_preds = self.discriminator(real_images)
real_targets = torch.ones(real_images.size(0), 1)
real_targets = real_targets.type_as(real_images)
real_loss = self.adversarial_loss(real_preds, real_targets)

```

In the preceding code, we are first passing the real image to the discriminator and saving the output as `real_preds`. Then, we are creating a dummy tensor with the values as all ones, calling it `real_targets`. The reason for setting all our real target values to ones is that we are passing the real images to the discriminator. We are also converting the type of the tensor for the real targets to be the same as the tensors for the real images. Finally, we are calculating our loss and calling it `real_loss`.

Now, the discriminator has been trained with the real images, and it's time to train it with the fake images that are being generated by the generator model. This step is similar to training our generator. So, we will create dummy random noise data, pass it to the generator for creating fake images, and then pass it to the discriminator for classifying it. The processing of training the discriminator with fake images is shown in the following code snippet:

```
            # Generate fake images
            real_random_noise = torch.randn(self.batch_size,
self.latent_size, 1, 1)
            real_random_noise = real_random_noise.type_as(real_
images)
            fake_images = self(real_random_noise) #self.
generator(latent)

            # Pass fake images through discriminator
            fake_targets = torch.zeros(fake_images.size(0), 1)
            fake_targets = fake_targets.type_as(real_images)
            fake_preds = self.discriminator(fake_images)
            fake_loss = self.adversarial_loss(fake_preds, fake_
targets)
```

```
            # fake_score = torch.mean(fake_preds).item()
            self.log('discriminator_loss', fake_loss, prog_
bar=True)
```

In the preceding code, we are first generating fake images by following the same steps we followed while training the generator. These fake images are stored as `fake_images`.

Next, we are creating a dummy tensor with the values as all zeros, calling it `fake_targets`. Then, we are converting the type of tensors for `fake_targets` to be the same as the tensors for `real_images`. Then, we are passing the fake images through the discriminator to make predictions and saving the predictions as `fake_preds`. Finally, we are calculating the loss by leveraging the `adversarial_loss` utility function, which takes in `fake_preds` and `fake_targets` as input to calculate the loss. This is also logged in the self-object to be called later for plotting the loss function using TensorBoard.

The final step in training the GAN model after training the discriminator is to calculate the total loss, which is the sum of the loss calculated when training the discriminator with real images and the fake loss, which is the loss calculated when training the discriminator with fake images. The following is the code snippet demonstrating this:

```
            # Update discriminator weights
            loss = real_loss + fake_loss
            self.log('total_loss', loss, prog_bar=True)
```

In the preceding code, we are adding `real_loss` and `fake_loss` to calculate the total loss and store it in the variable loss. This loss is also logged as the total loss to be called later for observation in TensorBoard.

Finally, we return the loss function and other attributes to log the loss values and show them in the progress bar. The following is the code snippet for returning loss and other attributes:

```

            tqdm_dict = {'d_loss': loss}
            output = OrderedDict({
                'loss': loss,
                'progress_bar': tqdm_dict,
                'log': tqdm_dict
            })
            return output
```

In the preceding code, we are saving the loss function and other attributes in a dictionary called `output`, which is then returned at the end of the training. Once this loss value is returned in the training step, the PyTorch Lightning module will take care of updating the weights. This will complete our training configuration.

To summarize the training loop, we are first getting the optimizer index and then training either the generator or the discriminator based on the index value and, finally, returning the loss value as an output.

> **Important Note**
>
> When the `optimizer_idx` value is `0`, the generator model is being trained, and when the value is `1`, the discriminator model is being trained.

Saving the generated fake images

It is also important to check how well our GAN model is being trained and improving over epochs and see whether it can generate any new food dishes. We can track our GAN model at every epoch by saving some images at the end of each epoch. This can be achieved by leveraging one of the PyTorch Lightning methods called `on_epoch_end()`. This method is called at the end of every epoch, so we will use it to save fake images that the GAN model has generated. The following is the code demonstrating this:

```
    def on_epoch_end(self):
        # import pdb;pdb.set_trace()
        z = self.validation.type_as(self.generator.model[0].
weight)
        sample_imgs = self(z) #self.current_epoch
        ALL_FOOD_IMAGES.append(sample_imgs.cpu())
        save_generated_samples(self.current_epoch, sample_imgs)
```

In the `on_epoch_end()` method, we are saving the weights of the generator model in the `z` variable and then using the `self` method to store the sample images as `sample_imgs`. Then, we are adding those sample images to the `ALL_FOOD_IMAGES` list. Finally, we are using our `save_generated_samples` utility function to save fake food images as `.png` files.

Training the GAN model

Finally, we are all set to train the GAN model. The following is the code for training our GAN model:

```
model = FoodGAN()
trainer = pl.Trainer( max_epochs=100, progress_bar_refresh_
rate=25, gpus=1)#gpus=1,
trainer.fit(model, food_train_dataloader)
```

In the preceding code, we are first initializing our `FoodGAN` model, saving it as `model`. Then, we are calling the `Trainer` method from the PyTorch Lightning package with a maximum number of 100 epochs and 1 GPU enabled. Finally, we are using the `fit` method to start training by passing our `FoodGAN` model, along with the data loader created earlier in this section.

The following is the output of training the GAN model:

```
GPU available: True, used: True
TPU available: False, using: 0 TPU cores
IPU available: False, using: 0 IPUs
LOCAL_RANK: 0 - CUDA_VISIBLE_DEVICES: [0]

  | Name          | Type              | Params
----------------------------------------------------
0 | generator     | FoodGenerator     | 4.9 M
1 | discriminator | FoodDiscriminator | 11.1 M
----------------------------------------------------
15.9 M    Trainable params
0         Non-trainable params
15.9 M    Total params
63.830    Total estimated model params size (MB)
Epoch 99: 100%
/usr/local/lib/python3.7/dist-packages/pytorch_lightning/loops/optimization/closure.py:36: LightningDeprecationWarning: One of the returned values {'progress_bar', 'log'} has a `grad_fn`. We will detach it automatically but this behaviour will change in v1.6. Please detach it manually:
  f"One of the returned values {set(extra.keys())} has a `grad_fn`. We will detach it automatically"
CPU times: user 30min 39s, sys: 1min 32s, total: 32min 12s
Wall time: 42min 29s
```

Figure 6.5 – Output of training the GAN model for 100 epochs

We can also visualize and observe the loss for the GAN model while it was training by leveraging TensorBoard, as shown here:

```
%load_ext tensorboard
%tensorboard --logdir lightning_logs/
```

This results in the following output:

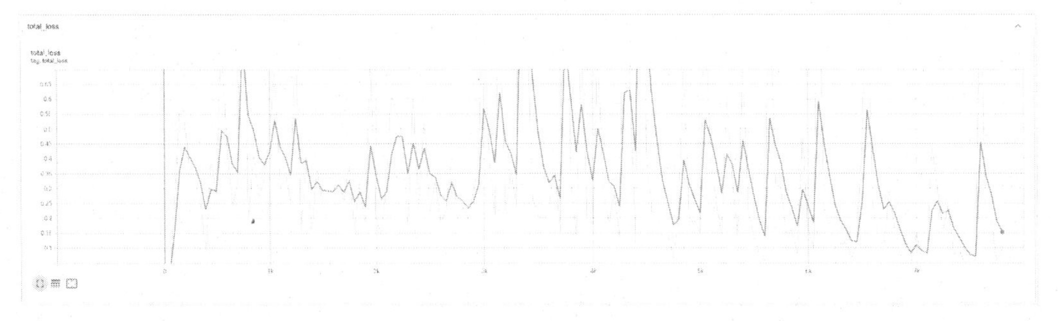

Figure 6.6 – Output for the total loss of the GAN model

We can also observe the generator loss and the discriminator loss (the full code and output is available in the GitHub repository).

The model output showing fake images

Here are some of the sample food images generated at different epochs.

We first train the model for `100` epochs but capture multiple results to show the progression:

Figure 6.7 – The generated images after 3 epochs

The following figure shows the progress after 9 epochs:

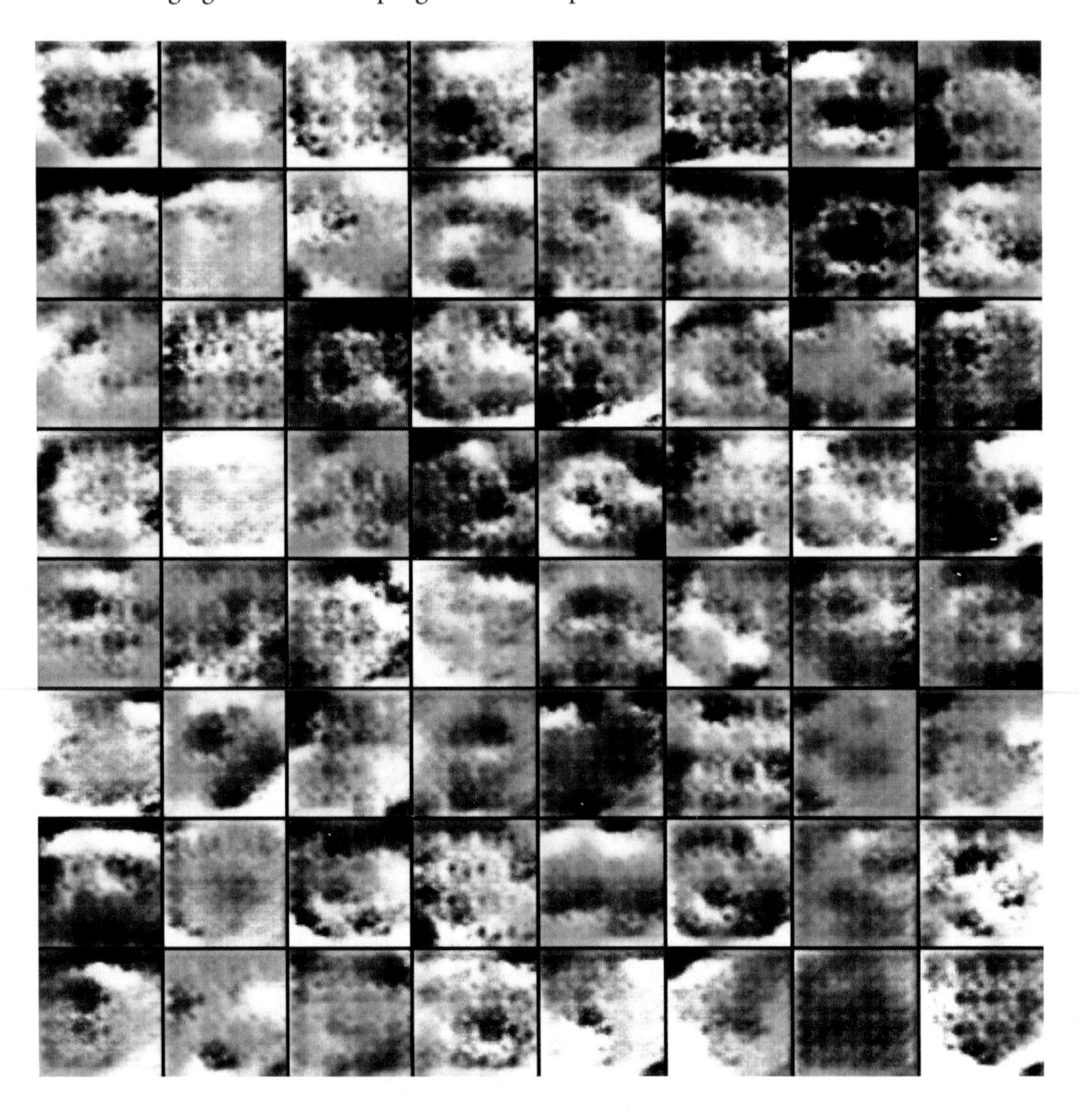

Figure 6.8 – The generated images after 9 epochs

The following figure shows the final output after 100 epochs:

Figure 6.9 – The fake food images at epoch 100

As you can see, we now have some food that doesn't exist in the original dataset, so they are fake food (at least until now based on the dataset, so you can try making those at home).

You can train the model for a greater number of epochs and the quality will continue to improve. For example, try training for `200`, `300`, `400`, and `500` epochs. (More results can be found on the GitHub page of our book.) There will always be some output that is completely noisy and looks like incomplete images.

A GAN is sensitive to batch size, latent size, and other hyperparameters. To improve the performance, you can try running the GAN model for a greater number of epochs and with different hyperparameters.

Creating new butterfly species using a GAN

In this section, we are going to use the same GAN model that we built in the previous section with a minor tweak to generate new species of butterflies.

Since we are following the same steps here, we will keep the description concise and observe the outputs. (The full code can be found in the GitHub repository for this chapter.)

We will first try with the previous architecture that we used for generating food images (which is 4 convolution, 1 fully connected layer, and 5 transposed convolution layers). We will then try another architecture with 5 convolution layers and 5 transposed convolution layers:

1. Download the dataset:

```
dataset_url =  'https://www.kaggle.com/gpiosenka/
butterfly-images40-species'
od.download(dataset_url)
```

2. Initialize the variables for the images:

```
image_size = 64
batch_size = 128
normalize = [(0.5, 0.5, 0.5), (0.5, 0.5, 0.5)]
latent_size = 256

butterfly_data_directory = "/content/butterfly-images40-
species/train"
```

3. Create a dataloader for the butterfly dataset:

```
butterfly_train_dataset = ImageFolder(butterfly_data_
directory, transform=T.Compose([
    T.Resize(image_size),
    T.CenterCrop(image_size),
    T.ToTensor(),
    T.Normalize(*normalize)]))

buttefly_train_dataloader = DataLoader(butterfly_train_
dataset, batch_size, num_workers=4, pin_memory=True,
shuffle=True)
```

4. Denormalise the images and display them.

In this section, we will do the following:

1. Define a utility function to denormalize the image tensors.
2. Define a utility function to load the display of the butterfly images.
3. Call the display images function to show the original butterfly images.

This code is the same as what we saw in the previous example, so you can reuse that. This will show the original images, as shown here:

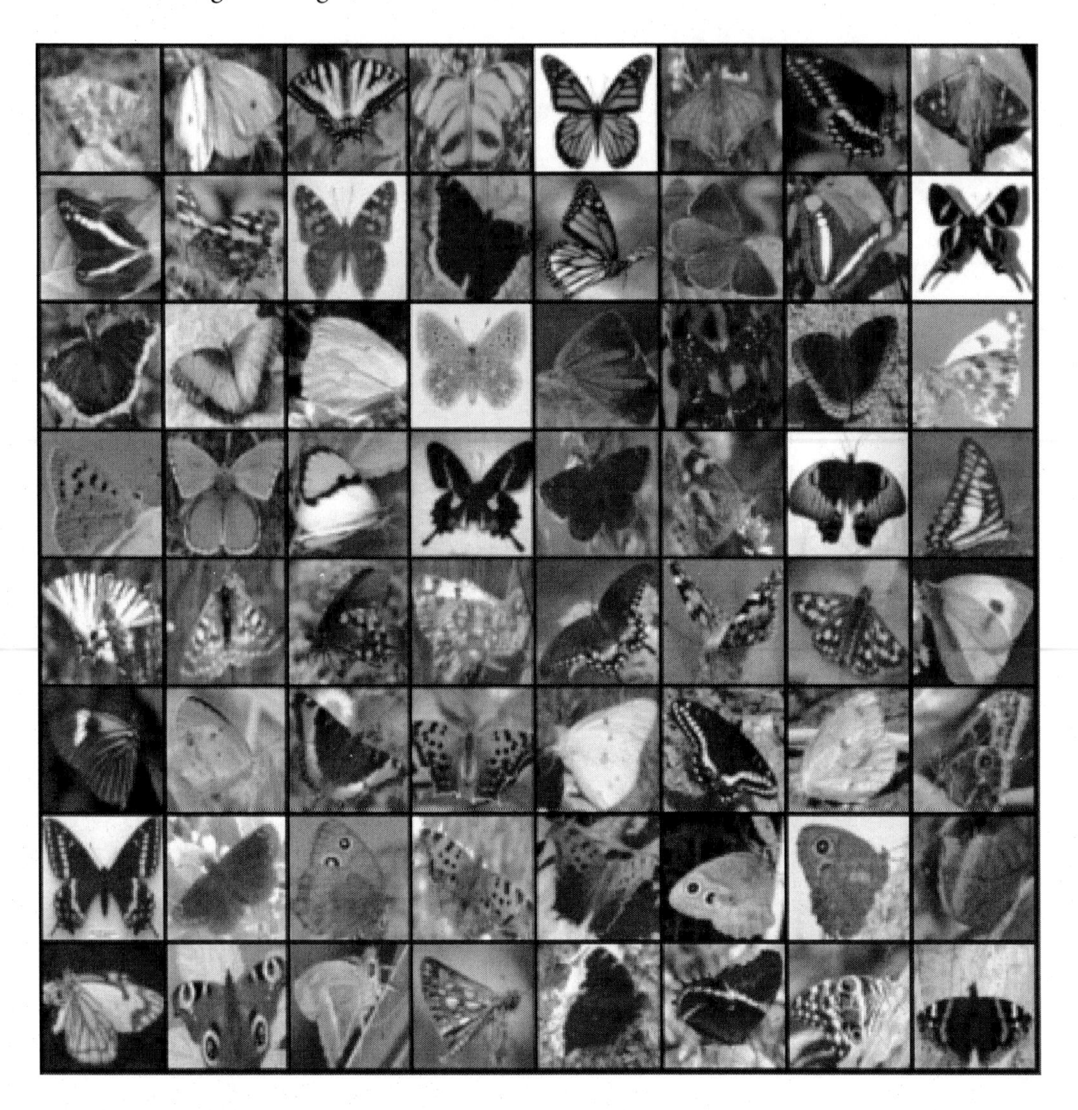

Figure 6.10 – The original butterfly images

Now, we can define the generator and discriminator module followed by the optimizer. The architecture is the same, so please feel free to repurpose the previous code. Once testing is done, you can train the model.

4. Train the butterfly GAN model:

```
model = ButterflyGAN()
trainer = pl.Trainer( max_epochs=100, progress_bar_
refresh_rate=25, gpus=1)#gpus=1,
trainer.fit(model, buttefly_train_dataloader)
```

In this code snippet we are training the Butterfly GAN model for 100 epochs

5. Generate the output of the butterfly GAN model:

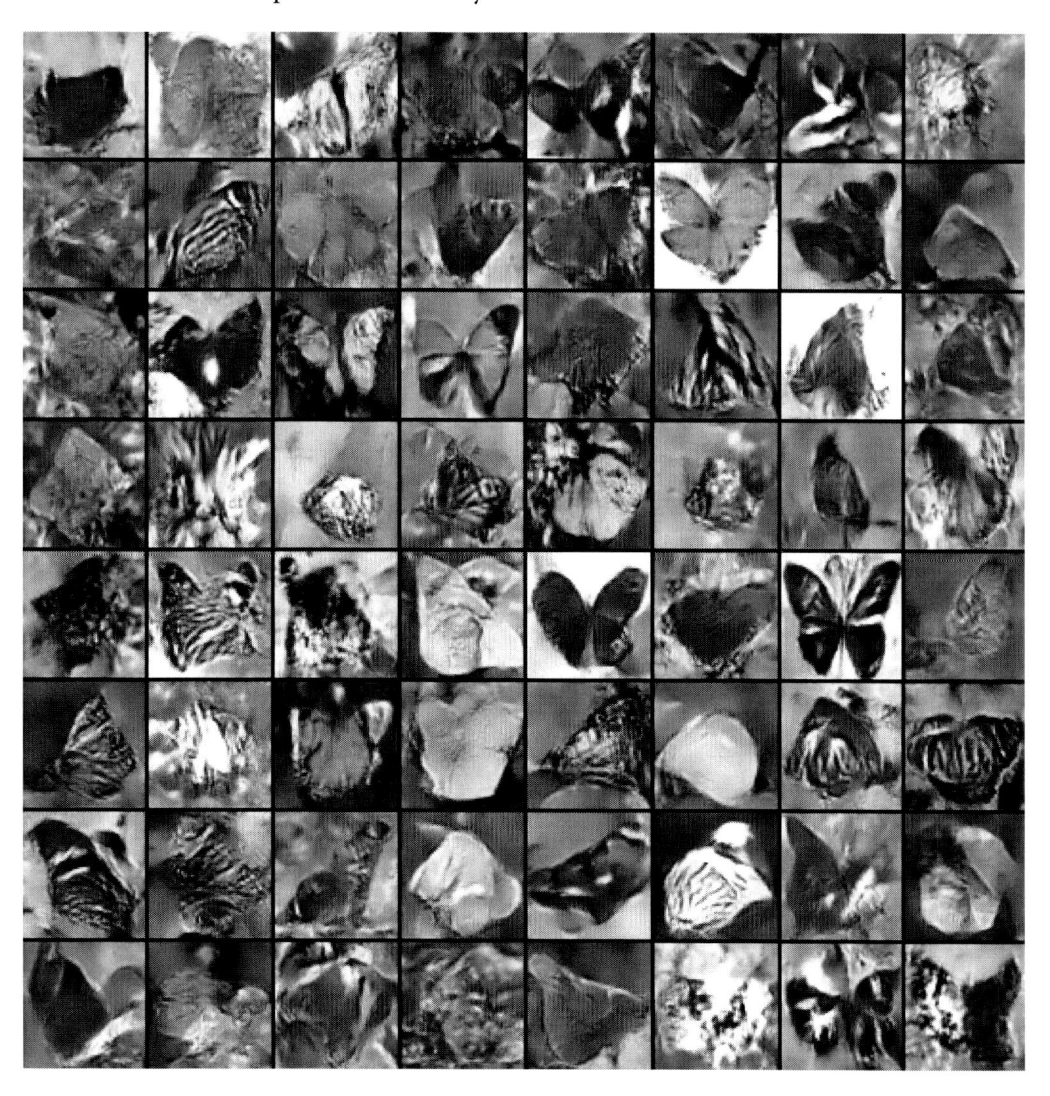

Figure 6.11 – Butterfly species generated from the GAN model

> **Important Note**
>
> Detecting GAN-generated fakes from real objects is a real challenge and an area of active research in Deep Learning community. It may be easy to detect fake butterflies here as some have weird colors, but not all. You may see some of the butterfly species as exotic Pacific butterflies, but make no mistake – all of them are totally fake. There are some tricks that you can use to identify fakes, such as a lack of symmetry or distorted colors. However, they are not foolproof, and more often than not, a human is deceived by a GAN-generated image.

GAN training challenges

A GAN model requires a lot of compute resources for training a model in order to get a good result, especially when a dataset is not very clean and representations in an image are not very easy to learn. In order to get a very clean output with sharp representations in our fake generated image, we need to pass a higher resolution image as input to our GAN model. However, the higher resolution means a lot more parameters are needed in the model, which in turn requires much more memory to train the model.

Here is an example scenario. We have trained our models using the image size of 64 pixels, but if we increase the image size to 128 pixels, then the number of parameters in the GAN model increases drastically from `15.9 M` to `93.4 M`. This, in turn, requires much more compute power to train the model, and with the limited resources in the Google Collab environment, you might get an error similar to this after 20–25 epochs:

```
RuntimeError: CUDA out of memory. Tried to allocate 64.00 MiB
(GPU 0; 15.78 GiB total capacity; 13.94 GiB already allocated;
50.75 MiB free; 14.09 GiB reserved in total by PyTorch) If
reserved memory is >> allocated memory try setting max_split_
size_mb to avoid fragmentation.  See documentation for Memory
Management and PYTORCH_CUDA_ALLOC_CONF
```

```
GPU available: True, used: True
TPU available: False, using: 0 TPU cores
IPU available: False, using: 0 IPUs
LOCAL_RANK: 0 - CUDA_VISIBLE_DEVICES: [0]

  | Name          | Type          | Params
------------------------------------------------
0 | generator     | Generator     | 48.8 M
1 | discriminator | Discriminator | 44.6 M
------------------------------------------------
93.4 M    Trainable params
0         Non-trainable params
93.4 M    Total params
373.537   Total estimated model params size (MB)
Epoch 11.0%                                    0/78 [00:00<?, ?it/s, loss=26, v_num=0, generator_loss=10.60, discriminator_loss=6.5e-5, total_loss=40.80]
/usr/local/lib/python3.7/dist-packages/pytorch_lightning/loops/optimization/closure.py:36: LightningDeprecationWarning: One of the returned values ('log', 'progress_bar') has a `grad_fn`. We will detach it au
  f"One of the returned values {set(extra.keys())} has a `grad_fn`. We will detach it automatically"
---------------------------------------------------------------------------
RuntimeError                              Traceback (most recent call last)
<ipython-input-19-0fca1cee60fe> in <module>()
----> 1 get_ipython().run_cell_magic('time', '', 'model = GAN()\n# ckpt_dir = "/content/gdrive/MyDrive/Colab Notebooks/gan"\n# latest_ckpt = "/content/gdrive/MyDrive/Colab Notebooks/gan/lightning_logs/version_9/checkpoints/epoch=89-step=7019.ckpt"\n# ckpt_callback = pl.callbacks.ModelCheckpoint(every_n_epochs=10, save_top_k=-1)\n# trainer = pl.Trainer(default_root_dir=ckpt_dir,\n#                    callbacks=[ckpt_callback], resume_from_checkpoint=latest_ckpt,\n#                    max_epochs=100, gpus=-1)\ntrainer = pl.Trainer(max_epochs=100, gpus=-1)\ntrainer.fit(model, veg_train_dataloader)')

                        41 frames
<decorator-gen-53> in time(self, line, cell, local_ns)

<timed exec> in <module>()

/usr/local/lib/python3.7/dist-packages/torch/nn/modules/conv.py in _conv_forward(self, input, weight, bias)
    441                             _pair(0), self.dilation, self.groups)
    442         return F.conv2d(input, weight, bias, self.stride,
--> 443                         self.padding, self.dilation, self.groups)
    444 
    445     def forward(self, input: Tensor) -> Tensor:

RuntimeError: CUDA out of memory. Tried to allocate 128.00 MiB (GPU 0; 15.78 GiB total capacity; 13.82 GiB already allocated; 104.75 MiB free; 14.03 GiB reserved in total by PyTorch) If reserved memory is >> allocated memory try setting max_split_size_mb to avoid fragmentation.  See documentation for Memory Management and PYTORCH_CUDA_ALLOC_CONF
```

Figure 6.12 – A memory error on higher resolution images

There are some tricks to reduce memory utilization, such as reducing the batch size or gradient accumulation. However, there are limitations to these workarounds as well. For example, if you reduce the batch size to 64 from 128, the model will take much longer to learn representations in the image. You can observe this in the generated image when you reduce the batch size and train your model.

The model oscillates when the batch size is low because the gradients are averages for a fewer number of data instances. In such cases, the gradient accumulation technique can be used, which adds gradients of the parameters for *n* number of batches. This can be achieved by using the `accumulate_grad_batches` argument in the `Trainer` instance, as shown here:

```
# Accumulate gradients for 16 batches
trainer = Trainer(accumulate_grad_batches=16)
```

Therefore, you can combine these two parameters, the batch size and `accumulate_grad_batches`, to get a similar effective batch size for training higher resolution images, as shown here:

```
batch_size = 8
trainer = pl.Trainer(max_epochs=100, gpus=-1, accumulate_grad_
batches=16)
```

This implies that the training will be done for an effective batch size of 128. However, the limitation is again the training time, so to train our model for much higher than 100 epochs in order to get a decent result using this technique while avoiding the out-of-memory error.

A lot of Deep Learning research areas are restricted by the amount of compute resources available to researchers. Most large tech companies (such as Google and Facebook) often come with new developments in the field, primarily due to their access to large servers and large datasets.

Creating images using DCGAN

A DCGAN is a direct extension of the GAN model discussed in the previous section, except that it explicitly uses the convolutional and convolutional-transpose layers in the discriminator and generator respectively. DCGAN was first proposed in a paper, *Unsupervised Representation Learning with Deep Convolutional Generative Adversarial Networks*, by Alec Radford, Luke Metz, and Soumith Chintala:

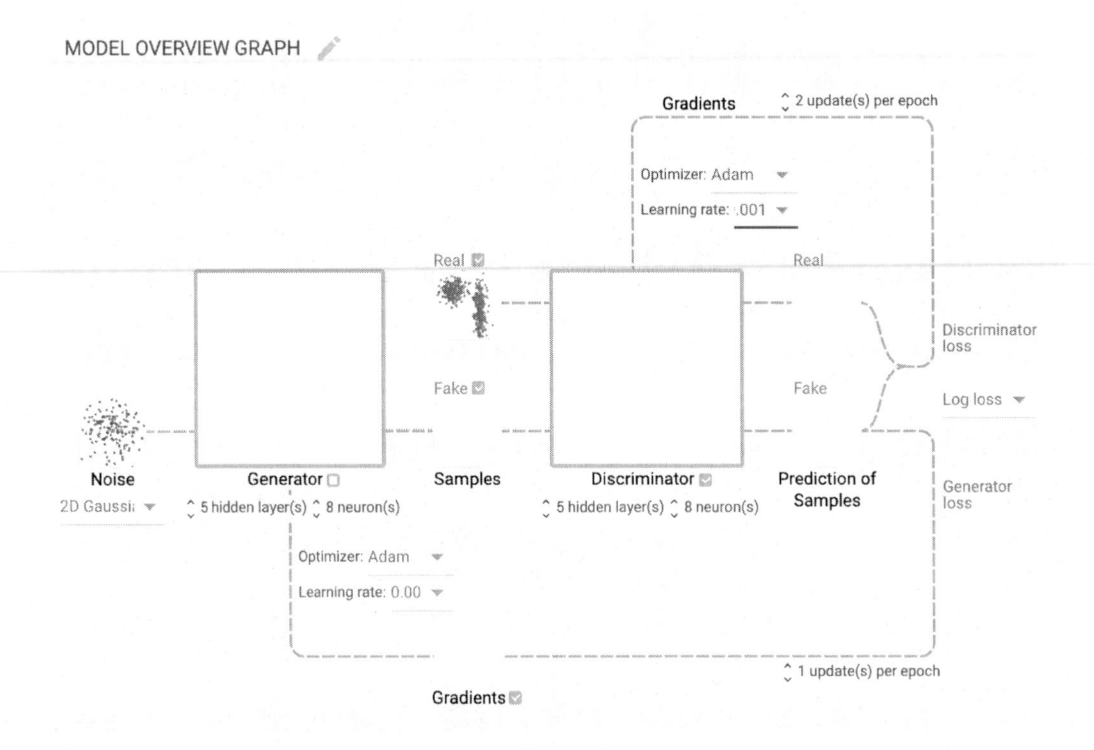

Figure 6.13 – A DCGAN architecture overview

The DCGAN architecture basically consists of **5 layers of convolution and 5 layers for transposed convolution**. There is no fully connected layer in this architecture. We will also use a learning rate of 0.0002 for training the model.

We can also take a more in-depth look at the generator architecture of the DCGAN to see how it works:

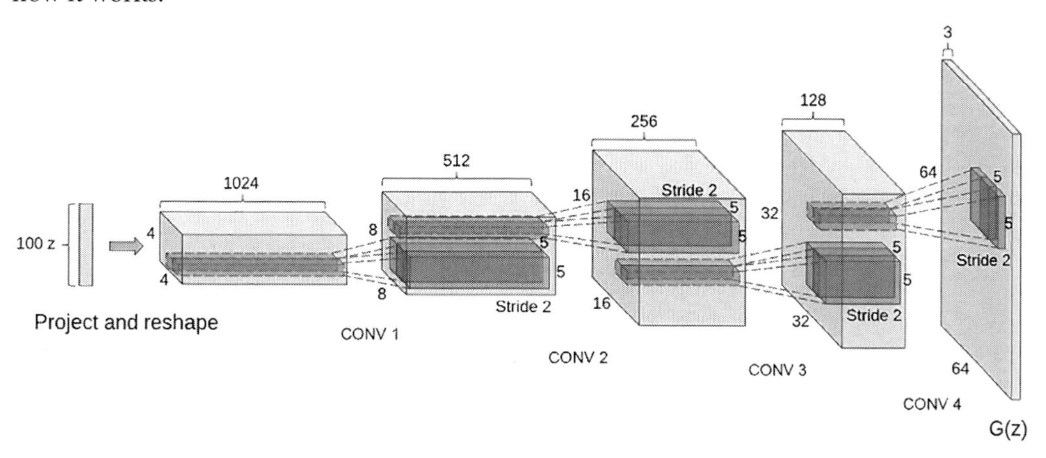

Figure 6.14 – The DCGAN generator architecture from the paper

It can be observed from the DCGAN generator architecture diagram that there are no fully connected or pooling layers used here. This is one of the architectural changes in the DCGAN model. The key advantage of DCGAN over GAN is its memory and compute efficiency. A tutorial for the DCGAN can be found on the PyTorch website.

We will use both the datasets (the food data and the butterfly data) on the same DCGAN model.

The code will consist of the following blocks:

1. Defining inputs
2. Loading data
3. Weights initialization
4. Discriminator model
5. Generator model
6. Optimizer
7. Training
8. Results

The code is very similar to the one we have just seen in the previous section. Please refer to the GitHub repository for this chapter for the full working code: `https://github.com/PacktPublishing/Deep-Learning-with-PyTorch-Lightning/tree/main/Chapter06`.

We trained the model for 100 epochs for both datasets, and the following is the loss we saw.

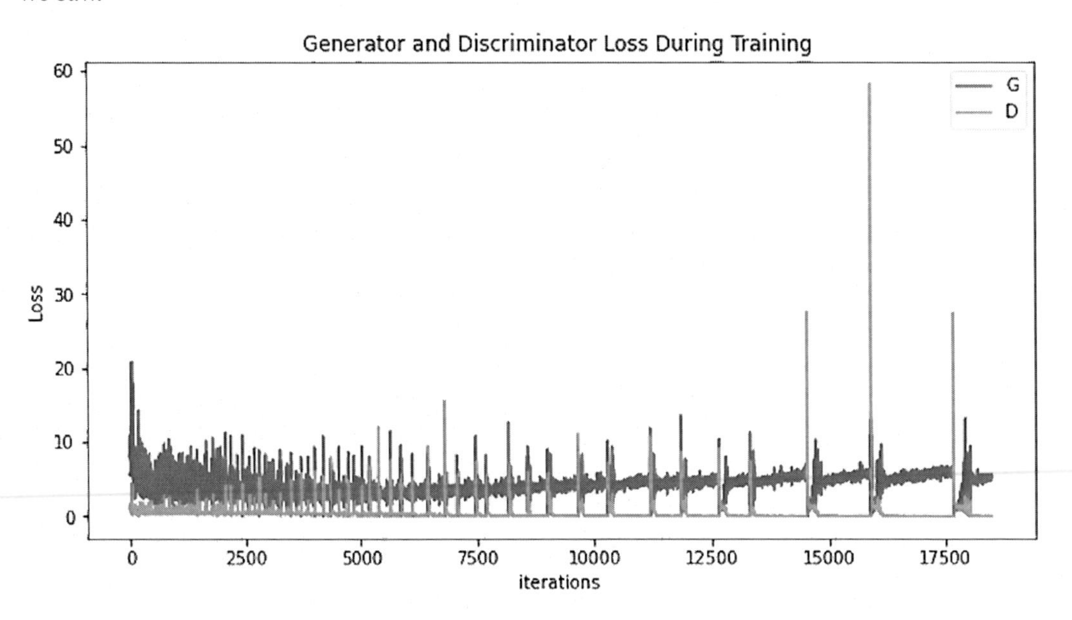

Figure 6.15 – Generator and discriminator loss during training of the DCGAN model

Based on the training, we get the following results for the food and butterfly datasets:

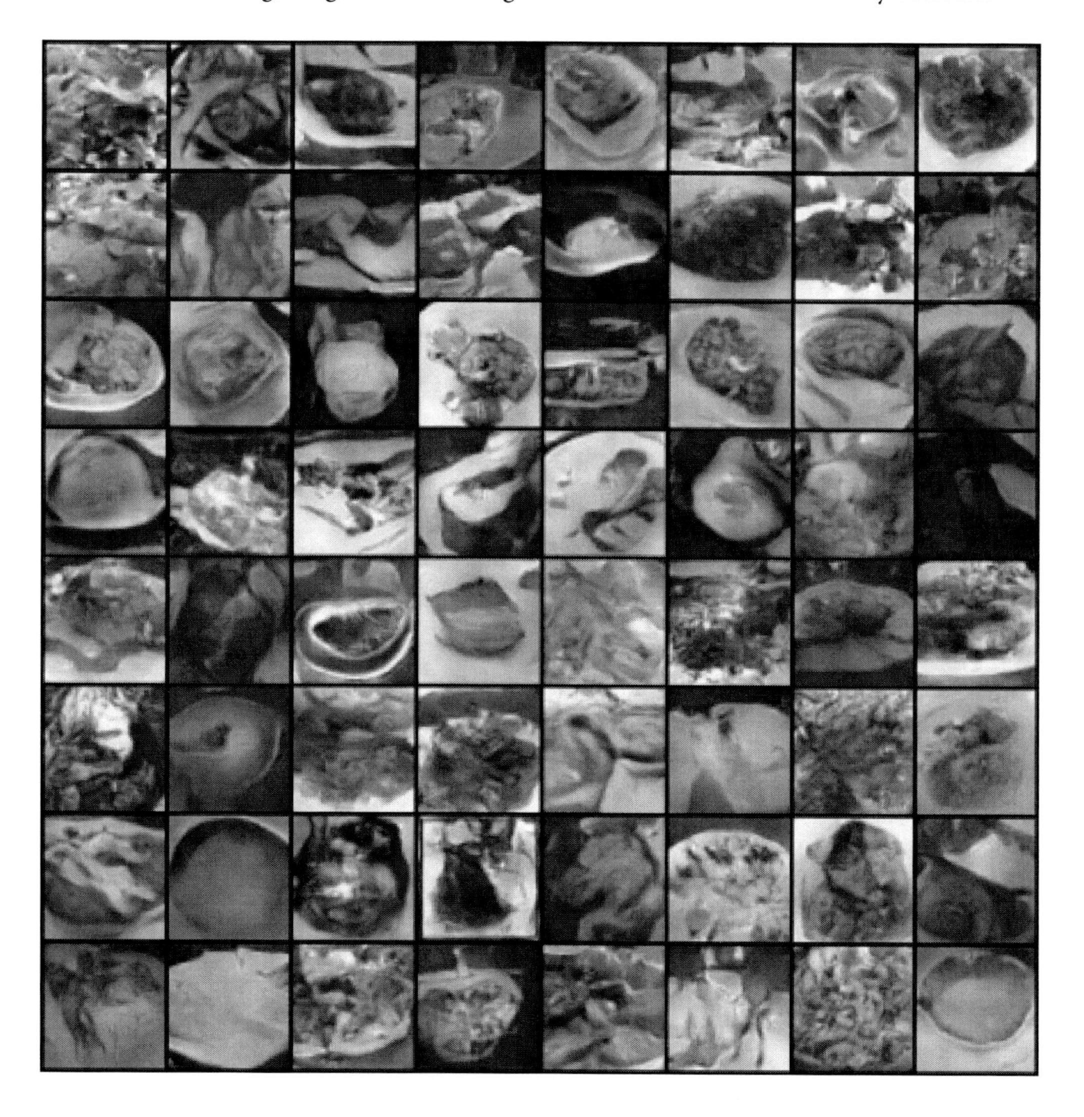

Figure 6.16 – Fake food images generated by the DCGAN model after 500 epochs

The following image shows the results for the butterfly dataset:

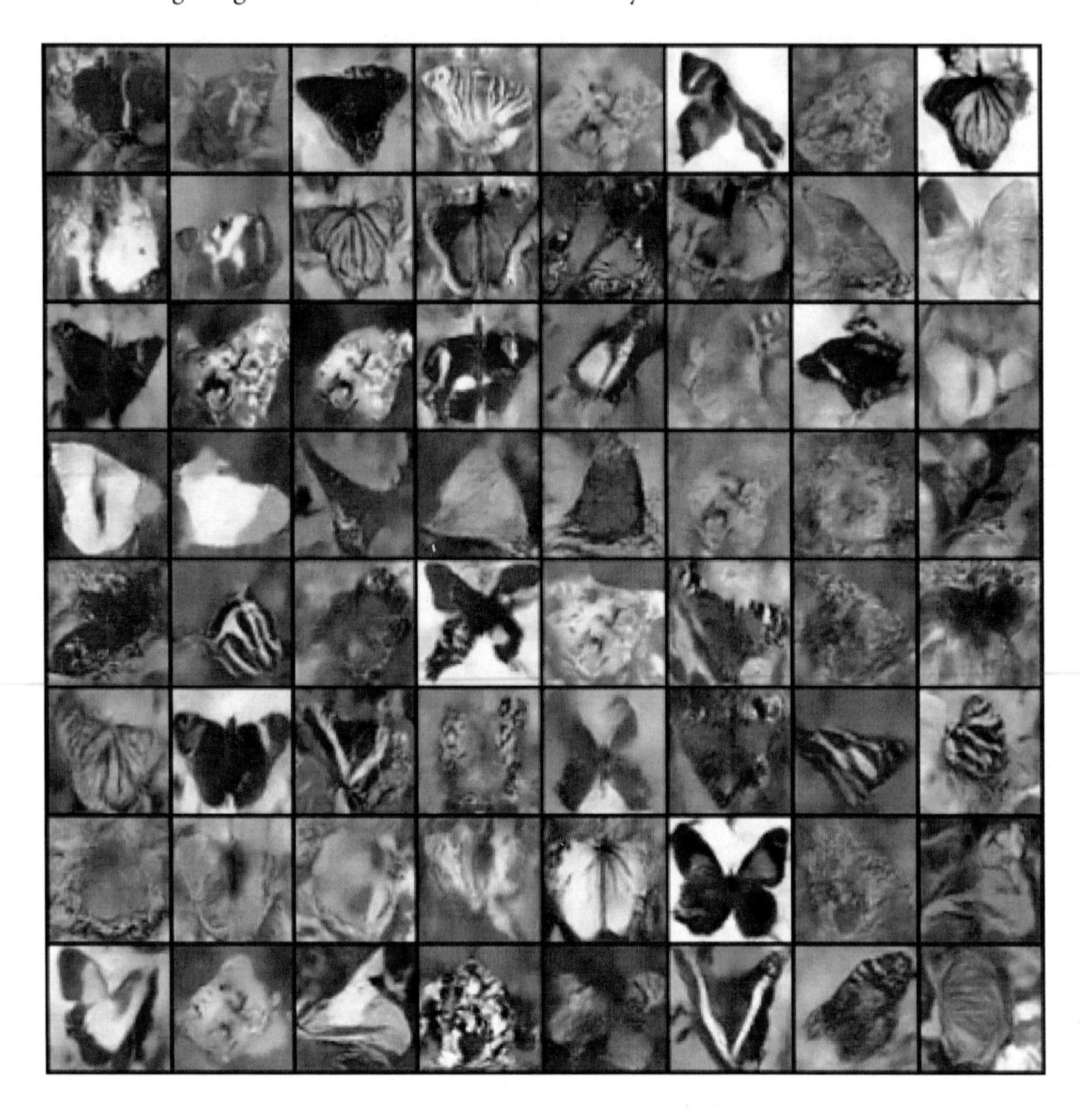

Figure 6.17 – Fake butterfly species generated by the DCGAN model after 500 epochs

As you will see, we get not just much better-quality results using DCGAN architecture but also with lesser epochs. The memory and compute requirements for the DCGAN were also lower than the vanilla GAN, and with the same amount of GPU, we could run the model for much longer. This is due to the inherent optimizations of the DCGAN, which makes it more efficient and effective.

Additional learning

- The first change that you can do to the model architecture is to change the number of convolutional and transposed convolutional layers. Most of the models use an eight-layer structure. You should change the preceding code to add more layers and compare the results.
- While we have used GAN and DCGAN architecture, you can also try other GAN architecture, such as BigGAN and StyleGAN.
- A GAN requires highly memory-intensive training. In order to reduce compute requirements, you can use pre-trained models. However, pre-trained models may only work with the original objects that they were trained for. As an example, you can generate new faces using a pre-trained StyleGAN model that was trained on a faces dataset. However, if there is no pre-trained model for butterflies (such as the dataset in this chapter), then it may not work well, and training from scratch may be the only option.
- Another option is to use a pre-trained model only for the discriminator. There are many papers that have used ImageNet pre-training for the discriminator only and got good results. You should try the same in this example as well.
- Lastly, go ahead and create anything new that you can dream of. GAN-created art is a new booming field. You can combine anything and generate anything. Who knows – your GAN art NFT may be auctioned at a high price one day!

Summary

GAN is a powerful method for generating not only images but also paintings, and even 3D objects (using newer variants of a GAN). We saw how, using a combination of discriminator and generator networks (each with five convolutional layers), we can start with random noise and generate an image that mimics real images. The play-off between the generator and discriminator keeps producing better images by minimizing the loss function and going through multiple iterations. The end result is fake pictures that never existed in real life.

It's a powerful method, and there are concerns about its ethical use. Fake images and objects can be used to defraud people; however, it also creates endless new opportunities. For example, imagine looking at a picture of fashion models while shopping for a new outfit. Instead of relying on endless image shoots, using a GAN (and DCGAN), you can generate realistic pictures of models with all body types, sizes, shapes, and colors, helping both companies and consumers. Fashion models are not the only example; imagine selling a home but having no furniture. Using a GAN, you can create realistic home furnishings – again, saving a lot of money for real estate developers. GANs are also a powerful source of data for augmentation and Deep Learning data generation purposes. Also, there are more possibilities for GANs that no one will have even thought of yet, and maybe you can come up with them by trying them out.

Next, we will continue our journey into generative modeling. Now that we have seen how to teach machines to generate images, we will try to teach machines how to write poems and generate text in the context of a given image. In the next chapter, we will explore **Semi-Supervised Learning**, where we will combine CNN and RNN architecture to generate *human-like* text, poems, or lyrics by making machines understand the context of what is inside an image.

7
Semi-Supervised Learning

Machine learning has been used for a long time to recognize patterns. However, recently the idea that machines can be used to *create* patterns has caught the imagination of everyone. The idea of machines being able to create art by mimicking known artistic styles or, given any input, provide a *human-like perspective* as output has become the new frontier in machine learning.

Most of the Deep Learning models we have seen thus far have been either about recognizing images (using the **Convolutional Neural Network** (**CNN**) architecture), generating text (with Transformers), or generating images (Generative Adversarial Networks). However, we as humans don't always view objects purely as text or images in real life but rather as a combination of them. For example, an image in a Facebook post or a news article will likely be accompanied by some comments describing it. Memes are a popular way of creating humor by combining catchy images with smart text. A music video is a combination of images, video, audio, and text, all combined together. If we want machines to truly be intelligent, they need to be smart enough to interpret content in media and explain it in such a way that humans understand it. Such *multimodal* learning is a holy grail of machine intelligence.

As mentioned earlier, ImageNet prompted the revolution in Deep Learning by achieving near-human performance in image recognition. It also opened the door for imagining new possibilities of what machines can achieve. One such prospect was to ask machines to not just recognize images but describe what is happening inside an image in layman's terms. This prompted the creation of a new crowdsourced project by Microsoft called **COCO**, which has human-curated captions for images. This created a set of models where we train machines how to write (such as teaching a child a language by showing them a picture of an apple and then writing the word *APPLE* on a blackboard and hoping that the child will use this skill to write new words). This also opened a new frontier in Deep Learning called **Semi-Supervised Learning**. This form of learning relies on human-provided input to begin training, so it has a supervised component to it; however, the initial input is not quite used as a ground truth or label. Rather, the output can be generated in an unsupervised manner with or without any prompt. It lies somewhere in the middle of the supervised-to-unsupervised spectrum and hence is called *Semi-Supervised Learning*. The biggest potential for semi-supervised learning, though, lies in the possibility of teaching machines the concept of *context* in an image. For example, an image of a car means a different thing depending on whether it's moving or parked or in a showroom, and making a machine understand those differences allows it to interpret what is happening inside the image.

In this chapter, we will see how PyTorch Lightning can be used to solve semi-supervised learning problems. We will focus on a solution that combines the **CNN** and **Recurrent Neural Network** (**RNN**) architectures.

We'll cover the following topics in this chapter:

- Getting started with Semi-Supervised Learning
- Going through the CNN–RNN architecture
- Generating captions for images

Technical requirements

In this chapter, we will primarily be using the following Python modules listed with their versions:

- PyTorch Lightning (version 1.5.2)
- NumPy (version 1.19.5)
- torch (version 1.10)
- torchvision (version 0.10.0)
- NLTK (version 3.2.5)
- Matplotlib (version 3.2.2)

In order to make sure that these modules work together and not go out of sync, we have used the specific version of `torch, torchvision, torchtext, torchaudio` with PyTorch Lightning 1.5.2. You can also use the latest version of PyTorch Lightning and torch compatible with each other. More details can be found on the GitHub link: `https://github.com/PacktPublishing/Deep-Learning-with-PyTorch-Lightning`.

```
!pip install torch==1.10.0 torchvision==0.11.1
torchtext==0.11.0 torchaudio==0.10.0 --quiet
```

```
!pip install pytorch-lightning==1.5.2 --quiet
```

Working code examples for this chapter can be found at this GitHub link: `https://github.com/PacktPublishing/Deep-Learning-with-PyTorch-Lightning/tree/main/Chapter07`.

The following source dataset is used in this chapter:

- The Microsoft **Common Objects in Context** (**COCO**) dataset, available at `https://cocodataset.org/#download`.

Getting started with semi-supervised learning

As we saw in the introduction, one of the most amazing applications of semi-supervised learning is the possibility to teach machines how to interpret images. This can be done not just to create captions for some given images but also to ask the machine to write a poetic description of how it *perceives* the images.

Check out the following results. On the left are some random images passed to the model and on the right are some poems generated by the model. The following results are interesting, as it is hard to identify whether these lyrical stanzas were created by a machine or a human:

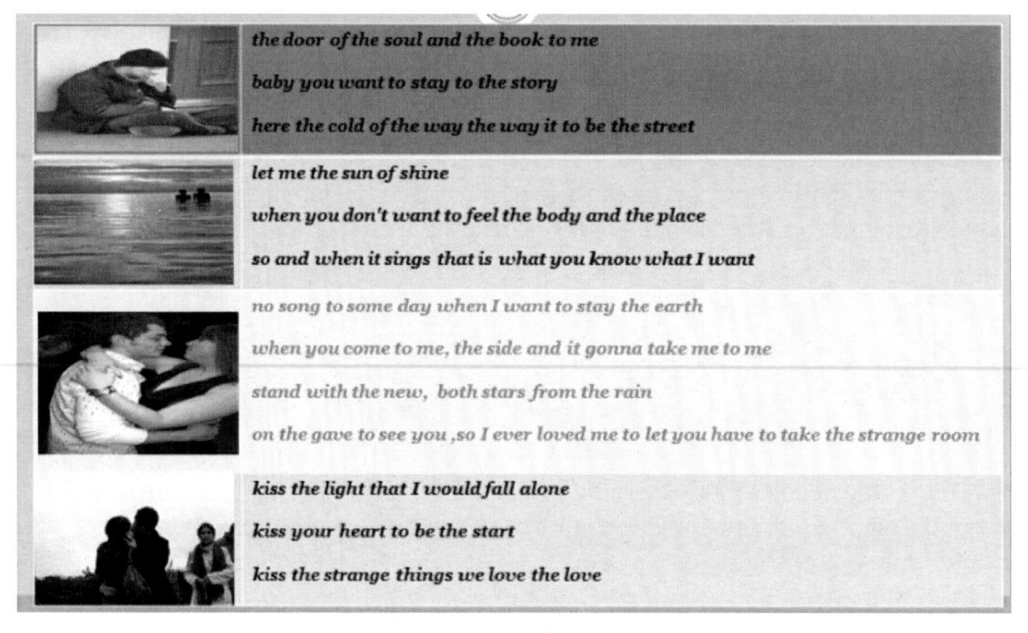

the door of the soul and the book to me
baby you want to stay to the story
here the cold of the way the way it to be the street
let me the sun of shine
when you don't want to feel the body and the place
so and when it sings that is what you know what I want
no song to some day when I want to stay the earth
when you come to me, the side and it gonna take me to me
stand with the new, both stars from the rain
on the gave to see you ,so I ever loved me to let you have to take the strange room
kiss the light that I would fall alone
kiss your heart to be the start
kiss the strange things we love the love

Figure 7.1 – Generating poems for a given image by analyzing context

For example, in the top image, the machine could detect the door and street and wrote a stanza about it. In the second image, it detected sunshine and wrote a lyrical stanza about sunsets and love. In the bottom image, the machine detected a couple kissing and wrote a few lines about kisses and love.

In this model, images and text are trained together so that by looking at an image, a machine can deduce the *context*. This internally uses various Deep Learning methods such as CNN and RNN with **Long Short-Term Memory** (**LSTM**). It gives a *perspective* prediction of the given object, based on the *style* of the trained data. For example, if there is an image of a *wall*, then we can use this to generate text, depending upon it may be spoken by Donald Trump or Hillary Clinton, or someone else. This fascinating new development brings machines closer to art and human perception.

To understand how this has been made possible, we need to understand the underlying neural network architecture. In *Chapter 2, Getting off the Ground with First Deep Learning Model*, we saw the CNN model, and in *Chapter 5, Time Series Models*, we saw an example of the LSTM model. We will be making use of both of them for this chapter.

Going through the CNN–RNN architecture

While there are many possible applications of semi-supervised learning and a number of possible neural architectures, we will start with one of the most popular, which is an architecture that combines CNN and RNN.

Simply put, we will be starting with an image, then use the CNN to recognize the image, and then pass the output of the CNN to an RNN, which in turn generates the text:

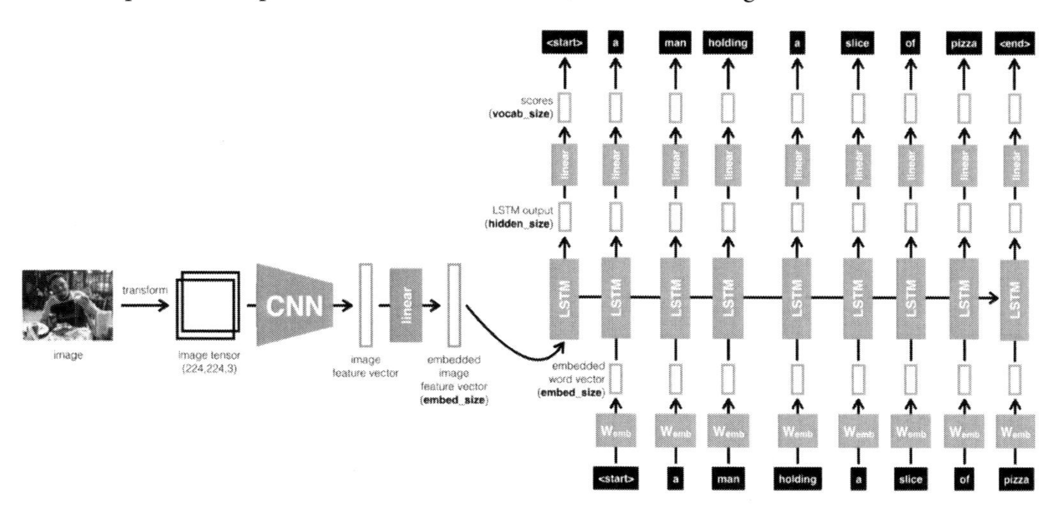

Figure 7.2 – CNN–RNN cascaded architecture

Intuitively speaking, the model is trained to recognize the images and their sentence descriptions so that it learns about the intermodal correspondence between language and visual data. It uses a CNN and a multimodal RNN to generate descriptions of the images. As mentioned above, LSTM is used for the implementation of the RNN.

This architecture was first proposed by Andrej Karpathy and his doctoral advisor Fei-Fei Li in their 2015 Stanford paper titled *Generative Text Using Images* and *Deep Visual-Semantic Alignments for Generating Image Descriptions*:

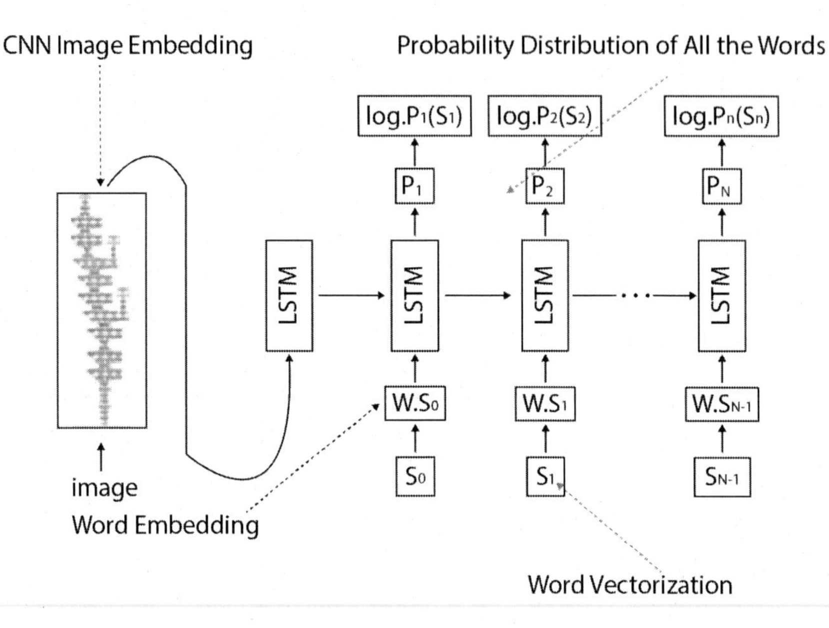

$$
\begin{aligned}
x_{-1} &= \text{CNN}(I) \\
x_t &= W_e S_t, \quad t \in \{0 \dots N-1\} \\
p_{t+1} &= \text{LSTM}(x_t), \quad t \in \{0 \dots N-1\}
\end{aligned}
$$

Figure 7.3 – LSTM and CNN working details (Image Credit- Andrej Karpathy)

Let's quickly go through the steps involved in the architecture described in the paper:

1. The dataset contains sentences that are written by people that describe what is happening in the images. The core idea relies on the fact that people will make frequent references to some objects but the context in which they occur. For example, the sentence *Man is sitting on the bench* has multiple parts, the *man* being the object, the *bench* being the location, and *sitting* being the action. Together, they define the context for the overall image.
2. Our objective is to generate text that describes what is happening in the image as a human would. In order to do so, we need to move the problem to a latent space and create a latent representation of image regions and words. Such a multimodal embedding will create a semantic map of similar contexts together and can generate text for unseen images.

3. In order to achieve it, we first use a CNN as an encoder and get a feature from the last layer before Softmax. In order to extract the relationship between the image and word, we will need to represent the words in the same form of image vector embedding. Thus, the tensor representation of an image is then passed on to an RNN modal.
4. The architecture uses an LSTM architecture to implement the RNN. The specific bidirectional RNN takes a sequence of words and transforms each word into a vector. The LSTM for text generation works a lot like what we saw for time series in *Chapter 5, Time Series Models*, by predicting the next word in a sentence. It does so by predicting each letter at a time given the entire history of previous letters, picking the letter with the maximum probability.
5. The LSTM activation function is set to a **Rectified Linear Unit** (**ReLU**), The training of the RNN is exactly the same as described in the previous model. Finally, an optimization method is used, which is the **Stochastic Gradient Descent** (**SGD**), with mini-batches to optimize the model.
6. Finally, in order to generate descriptive text or caption for unseen images, the model works by first using a CNN image recognition model to detect object areas and identify the objects. These objects then become a primer or a seed to our LSTM model and the model predicts the sentence. The sentence prediction happens one character at a time by picking up the maximum probability (Softmax) of a character over the distribution. The vocabulary supplied plays a key part in what text can be generated.
7. And if you change the vocabulary from, say, a caption to poems, then the model will learn to generate the poems. If you give it Shakespeare, it will generate sonnets, and whatever you can imagine!

Generating captions for images

This model will involve the following steps:

1. Downloading the dataset
2. Assembling the data
3. Training the model
4. Generating the caption

Downloading the dataset

In this step, we will download the COCO dataset that we will use to train our model.

COCO dataset

The COCO dataset *is a large-scale object detection, segmentation, and captioning dataset* (`https://cocodataset.org`). It has 1.5 million object instances, 80 object categories, and 5 captions per image. You can explore the dataset at `https://cocodataset.org/#explore` by filtering on one or more object types, such as the images of dogs shown in the following screenshot. Each image has tiles above it to show/hide URLs, segmentations, and captions:

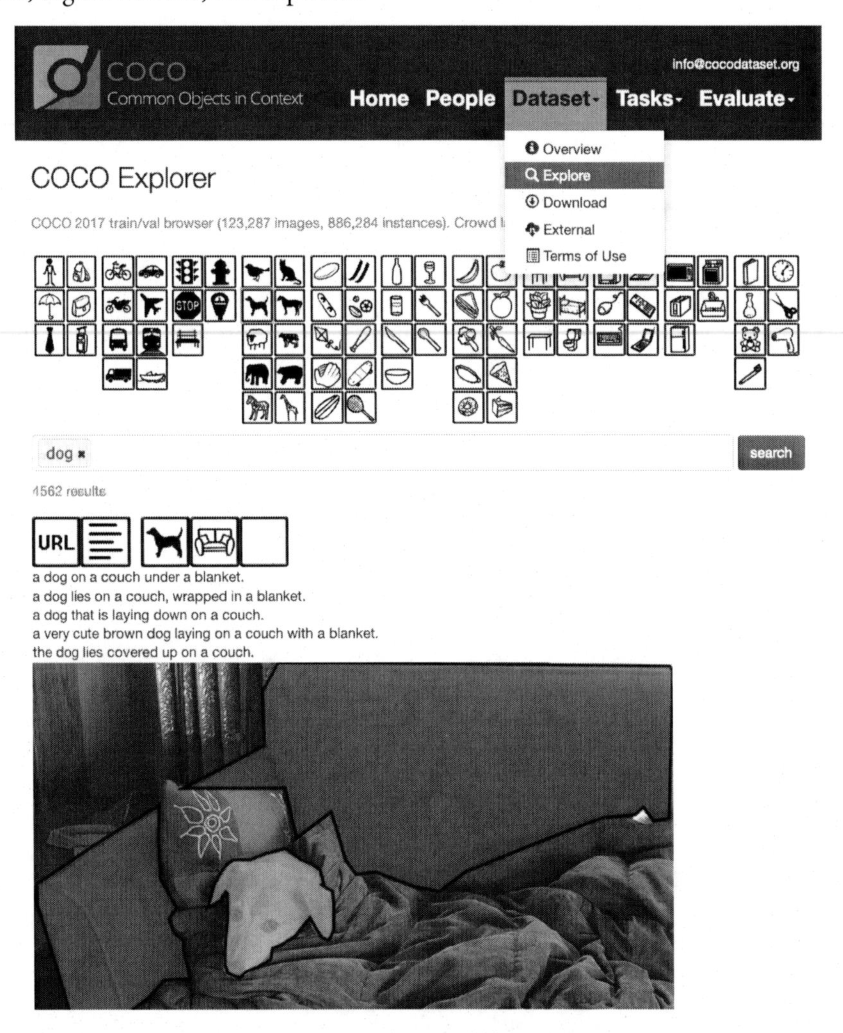

Figure 7.4 – COCO dataset

Here are a few more images from the dataset:

Figure 7.5 – Random dataset examples from the COCO website home page

Extracting the dataset

In this chapter, we will train our hybrid CNN–RNN model using 4,000 images in the COCO 2017 training dataset along with the captions for those images. The COCO 2017 dataset contains more than 118,000 images and more than 590,000 captions. Training a model using such a big dataset takes a very long time, so we filter out 4,000 images and their associated captions, which we will describe later. But first, the following are the steps in code (`Downloading_the_dataset.ipynb` notebook) for downloading all the images and captions to a folder named `coco_data`:

```
!wget http://images.cocodataset.org/zips/train2017.zip
!wget http://images.cocodataset.org/annotations/annotations_
trainval2017.zip

!mkdir coco_data

!unzip ./train2017.zip -d ./coco_data/
!rm ./train2017.zip

!unzip ./annotations_trainval2017.zip -d ./coco_data/
!rm ./annotations_trainval2017.zip
!rm ./coco_data/annotations/instances_val2017.json
!rm ./coco_data/annotations/captions_val2017.json
!rm ./coco_data/annotations/person_keypoints_train2017.json
!rm ./coco_data/annotations/person_keypoints_val2017.json
```

In the preceding code snippet, we download the ZIP files from the COCO website using the `wget` command. This is equivalent to downloading the files, marked using red arrows in the following screenshot, taken from the download page of the COCO website (`https://cocodataset.org/#download`):

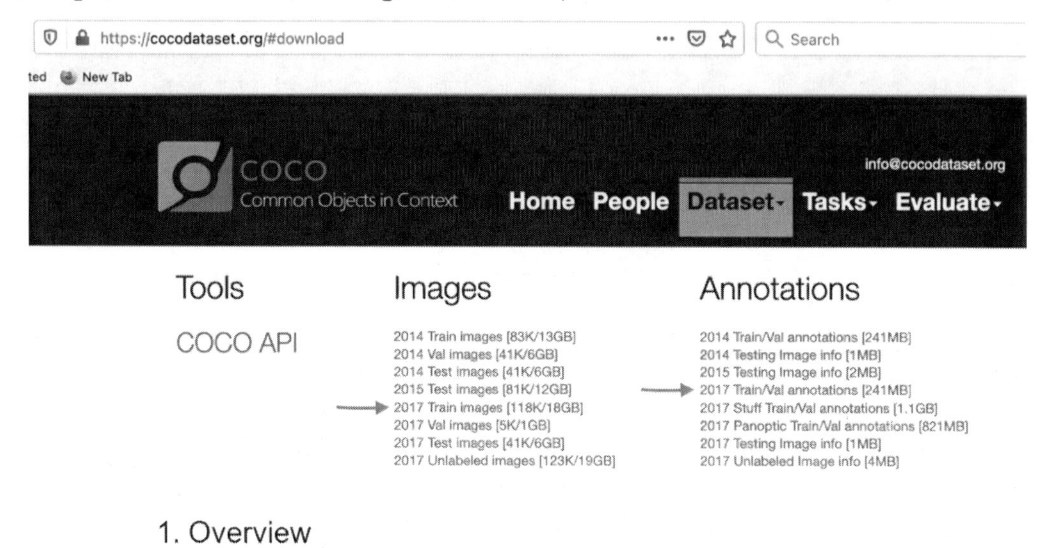

Figure 7.6 – Download page from the COCO website

We unzip the ZIP files and then delete them. We also delete some extracted files that we are not going to use, such as the files containing validation data.

The following screenshot shows the contents of the `coco_data` directory after running the code snippet:

```
!ls ./coco_data

annotations  train2017

!ls ./coco_data/annotations

captions_train2017.json  instances_train2017.json

!ls ./coco_data/train2017

000000120643.jpg  000000267049.jpg  000000411223.jpg  000000557785.jpg
000000120644.jpg  000000267055.jpg  000000411225.jpg  000000557794.jpg
000000120645.jpg  000000267059.jpg  000000411226.jpg  000000557804.jpg
000000120648.jpg  000000267064.jpg  000000411238.jpg  000000557811.jpg
000000120655.jpg  000000267067.jpg  000000411241.jpg  000000557812.jpg
```

Figure 7.7 – Downloaded and extracted COCO data

Assembling the data

While Deep Learning usually involves large datasets, such as all images and captions in COCO 2017, training a model using such a big dataset requires powerful machines and lots of time. We limit the dataset to 4,000 images and their captions so that the model described in this chapter can be trained in days rather than weeks.

In this section, we will describe how we process the COCO 2017 data in order to filter out 4,000 images and their captions, resize the images, and create the vocabulary from the captions. We will work in the `Assembling_the_data.ipynb` notebook. We import the necessary packages into the first cell of the notebook, as shown in the following code block:

```
import os
import json
import random
import nltk
import pickle
from shutil import copyfile
from collections import Counter
from PIL import Image
from vocabulary import Vocabulary
```

Filtering the images and their captions

As mentioned in the previous section, we limit the size of the training dataset by filtering out 1,000 images each for four categories: *motorcycle*, *airplane*, *elephant*, and *tennis racket*. We also filter out captions for those images.

First, we process annotations in the `instances_train2017.json` metadata file. This file has the *object detection* information (you can refer to details of this and other COCO dataset annotations at the following web page: `https://cocodataset.org/#format-data`). We use `category_id`, `image_id`, and `area` fields in an object detection annotation for the following two purposes:

- To list various categories that are present in an image.

- To sort categories in an image in decreasing order of their areas. This helps us determine during filtering whether a category is prominent in an image or not. For example, the tennis racket marked in green color in the following figure in the COCO dataset is not as prominent as the people, cars, luggage, and so on. So captions for the image don't mention the tennis racket:

Figure 7.8 – Non-predominant category

Selecting images by categories

In the following code snippet, we start by reading the JSON file and initializing variables:

```
obj_fl = "./coco_data/annotations/instances_train2017.json"
with open(obj_fl) as json_file:
  object_detections = json.load(json_file)
CATEGORY_LIST = [4, 5, 22, 43]
COUNT_PER_CATEGORY = 1000
category_dict = dict()
```

```
for category_id in CATEGORY_LIST:
  category_dict[category_id] = dict()
all_images = dict()
filtered_images = set()
```

For CATEGORY_LIST, we manually looked up id of the four categories in the *categories* array in the JSON. For example, the following is an entry for a category (you can select any categories that you wish):

```
{"supercategory": "vehicle","id": 4,"name": "motorcycle"}
```

Then, we use the for loop in the following code block to populate the all_images and category_dict dictionaries:

```
for annotation in object_detections['annotations']:
  category_id = annotation['category_id']
  image_id = annotation['image_id']
  area = annotation['area']
  if category_id in CATEGORY_LIST:
    if image_id not in category_dict[category_id]:
      category_dict[category_id][image_id] = []
  if image_id not in all_images:
    all_images[image_id] = dict()
  if category_id not in all_images[image_id]:
    all_images[image_id][category_id] = area
  else:
    current_area = all_images[image_id][category_id]
    if area > current_area:
      all_images[image_id][category_id] = area
```

After execution of this for loop, the dictionaries are as follows:

- The all_images dictionary contains categories and their areas for each image in the dataset.
- The category_dict dictionary contains all images that have one or more of the four categories that we are interested in.

If COUNT_PER_CATEGORY is set to -1, it means that you want to filter *all* images of the categories specified in CATEGORY_LIST. So, in the if block, we just use category_dict to get images.

Otherwise, in the else block, we filter out the COUNT_PER_CATEGORY number of *prominent* images for each of the four categories. We use two for loops in the else block. The first for loop, shown in the following code block, uses image-specific categories and areas information in the all_images dictionary to sort category_ids for each image in *decreasing* order of their areas. In other words, after this for loop, a value in the dictionary is a list of categories in decreasing order of their *prominence* in the image:

```
for image_id in all_images:
    areas = list(all_images[image_id].values())
    categories = list(all_images[image_id].keys())
    sorted_areas = sorted(areas, reverse=True)
    sorted_categories = []
    for area in sorted_areas:
      sorted_categories.append(categories[areas.index(area)])
    all_images[image_id] = sorted_categories
```

The second for loop in the else block iterates over images for the four categories stored in category_dict and uses the information stored in the all_images dictionary to filter out the COUNT_PER_CATEGORY number of most prominent images. This for loop prints the following results:

```
Processing category 4
  Added 1000 images at prominence_index 0 out of 2134 images
  Completed filtering of total 1000 images of category 4
Processing category 5
  Added 1000 images at prominence_index 0 out of 2707 images
  Completed filtering of total 1000 images of category 5
Processing category 22
  Added 1000 images at prominence_index 0 out of 1981 images
  Completed filtering of total 1000 images of category 22
Processing category 43
  Added all 30 images at prominence_index 0
  Added 970 images at prominence_index 1 out of 2621 images
  Completed filtering of total 1000 images of category 43
Processed all categories. Number of filtered images is 4000
```

Figure 7.9 – Output from the image filtering code

Selecting captions

In the next cell of the notebook, we start working with the captions stored in the `captions_train2017.json` metadata file. We separate out captions associated with the images that we filtered in the preceding notebook cell, as shown in the following code block:

```
filtered_annotations = []
for annotation in captions['annotations']:
  if annotation['image_id'] in filtered_images:
    filtered_annotations.append(annotation)
captions['annotations'] = filtered_annotations
```

In the JSON file, captions are stored in an array named `annotations`. A caption entry in the array looks like this:

```
{"image_id": 173799,"id": 665512,"caption": "Two men herding a pack of elephants across a field."}
```

We separate out captions whose `image_id` value is in the `filtered_images` set.

The `captions` JSON file also has an array named `images`. In the next `for` loop, we shorten the images array to store entries for only the filtered images:

```
images = []
filtered_image_file_names = set()
for image in captions['images']:
  if image['id'] in filtered_images:
    images.append(image)
    filtered_image_file_names.add(image['file_name'])
captions['images'] = images
```

Finally, we save the filtered captions in a new file named `coco_data/captions.json` and we copy filtered image files (using the `copyfile` function) to a new directory named `coco_data/images`:

```
Number of filtered annotations is 20007
Expected number of filtered images is 4000, actual number is 4000
```

Figure 7.10 – Output from the image filtering code

This completes our data assembly step and gives us a training dataset of 4,000 images and 20,000 captions across 4 categories.

Resizing the images

All images in the COCO dataset are colored, but they can be of various sizes. As described next, all the images are transformed to a uniform size of 3 x 256 x 256 and stored in a folder named `images`. The following code block is from the `resize_images` function defined in the `Assembling_the_data.ipynb` notebook:

```
def resize_images(input_path, output_path, new_size):
    if not os.path.exists(output_path):
        os.makedirs(output_path)
    image_files = os.listdir(input_path)
    num_images = len(image_files)
    for i, img in enumerate(image_files):
        img_full_path = os.path.join(input_path, img)
        with open(img_full_path, 'r+b') as f:
            with Image.open(f) as image:
                image = image.resize(new_size, Image.ANTIALIAS)
                img_sv_full_path = os.path.join(output_path, 
img)
                image.save(img_sv_full_path, image.format)
        if (i+1) % 100 == 0 or (i+1) == num_images:
            print("Resized {} out of {} total 
images.".format(i+1, num_images))
```

We pass the following arguments to the `resize_images` function shown in the preceding code block:

- `input_path`: the `coco_data/images` folder where we saved 4,000 filtered images from the COCO 2017 training dataset
- `output_path`: the`coco_data/resized_images` folder
- `new_size`: dimensions [256 x 256]

In the preceding code snippet, we iterate over all images in `input_path` and resize each image by calling its `resize` method. We save each resized image to the `output_path` folder.

Here are the print messages emitted by the `resize_images` function:

```
Resized 2900 out of 4000 total images.
Resized 3000 out of 4000 total images.
Resized 3100 out of 4000 total images.
Resized 3200 out of 4000 total images.
Resized 3300 out of 4000 total images.
Resized 3400 out of 4000 total images.
Resized 3500 out of 4000 total images.
Resized 3600 out of 4000 total images.
Resized 3700 out of 4000 total images.
Resized 3800 out of 4000 total images.
Resized 3900 out of 4000 total images.
Resized 4000 out of 4000 total images.
```

Figure 7.11 – Output for image resizing

Then, in that same notebook cell, we use the following commands to move the resized images into the `coco_data/images` directory:

```
!rm -rf ./coco_data/images
!mv ./coco_data/resized_images ./coco_data/images
```

After the images are resized, we build the vocabulary.

Building the vocabulary

In the last cell of the `Assembling_the_data.ipynb` notebook, we process the captions associated with the filtered COCO dataset images using the `build_vocabulary` function. This function creates an instance of the `Vocabulary` class. The `Vocabulary` class is defined in a separate file, `vocabulary.py`, so that the definition can be reused during the training and the prediction phases, as described later. This is why we have added the `from vocabulary import Vocabulary` statement in the first cell of this notebook.

The following code block shows the `Vocabulary` class definition in the `vocabulary.py` file:

```
class Vocabulary(object):
  def __init__(self):
    self.token_to_int = {}
    self.int_to_token = {}
```

```
        self.current_index = 0

    def __call__(self, token):
        if not token in self.token_to_int:
            return self.token_to_int['<unk>']
        return self.token_to_int[token]

    def __len__(self):
        return len(self.token_to_int)

    def add_token(self, token):
        if not token in self.token_to_int:
            self.token_to_int[token] = self.current_index
            self.int_to_token[self.current_index] = token
            self.current_index += 1
```

We map each unique word – called a **token** – in the captions to an integer. The `Vocabulary` object has a dictionary named `token_to_int` to retrieve the integer corresponding to a token and a dictionary named `int_to_token` to retrieve the token corresponding to an integer.

The following code snippet shows the definition of the `build_vocabulary` function in the last cell of the `Assembling_the_data.ipynb` notebook:

```
def build_vocabulary(json_path, threshold):
    with open(json_path) as json_file:
        captions = json.load(json_file)
    counter = Counter()
    i = 0
    for annotation in captions['annotations']:
        i = i + 1
        caption = annotation['caption']
        tokens = nltk.tokenize.word_tokenize(caption.lower())
        counter.update(tokens)
        if i % 1000 == 0 or i == len(captions['annotations']):
            print("Tokenized {} out of total {} captions.".format(i,
len(captions['annotations'])))

```

```
    tokens = [tkn for tkn, i in counter.items() if i >=
threshold]

    vocabulary = Vocabulary()
    vocabulary.add_token('<pad>')
    vocabulary.add_token('<start>')
    vocabulary.add_token('<end>')
    vocabulary.add_token('<unk>')

    for i, token in enumerate(tokens):
        vocabulary.add_token(token)
    return vocabulary

vocabulary = build_vocabulary(json_path='coco_data/captions.
json', threshold=4)
vocabulary_path = './coco_data/vocabulary.pkl'
with open(vocabulary_path, 'wb') as f:
    pickle.dump(vocabulary, f)
print("Total vocabulary size: {}".format(len(vocabulary)))
```

We pass the location of the `captions` JSON (`coco_data/captions.json`) as the `json_path` argument to the function and the `4` value as the `threshold` argument.

First, we use `json.load` to load the JSON. `nltk` stands for **Natural Language Toolkit**. We use NLTK's `tokenize.word_tokenize` method to split caption sentences into words and punctuation. We use the `collections.Counter` dictionary object to count the number of occurrences for each token. After processing all captions inside the `for` loop, we discard the tokens that appear less frequently than the threshold.

We then instantiate the `Vocabulary` object and add some special tokens to it – `<start>` and `<end>` for the start and end of a sentence, `<pad>` for padding, and `<unk>`, which is used as the return value when the `__call__` method of the `Vocabulary` object is asked to return an integer for a token that doesn't exist in the `token_to_int` dictionary. We then add the rest of the tokens to `Vocabulary` in a `for` loop.

> **Important Note**
>
> It is important to add the <pad> token to the vocabulary before any other tokens are added because it ensures that 0 is assigned as the integer value for that token. This makes the definition of the <pad> token consistent with the programming logic in coco_collate_fn, where zeros are directly used (torch.zeros()) when creating a batch of padded captions.

Finally, the vocabulary is persisted in the coco_data directory using the pickle.dump method.

Here are the print messages emitted by the build_vocabulary function:

```
Tokenized 12000 out of total 20012 captions.
Tokenized 13000 out of total 20012 captions.
Tokenized 14000 out of total 20012 captions.
Tokenized 15000 out of total 20012 captions.
Tokenized 16000 out of total 20012 captions.
Tokenized 17000 out of total 20012 captions.
Tokenized 18000 out of total 20012 captions.
Tokenized 19000 out of total 20012 captions.
Tokenized 20000 out of total 20012 captions.
Tokenized 20012 out of total 20012 captions.
Total vocabulary size: 1687
```

Figure 7.12 – Output of tokenization

After this step, we are ready to start training the model.

> **Important Note**
>
> Downloading the dataset and assembling the data are one-time processing steps. If you are rerunning the model to resume or restart the training, then you do not need to repeat the steps up to this point and can start beyond this point.

Training the model

In this section, we describe the model training. It involves loading data using the torch.utils.data.Dataset and torch.utils.data.DataLoader classes, defining the model using the pytorch_lightning.LightningModule class, setting the training configuration, and launching the training process using the PyTorch Lightning framework's Trainer. We will work in the Training_the_model.ipynb notebook and the model.py file in this section.

We import the necessary packages into the first cell of the `Training_the_model.ipynb` notebook, as shown in the following code block:

```
import os
import json
import pickle
import nltk
from PIL import Image

import torch
import torch.utils.data as data
import torchvision.transforms as transforms

import pytorch_lightning as pl

from model import HybridModel
from vocabulary import Vocabulary
```

Dataset

Next, we define the `CocoDataset` class, which extends the `torch.utils.data.Dataset` class. `CocoDataset` is a map-style dataset, so we define the `__getitem__()` and `__len__()` methods in the class. The `__len__()` method returns a total number of samples in the dataset, whereas the `__getitem__()` method returns a sample at a given index (the `idx` parameter of the method, as shown in the following code block):

```
class CocoDataset(data.Dataset):
    def __init__(self, data_path, json_path, vocabulary,
transform=None):
        self.image_dir = data_path
        self.vocabulary = vocabulary
        self.transform = transform
        with open(json_path) as json_file:
            self.coco = json.load(json_file)
        self.image_id_file_name = dict()
        for image in self.coco['images']:
```

```
            self.image_id_file_name[image['id']] = image['file_
name']

    def __getitem__(self, idx):
        annotation = self.coco['annotations'][idx]
        caption = annotation['caption']
        tkns = nltk.tokenize.word_tokenize(str(caption).
lower())
        caption = []
        caption.append(self.vocabulary('<start>'))
        caption.extend([self.vocabulary(tkn) for tkn in tkns])
        caption.append(self.vocabulary('<end>'))

        image_id = annotation['image_id']
        image_file = self.image_id_file_name[image_id]
        image_path = os.path.join(self.image_dir, image_file)
        image = Image.open(image_path).convert('RGB')
        if self.transform is not None:
            image = self.transform(image)

        return image, torch.Tensor(caption)

    def __len__(self):
        return len(self.coco['annotations'])
```

As described later in this section, `__init__` receives the `images` directory (`coco_data/images`) as the `data_path` parameter and the `captions` JSON (`coco_data/captions.json`) as the `json_path` parameter. It also receives the `Vocabulary` object. The `captions` JSON is loaded using `json.load` and stored in the `self.coco` variable. The `for` loop in `__init__` creates a dictionary named `self.image_id_file_name` that maps the image ID to a filename.

`__len__()` returns the total length of the dataset, as shown previously.

> **Important Note**
>
> The COCO dataset has five captions per image. Since our model processes each image-caption pair, the length of the dataset equals the total number of captions, not the total number of images.

The `__getitem__()` method in the preceding code block returns an image–caption pair for a given index. It retrieves the caption corresponding to the `idx` index, tokenizes the captions, and uses `vocabulary` to convert the tokens into their corresponding integers. Then, it retrieves the image ID corresponding to `idx`, uses the `self.image_id_file_name` dictionary to get the image's filename, loads the image from the file, and transforms the image based on the `transforms` parameter.

The `CocoDataset` object is passed as an argument to `DataLoader`, as described later in this section. But `DataLoader` also requires a `collate` function, which we will describe next.

The collate function

We define the collate function named `coco_collate_fn()` in the next cell of the `Training_the_model.ipynb` notebook. As shown in the following code snippet, `coco_collate_fn()` receives a batch of images and their corresponding captions as input, named `data_batch`. It adds padding to the captions in the batch:

```
def coco_collate_fn(data_batch):
  data_batch.sort(key=lambda d: len(d[1]), reverse=True)
  imgs, caps = zip(*data_batch)

  imgs = torch.stack(imgs, 0)

  cap_lens = [len(cap) for cap in caps]
  padded_caps = torch.zeros(len(caps), max(cap_lens)).long()
  for i, cap in enumerate(caps):
    end = cap_lens[i]
    padded_caps[i, :end] = cap[:end]
  return imgs, padded_caps, cap_lens
```

We first sort `data_batch` by caption length in descending order, and then we separate the image (`imgs`) and caption (`caps`) lists.

Let's denote the length of the imgs list using <batch_size>. It contains 3 x 256 x 256-dimensional images. It is converted into a single tensor of <batch_size> x 3 x 256 x 256 size using the torch.stack() function.

Similarly, the caps list has a total of <batch_size> number of entries and it contains captions of various length. Let's denote the length of the longest caption in a batch using <max_caption_length>. The for loop converts the caps list into a single tensor named padded_caps of <batch_size> x <max_caption_length> size. Captions that are shorter than <max_caption_length> get padded with zeros.

Finally, the function returns imgs, padded_caps, and cap_lens; the cap_lens list contains actual (non-padded) lengths of captions in the batch.

The CocoDataset object and coco_collate_fn() are passed as arguments to DataLoader, as described in the next section.

DataLoader

The get_loader() function is defined in the next cell of the Training_the_model.ipynb notebook, as shown in the following code block:

```
def get_loader(data_path, json_path, vocabulary, transform,
batch_size, shuffle, num_workers=0):
    coco_ds = CocoDataset(data_path=data_path,
                          json_path=json_path,
                          vocabulary=vocabulary,
                          transform=transform)
    coco_dl = data.DataLoader(dataset=coco_ds,
                              batch_size=batch_size,
                              shuffle=shuffle,
                              num_workers=num_workers,
                              collate_fn=coco_collate_fn)
    return coco_dl
```

The function instantiates a CocoDataset object named coco_ds and passes it, as well as the coco_collate_fn function, as arguments during the instantiation of an object named coco_dl of torch.utils.data.DataLoader type. Finally, the function returns the coco_dl object.

Hybrid CNN–RNN model

The model is defined in a separate file named `model.py` so that we can reuse the code during the prediction step, as described later. As can be seen in the `model.py` file, first we import the necessary packages:

```
import torch
import torch.nn as nn
from torch.nn.utils.rnn import pack_padded_sequence as pk_pdd_
seq
import torchvision.models as models

import pytorch_lightning as pl
```

As always, our `HybridModel` class extends `LightningModule`. In the rest of this section, we will describe the CNN and RNN layers, as well as training configurations such as optimizer settings, learning rate, training loss, and batch size.

CNN and RNN layers

Our model is a hybrid of a CNN model and an RNN model. We define sequential layers of both models in `__init__()` of our `HybridModel` class definition, as shown in the following code block:

```
def __init__(self, cnn_embdng_sz, lstm_embdng_sz, lstm_hidden_
lyr_sz, lstm_vocab_sz, lstm_num_lyrs, max_seq_len=20):
    super(HybridModel, self).__init__()
    resnet = models.resnet152(pretrained=False)
    module_list = list(resnet.children())[:-1]
    self.cnn_resnet = nn.Sequential(*module_list)
    self.cnn_linear = nn.Linear(resnet.fc.in_features,
                                   cnn_embdng_sz)
    self.cnn_batch_norm = nn.BatchNorm1d(cnn_embdng_sz,
                                           momentum=0.01)

    self.lstm_embdng_lyr = nn.Embedding(lstm_vocab_sz,
                                          lstm_embdng_sz)
    self.lstm_lyr = nn.LSTM(lstm_embdng_sz,
                              lstm_hidden_lyr_sz,
                              lstm_num_lyrs,
```

```
                                batch_first=True)
        self.lstm_linear = nn.Linear(lstm_hidden_lyr_sz,
                                     lstm_vocab_sz)
        self.max_seq_len = max_seq_len
        self.save_hyperparameters()
```

For the CNN portion, we use the **ResNet-152** architecture. We will use a readily available `torchvision.models.resnet152` model. However, for output from the CNN model, we don't want a probability prediction that an image is of a given class type such as an elephant or an airplane. Rather, we will use the learned representation of an image output by the CNN, and then it will be passed on as input to the RNN model.

Thus, we remove the last **Fully Connected** (**FC**) Softmax layer of the model using the `list(resnet.children())[:-1]` statement, and then we reconnect all other layers using `nn.Sequential()`. Then, we add a linear layer named `self.cnn_linear`, followed by a batch normalization layer named `self.cnn_batch_norm`. Batch normalization is used as a regularization technique to avoid overfitting and to make the model layers more stable.

> **Important Note**
>
> Note that we pass `pretrained=False` when instantiating the predefined `torchvision.models.resnet152` model in the preceding code snippet. This is because the pretrained ResNet-152 has been trained using the ImageNet dataset, not the COCO dataset, as documented under the ResNet section here: `https://pytorch.org/vision/stable/models.html#id10`.
>
> You can definitely try using the `pretrained=True` option as well and explore the accuracy of the model. While a model trained on ImageNet may extract some classes, as shared in *Chapter 3, Transfer Learning Using Pre-Trained Models*, the overall accuracy may suffer as the complexity of images is quite different in the two datasets. In this section, we have decided to train the model from scratch by using `pretrained=False`.

For the RNN portion of `__init__()`, we define LSTM layers, as shown in the preceding code block. The LSTM layers take an encoded image representation from the CNN and output a sequence of words – a sentence containing at most `self.max_seq_len` words. We use the default value of `20` for the `max_seq_len` parameter.

Next, we describe the training configuration defined in the `HybridModel` class in the `model.py` file.

Optimizer setting

The `torch.optim.Adam` optimizer is returned by the `configure_optimizers` method of the `HybridModel` class, as shown in the following code snippet:

```
def configure_optimizers(self):
    params = list(self.lstm_embdng_lyr.parameters()) + \
             list(self.lstm_lyr.parameters()) + \
             list(self.lstm_linear.parameters()) + \
             list(self.cnn_linear.parameters()) + \
                 list(self.cnn_batch_norm.parameters())
    optimizer = torch.optim.Adam(parameters, lr=0.0003)
    return optimizer
```

We pass `lr=0.0003` as an argument when instantiating the `torch.optim.Adam` optimizer. `lr` stands for **learning rate**.

> **Important Note**
>
> There are dozens of optimizers you can use. The choice of an optimizer is a very important hyperparameter and has a big impact on how a model is trained. Getting stuck in local minima is often a problem, and a change of optimizer is the first thing to try in such cases. You can find a list of all supported optimizers here: `https://pytorch.org/docs/stable/optim.html`

Changing to an RMSprop optimizer

You can also change the `Adam` optimizer in the preceding statement to `RMSprop`, as shown in the following:

```
optimizer = torch.optim.RMSprop(parameters, lr=0.0003)
```

`RMSprop` has a special relationship with sequence generation models such as this one. The centered version first appears in a paper by Geoffrey Hinton titled *Generating Sequences With Recurrent Neural Networks* (`https://arxiv.org/pdf/1308.0850v5.pdf`) and has given really good results for caption generation-type problems. It works great in avoiding the local minima for this kind of model. The implementation takes the square root of the gradient average before adding `epsilon`.

Why one optimizer works better in some cases than others is still a bit of mystery in Deep Learning. In this chapter, for your learning, we have implemented the training using both **Adam** and `RMSprop` optimizers. This should prepare you for future endeavors and when trying out various other optimizers.

Training loss

Now, we will define the training loss, for which we will use the cross-entropy loss function.

The `training_step()` method of the `HybridModel` class uses `torch.nn.CrossEntropyLoss` to calculate the loss, as shown in the following code block:

```
def training_step(self, batch, batch_idx):
    loss_criterion = nn.CrossEntropyLoss()
    imgs, caps, lens = batch
    outputs = self(imgs, caps, lens)
    targets = pk_pdd_seq(caps, lens, batch_first=True)[0]
    loss = loss_criterion(outputs, targets)
    self.log('train_loss', loss, on_epoch=True)
    return loss
```

The `batch` parameter of the `training_step()` method is nothing but the values returned by `coco_collate_fn` described earlier, so we assign those values as such. They are then passed to the `forward` method to generate the outputs, as can be seen in the `outputs = self(imgs, caps, lens)` statement. The `targets` variable is used to calculate the loss.

The `self.log` statement uses the logging feature of the PyTorch Lightning framework to record the loss. That is how we are able to retrieve the loss curve, shown later when we describe the training process.

> **Important Note**
> Refer to the *Managing training* section of *Chapter 10, Scaling and Managing Training* for details of how the loss curve is visualized in TensorBoard.

Learning rate

As we mentioned earlier, you can change the `lr` learning rate in the following statement in the `configure_optimizers()` method of the `HybridModel` class:

```
optimizer = torch.optim.Adam(params, lr=0.0003)
```

> **Important Note**
>
> As documented at `https://pytorch.org/docs/stable/generated/torch.optim.Adam.html#torch.optim.Adam`, the default `lr` value is `1e-3`, that is, `0.001`. We have changed the `lr` value to `0.0003` to converge better.

Batch size

On the other hand, using a bigger batch size enables you to use a higher learning rate that reduces the training time. You can change the batch size at the following statement in `Training_the_model.ipynb` where the `get_loader()` function is used to instantiate `DataLoader`:

```
coco_data_loader = get_loader('coco_data/images',
                              'coco_data/captions.json',
                              vocabulary,
                              transform,
                              256,
                              shuffle=True,
                              num_workers=4)
```

The batch size in the preceding code snippet is `256`.

The sentence output by the LSTM should ideally describe the image input to the CNN after `HybridModel` is trained. In the next step, we describe how the `Trainer` provided by the PyTorch Lightning framework is used to launch model training. We also describe how `coco_data_loader`, described in the preceding code snippet, is passed as an argument to `Trainer`.

Launching model training

We worked on the `model.py` file in the previous section regarding the `HybridModel` class. Now, back in the `Training_the_model.ipynb` notebook, we will work in the last cell of the notebook, as shown in the following code block:

```
transform = transforms.Compose([
    transforms.RandomCrop(224),
    transforms.RandomHorizontalFlip(),
    transforms.ToTensor(),
    transforms.Normalize((0.485, 0.456, 0.406),
```

```
                                  (0.229, 0.224, 0.225))])

with open('coco_data/vocabulary.pkl', 'rb') as f:
    vocabulary = pickle.load(f)

coco_data_loader = get_loader('coco_data/images',
                              'coco_data/captions.json',
                              vocabulary,
                              transform,
                              128,
                              shuffle=True,
                              num_workers=4)

hybrid_model = HybridModel(256, 256, 512,
                           len(vocabulary), 1)
trainer = pl.Trainer(max_epochs=5)
trainer.fit(hybrid_model, coco_data_loader)
```

During training, image preprocessing and normalization transforms specified in the `transform` variable are performed as required for the pretrained ResNet CNN model. The `transform` variable is passed as an argument to the `get_loader()` function that we described in a previous section.

Then, `Vocabulary`, persisted using `pickle`, is loaded from the `coco_data/vocabulary.pkl` file.

Next, a `DataLoader` object named `coco_data_loader` is created by calling the `get_loader` function described earlier.

Then, an instance of `HybridModel` named `hybrid_model` is created, and the model training is kicked off using `trainer.fit()`. As shown in the preceding code block, we pass `hybrid_model` as well as `coco_data_loader` as arguments to the `fit` method. The following is a screenshot of output produced by PyTorch Lightning during the training:

```
coco_data_loader = get_loader('coco_data/images', 'coco_data/captions.json', vocabulary,
                          transform, 128,
                          shuffle=True, num_workers=4)

hybrid_model = HybridModel(256, 256, 512, len(vocabulary), 1)
trainer = pl.Trainer(max_epochs=5)
trainer.fit(hybrid_model, coco_data_loader)

GPU available: False, used: False
TPU available: False, using: 0 TPU cores
IPU available: False, using: 0 IPUs

  | Name            | Type        | Params
-------------------------------------------------
0 | cnn_resnet      | Sequential  | 58.1 M
1 | cnn_linear      | Linear      | 524 K
2 | cnn_batch_norm  | BatchNorm1d | 512
3 | lstm_embdng_lyr | Embedding   | 441 K
4 | lstm_lyr        | LSTM        | 1.6 M
5 | lstm_linear     | Linear      | 885 K
-------------------------------------------------
61.6 M    Trainable params
0         Non-trainable params
61.6 M    Total params
246.292   Total estimated model params size (MB)
Epoch 0: 64%                                          100/157 [31:03<17:31, 18.45s/it, loss=3.7, v_num=0]
```

Figure 7.13 – Training output

> **Important Note**
>
> As you may have noticed, we only train the model for five epochs by setting `max_epochs=5` during instantiation of `pl.Trainer`, as shown in the preceding code snippet. For realistic results, the model would need to be trained for thousands of epochs on a GPU machine in order to converge, as shown in the next section.

Training progress

In order to boost the speed of model training, we used GPUs and turned on the 16-bit precision setting of the PyTorch Lightning `Trainer`, as shown in the following code statement. If your underlying infrastructure has GPUs, then that option can be enabled using the `gpu=n` option where `n` is the number of GPUs to be used. To use all available GPUs, specify `gpu=-1`, as shown here:

```
trainer = pl.Trainer(max_epochs=50000,
                     precision=16, gpus=-1)
```

Using a lower learning rate helps the model train better, but training takes more time. The following chart shows the loss curve for `lr=0.0003` using black- colored arrows, compared to the other curve for `lr=0.001`:

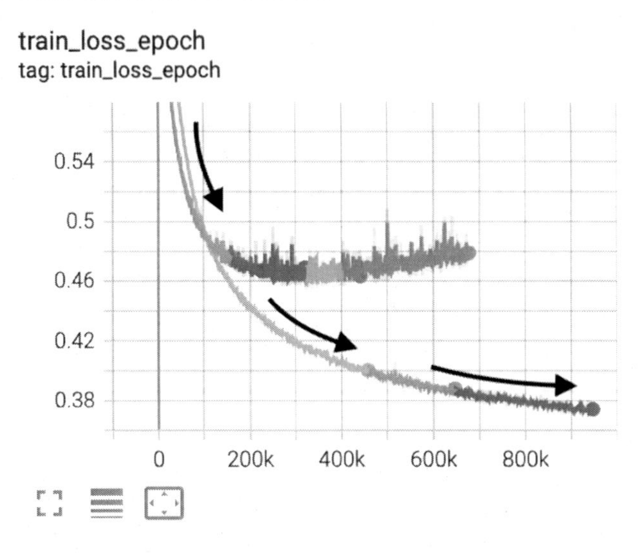

Figure 7.14 – Loss trajectory with different learning rates – the lower the better

Training with the RMSprop optimizer shows us a good decline in the loss rate, as shown in the following chart:

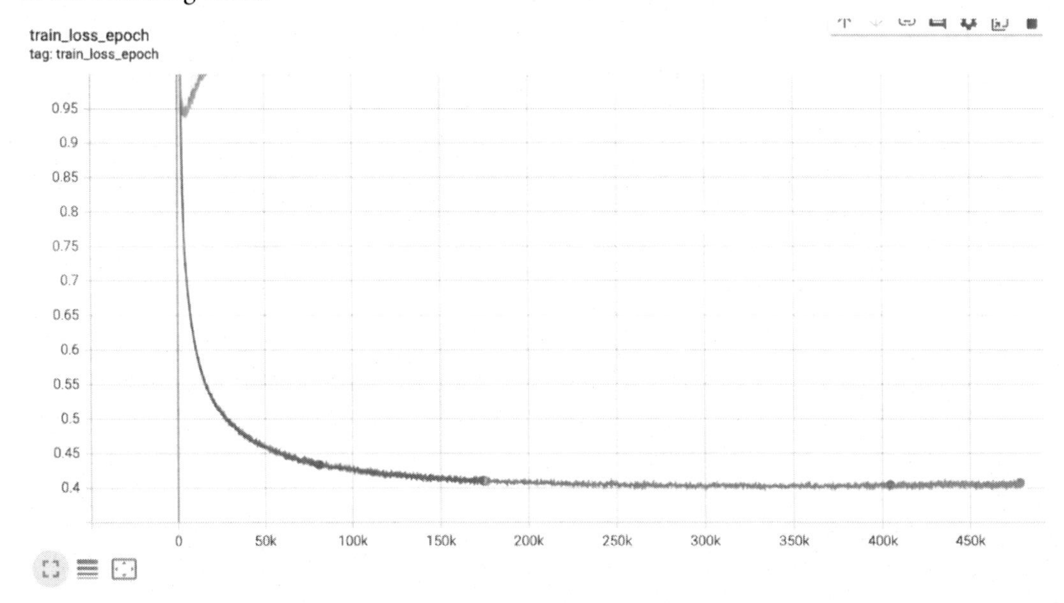

Figure 7.15 – Training loss with RMSprop

Generating the caption

Our HybridModel definition in the model.py file has a couple of peculiar implementation details necessary for it to be used for prediction. We will describe those peculiarities first, and then we will describe the code in the Generating_the_caption.ipynb notebook.

There is the get_caption method in the HybridModel class, which will be called to generate a caption for an image. This method takes an image as input, makes a forward pass through the CNN to generate the input features for LSTM, and then uses a greedy search to generate the caption with the maximum probability:

```
def get_caption(self, img, lstm_sts=None):
  """CNN"""
  features = self.forward_cnn_no_batch_norm(img)
  """LSTM: Generate captions using greedy search."""
  token_ints = []
  inputs = features.unsqueeze(1)
  for i in range(self.max_seq_len):
    hddn_vars, lstm_sts = self.lstm_lyr(inputs, lstm_sts)
    model_outputs = self.lstm_linear(hddn_vars.squeeze(1))
    _, predicted_outputs = model_outputs.max(1)
    token_ints.append(predicted_outputs)
    inputs = self.lstm_embdng_lyr(predicted_outputs)
    inputs = inputs.unsqueeze(1)
  token_ints = torch.stack(token_ints, 1)
  return token_ints
```

Also, we have separated part of the CNN's forward logic in a separate method named forward_cnn_no_batch_norm() in the HybridModel class. As shown in the preceding code snippet, this is the method that get_caption uses for the forward pass through CNN in order to generate the input features for LSTM because the cnn_batch_norm module is to be omitted during the prediction phase of a CNN:

```
def forward_cnn_no_batch_norm(self, input_images):
    with torch.no_grad():
        features = self.cnn_resnet(input_images)
    features = features.reshape(features.size(0), -1)
    return self.cnn_linear(features)
```

For the remainder of this section, we will work in the `Generating_the_caption.ipynb` notebook. First, we import the necessary packages in the first cell of the notebook, as shown in the following code block:

```
import pickle
import numpy as np
from PIL import Image
import matplotlib.pyplot as plt

import torchvision.transforms as transforms

from model import HybridModel
from vocabulary import Vocabulary
```

In the second cell of the notebook, we use the `load_image` function to load the image, transform it, and display it, as shown in the following code snippet:

```
def load_image(image_file_path, transform=None):
    img = Image.open(image_file_path).convert('RGB')
    img = img.resize([224, 224], Image.LANCZOS)
    plt.imshow(np.asarray(img))
    if transform is not None:
        img = transform(img).unsqueeze(0)
    return img

# Prepare an image
image_file_path = 'sample.png'
transform = transforms.Compose([
    transforms.ToTensor(),
    transforms.Normalize((0.485, 0.456, 0.406),
                         (0.229, 0.224, 0.225))])
img = load_image(image_file_path, transform)
```

Then, we create an instance of `HybridModel` by passing the checkpoint to `HybridModel.load_from_checkpoint()`, as shown in the following code block:

```
hybrid_model = HybridModel.load_from_checkpoint("lightning_
logs/version_0/checkpoints/epoch=4-step=784.ckpt")
token_ints = hybrid_model.get_caption(img)
token_ints = token_ints[0].cpu().numpy()

# Convert ints to strings
with open('coco_data/vocabulary.pkl', 'rb') as f:
    vocabulary = pickle.load(f)
predicted_caption = []
for token_int in token_ints:
    token = vocabulary.int_to_token[token_int]
    predicted_caption.append(token)
    if token == '<end>':
        break
predicted_sentence = ' '.join(predicted_caption)

# Print out the generated caption
print(predicted_sentence)
```

We pass the transformed image to the `get_caption` method of the model. The `get_caption` method returns integers corresponding to tokens in the caption, so we use `vocabulary` to get the tokens and generate the caption sentence. We finally print the caption.

Image caption predictions

Now we can pass an unseen image (which was not part of the training set) and ask the model to generate the caption for us. While the sentence generated by our model is not yet perfect (it might take tens of thousands of epochs to converge), a quick search in the `captions.json` file for this entire sentence reveals that the model created the sentence on its own. The sentence is not part of the input data that we used to train the model.

Intermediate results

The model works by understanding classes from the image and then generating the text using the RNN LSTM model for those classes and subclass actions. You will notice some noise in earlier predictions.

The following are the results after 200 epochs:

```
<start> chinese <unk> next to a large military aircraft . <end>
```

Figure 7.16 – Results after 200 epochs

The following are the results after 1,000 epochs:

`<start> a large airplane and a truck next to a building . <end>`

Figure 7.17 – Results after 1,000 epochs

The following are the results after 2,000 epochs:

`teen black-and-white rared baby elephant on its head in front of another small elephant . <end>`

Figure 7.18 – Additional results after 2000 epochs

Results

You may find that after 10,000 epochs, generated captions start getting more *human-like*. The results will continue to get better with even more epochs. However, don't forget that we have trained this model on only a 4,000-image set. That limits the scope of all the contexts and English vocabulary it can learn from. If this were to train on millions of images, then results on unseen images would be much better.

We trained this model on a GPU server and it took us over 4 days to complete. Here are some caption predictions on RMSprop after 7,000 epochs with a batch size of 256 and learning rate of `0.001`:

```
<start> the jet is flying <unk> with the sky behind it . <end>
```

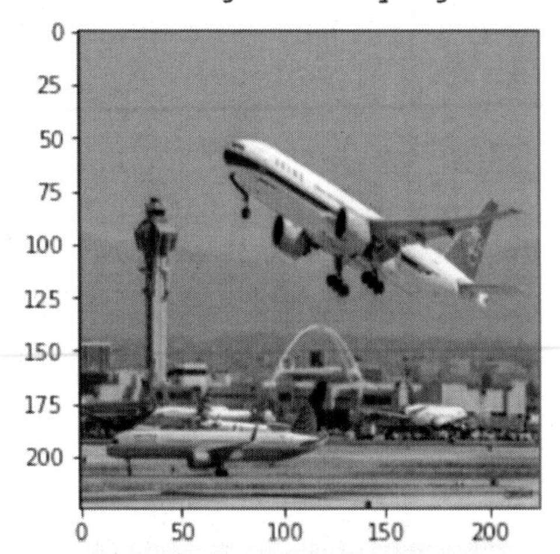


```
<start> a man swinging a tennis racquet at a tennis ball . <end>
```

Figure 7.19 – Results after 7000 epochs with RMSprop

The results for the same after 10,000 epochs comes out to be the following:

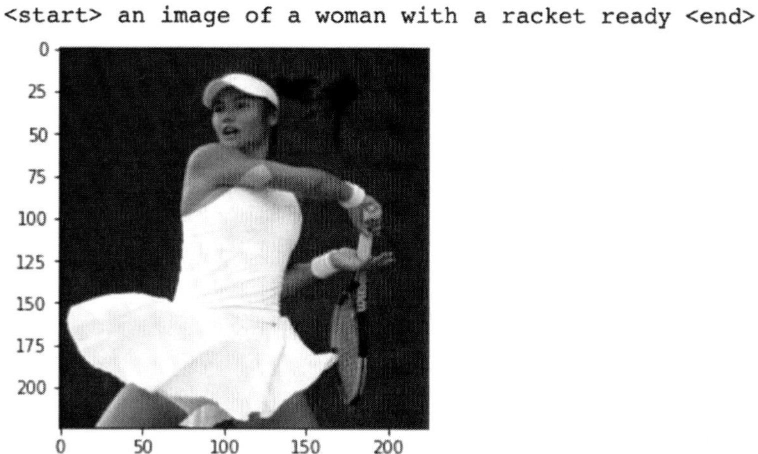

Figure 7.20 – Results after 10,000 epochs

As you can see, we are getting interesting results for our model, especially with higher epochs. Now we can ask the machine to generate captions as a *human* would.

Next steps

Now that we have shown how a machine can generate captions for images, as an additional exercise, you can try the following to improve your skills:

- Try various other training parameter combinations, such as a different optimizer, learning rate, or a number of epochs.
- Try changing the CNN architecture from ResNet-152 to ResNet-50 or other like AlexNet or VGGNet.
- Try the project with a different dataset. There are other datasets available in the semi-supervised domain with application-specific captions, such as the manufacturing sector or medical images.
- As shown in an earlier section regarding the introduction of semi-supervised learning, instead of generating captions in *plain* English, you can use any style, such as poems or texts by Shakespeare, by first training the model on those texts and then using a style-transfer mechanism to generate the caption. To recreate the results shown earlier, you could train on a lyrics dataset and ask machine to emulate their poetic style.

- Finally, to expand your horizons even more, you could try combining other models. Audio is also a form of sequence, and you can try models that generate audio commentary automatically for some given images.

Summary

We have seen in this chapter how PyTorch Lightning can be used to create semi-supervised learning models easily with a lot of out-of-the-box capabilities. We have seen an example of how to use machines to generate the captions for images as if they were written by *humans*. We have also seen an implementation of code for an advanced neural network architecture that combines the CNN and RNN architectures.

Creating art using machine learning algorithms opens new possibilities for what can be done in this field. What we have done in this project is a modest wrapper around recently developed algorithms in this field, extending them to different areas. One challenge in generated text that often comes up is a *contextual accuracy parameter*, which measures the accuracy of created lyrics based on the question, *does it make sense to humans?* The proposal of some sort of technical criterion to be used to measure the accuracy of such models in this regard is a very important area of research for the future.

This idea of multi-modal learning can also be extended to video with audio. There is a strong correlation in movies between the action taking place onscreen (such as a fight, romance, violence, or comedy) and the background music played. Eventually, it should be possible to extend multimodal learning into the audiovisual domain, predicting/generating background musical scores for short videos (maybe even recreating a Charlie Chaplin movie with its background score generated by machine learning!).

In the next chapter, we will see the newest and perhaps the most advanced learning method, called **Self-Supervised Learning**. This method makes it possible to do machine learning even on unlabeled data by self-generating its own labels and thereby opening up a whole new frontier in the domain. PyTorch Lightning is perhaps the first framework to have built-in support for Self-Supervised Learning models to make them easily accessible to the data science community, as we will see in the next chapter.

8 Self-Supervised Learning

Since the dawn of Machine Learning, the field has been neatly divided into two camps: supervised learning and unsupervised learning. In supervised learning, there should be a labeled dataset available, and if that is not the case, then the only option left is unsupervised learning. While unsupervised learning may sound great as it can work without labels, in practice, the applications of unsupervised methods such as clustering are quite limited. There is also no easy option to evaluate the accuracy of unsupervised methods or to deploy them.

The most practical Machine Learning applications tend to be supervised learning applications (for example, recognizing objects in images, predicting future stock prices or sales, or recommending the right movie to you on Netflix). The trade-off for supervised learning is the necessity for well-curated and high-quality trustworthy labels. Most datasets are not born with labels and getting such labels can be quite costly or at times downright impossible. One of the most popular Deep Learning datasets, ImageNet, consists of over 14 million images, with each label identifying an object in that image. As you may have guessed, the source images didn't come with those nice labels, so an army of 149,000 workers (mostly grad students) using Amazon's Mechanical Turk app spent over 19 months manually labeling each image. There are many datasets, such as medical X-ray images/CT scans for brain tumors, where doing this is simply impossible as it needs trained doctors, and there aren't many expert doctors available to label every image.

This begs the question, what if we can come up with a new method that can work without needing so many labels, such as unsupervised learning, but gives output that is as high-impact as supervised learning? That is exactly what Self-Supervised Learning promises to do.

Self-Supervised Learning is the latest paradigm in Machine Learning and is the most advanced frontier. While it has been theorized for a few years, it's only in the last year that it has been able to show results comparable to supervised learning and has become touted as the future of Machine Learning. The foundation of Self-Supervised Learning for images is that we can make machines learn a *true representation* even without labels. With a minuscule number of labels (as low as 1% of the dataset), we can achieve as good results as supervised models can. This unlocks the untapped potential in millions of datasets that are sitting unused due to the lack of high-quality labels.

In this chapter, we will get an introduction to Self-Supervised Learning and then go through one of the most widely used architectures in Self-Supervised Learning for image recognition known as **contrastive representative learning**. In this chapter, we will cover the following topics:

- Getting started with Self-Supervised Learning
- What is Contrastive learning?
- SimCLR architecture
- SimCLR contrastive learning model for image recognition

Technical requirements

In this chapter, we will be primarily using the following Python modules:

- NumPy (version 1.21.5)
- `torch` (version 1.10)
- `torchvision` (version 0.11.1)
- `PyTorch Lightning` (version 1.5.2)

Please check the correct version of the packages before running the code.

In order to make sure that these modules work together and not go out of sync, we have used the specifi c version of torch, torchvision, torchtext, torchaudio with PyTorch Lightning 1.5.2. You can also use the latest version of PyTorch Lightning and torch compatible with each other. More details can be found on the GitHub link:

`https://github.com/PacktPublishing/Deep-Learning-with-PyTorch-Lightning`.

```
!pip install torch==1.10.0 torchvision==0.11.1
torchtext==0.11.0 torchaudio==0.10.0 --quiet
```

```
!pip install pytorch-lightning==1.5.2 --quiet
```

Working examples for this chapter can be found at this GitHub link: `https://github.com/PacktPublishing/Deep-Learning-with-PyTorch-Lightning/tree/main/Chapter08`.

STL-10 source datasets can be found at `https://cs.stanford.edu/~acoates/stl10/`.

Figure 8.1 – A snapshot of STL-10 dataset

The STL-10 dataset is an image recognition dataset for developing Self-Supervised Learning algorithms. It is similar to CIFAR-10, but with a very important difference: each class has fewer labeled training examples than CIFAR-10, but a very large set of unlabeled examples is provided in order to learn image representations prior to supervised training.

Getting started with Self-Supervised Learning

The future of Machine Learning has been hotly contested given the spectacular success of Deep Learning methods such as CNN and RNN in recent years. While CNNs can do amazing things, such as image recognition, and RNNs can generate text, and other advanced NLP methods, such as the Transformer, can achieve marvelous results, all of them have serious limitations when compared to human intelligence. They don't compare very well to humans on tasks such as reasoning, deduction, and comprehension. Also, most notably, they require an enormous amount of well-labeled training data to learn even something as simple as image recognition.

Figure 8.2 – A child learns to classify objects with very few labels

Unsurprisingly, that is not the way humans learn. A child does not need millions of labeled images as input before it can recognize objects. The incredible ability of the human brain to generate its own new labels based on a minuscule amount of initial information is unparalleled when compared to Machine Learning.

In order to expand the potential of AI, various other methods have been tried. The quest for achieving near-human intelligence performance led to two distinct methods, namely, **Reinforcement learning** and **Self-supervised learning**.

In Reinforcement Learning, the focus is on constructing a game-like environment and making a machine learn how to navigate through the environment without explicit directions. Each system is configured to maximize the reward function and, slowly, agents learn by making mistakes in each game event and then minimize those mistakes in the next event. Doing so requires a model to be trained for millions of cycles, which sometimes translates to thousands of years of human time. While this method has beaten humans at very difficult games such as *Go* and set a new benchmark for machine intelligence, clearly this is not how humans learn. We don't practice a game for thousands of years before being able to play it. Also, so many trials make it too slow to learn for any practical industrial applications.

In *Self-Supervised Learning*, however, the focus is on making the machine learn a bit like a human by trying to create its own labels and continue to learn adaptively. The term **Self-Supervised Learning** is the brainchild of Yann LeCun, one of the Turing Award recipients (the equivalent of the Nobel Prize for computing) for making a foundational contribution to Deep Learning. He also laid the groundwork for Self-Supervised Learning as well and conducted a lot of research using energy modeling methods.

Figure 8.3 – Future belongs to "Self-Supervised Learning"

Most notably, Yann LeCun argued that the future of AI will neither be supervised nor reinforced, but will be self-supervised! This is arguably the most important area, with the potential to disrupt the way we know Machine Learning.

So, what does it mean to be Self-Supervised?

The core concept is that we can learn in multiple dimensions of data. In supervised learning, we have data (x) and labels (y), and we can do a lot of things, such as prediction, classification, and object detection, whereas, in unsupervised learning, we only have data (x), and we can only do clustering types of models. In unsupervised learning, we have the advantage that we don't need costly labels, but the kinds of models we can build are limited. What if we start in an unsupervised manner (with only x and then somehow generate labels (y) for the dataset) and then move on to supervised learning?

In other words, what if we can make the machine learn to generate its own labels as it goes along? Currently, say I have an image dataset such as CIFAR-10 that consists of 10 classes of images (classes such as bird, airplane, dog, and cat) spread over 65,000 labels. This is what machine needs to learn to recognize those 10 classes. What if, instead of supplying 65,000 labels, as we did for this dataset, I supply only 10 labels (one for each class) and then the machine finds images similar to those classes and adds labels to them? If we can do that, then the machine is self-supervising its learning process, and it will be able to scale to solve previously unsolved problems.

What I have provided here is a rather simplistic definition of Self-Supervised Learning. Yann LeCun defined Self-Supervised Learning mostly in the context of **Energy Modelling** as a model that can learn not just forward from backward but in any direction. Energy modeling is an area of active research in the Deep Learning community. Ideas such as **Concept Learning**, whereby a model learns a concept of *image and label* together, may be revolutionary in the future. Also, there is one Self-Supervised Learning application you may have already heard of. NLP models such as GPT3 and Transformers have been trained with no labels and still can be fine-tuned or adjusted easily for any task. You can appreciate that language is a unidimensional data structure as data normally flows in one direction (backward to forward, as we read English from left to right), and so it's easy to learn structure without any labels being associated with it.

In other areas, such as images or structured data, learning without labels or with a very limited number of labels has proven to be challenging. One area that we will focus on in this chapter that has got very interesting results in recent months is **contrastive learning**, in which we can find similar images from dissimilar images without having any labels associated with them.

> **Important Note**
>
> To learn more about energy modeling, it is advisable to go through lectures focusing on them. Refer to the online lecture entitled "A Tutorial on Energy-Based Learning," by Yann LeCun: `https://training.incf.org/lesson/energy-based-models-i`.

What is Contrastive Learning?

The idea of understanding an image is to get an image of a particular kind (say a *dog*) and then we can recognize all other dogs by reasoning that they share the same representation or structure. For example, if you show a child who is not yet able to talk or understand language (say, less than 2 years old) a picture of a *dog* (or a real dog for that matter) and then give them a pack of cards with a collection of animals, which includes dogs, cats, elephants, and birds, and ask the child which picture is similar to the first one, it is most likely that the child could easily pick the card with a dog on it. And the child would be able to do so even without you explaining that this picture equals *"dog"* (in other words, without supplying any new labels).

You could say that a child learned to recognize *all dogs* in a single instance and with a single label! Wouldn't it be awesome if a machine could do that as well? That is exactly what contrastive learning is!

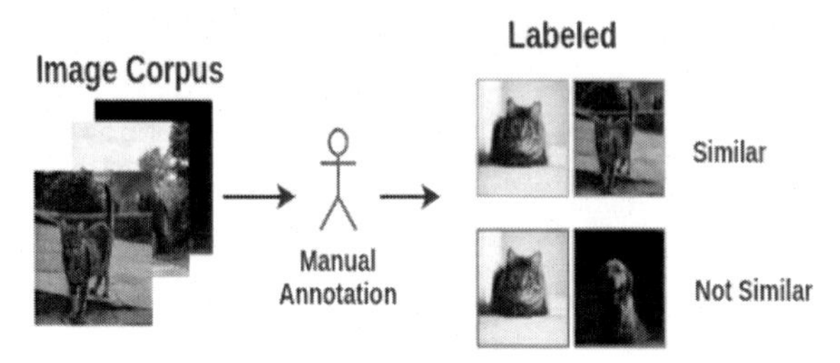

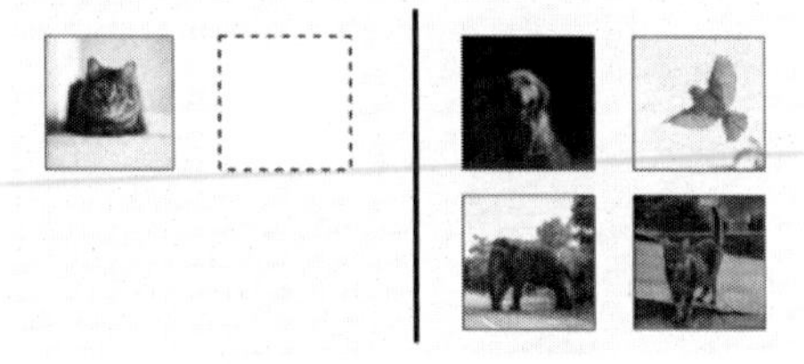

Figure 8.4 – How contrastive learning differs from supervised learning (Source: `https://amitness.com/2020/03/illustrated-simclr/`)

What is happening here is a form of **representation learning**. In fact, the full name of this method is **contrastive representation learning**. The child has understood that a dog has a certain type of representation (a tail, four legs, eyes, and so on) and then is able to find similar representations. Astonishingly, the human brain does this with a surprisingly minuscule amount of data (even a single image is enough to teach someone a new object). In fact, child development experts have theorized that when the child is barely a few months old, it begins to recognize its mother and father and other familiar objects purely by creating loose representations (like silhouettes). This is one of the key development stages when it begins to accept new visual data and start the process of recognition and classification. This visual ability, which makes us see as opposed to just look at objects, is very crucial in our intellectual development. Similarly, the ability to make a machine learn how images differ from each other without passing any labels is an important milestone in the development of AI.

There have been various proposed architectures for contrastive learning that have had spectacular results. Some popular ones are SimCLR, CPC, YADIM, and NOLO. In this chapter, we will see the architecture that is fast becoming a de facto standard for contrastive learning – SimCLR.

SimCLR architecture

SimCLR stands for **Simple Contrastive Learning Architecture**. This architecture is based on the paper *"A Simple Framework for Contrastive Learning of Visual Representations"*, published by Geoffrey Hinton and Google Team. Geoffrey Hinton (just like Yann LeCun) is a co-recipient of the Turing Award for his work on Deep Learning. There are SimCLR and SimCLR2 versions. SimCLR2 is a larger and denser network than SimCLR. At the time of writing, SimCLR2 was the best architecture update available, but don't be surprised if there is a SimCLR3 soon that is even denser and better than the previous one.

The architecture has shown in relation to the ImageNet dataset that we can achieve 93% accuracy with just 1% of labels. This is a truly remarkable result considering that it took over 2 years and a great deal of effort from over 140,000 labelers (mostly graduate students) on Mechanical Turk to label ImageNet by hand. It was a massive undertaking carried out on a global scale. Apart from the sheer amount of time it took to label that dataset, it also became clear that without the backing of big companies such as Google, such an endeavor is difficult. It may come as no surprise to you that many datasets are lying unused simply because they are not properly labeled. If we can achieve comparable results with just 1% of labels, it would open the previously unopened doors in what Deep Learning can do!

How does SimCLR work?

Let's have a quick overview of how SimCLR works. We urge you to read the full paper mentioned in the previous section for more details.

The idea behind contrastive learning is that we want to group similar images while differentiating them at the same time from dissimilar images. This process takes place on an unlabeled set of images.

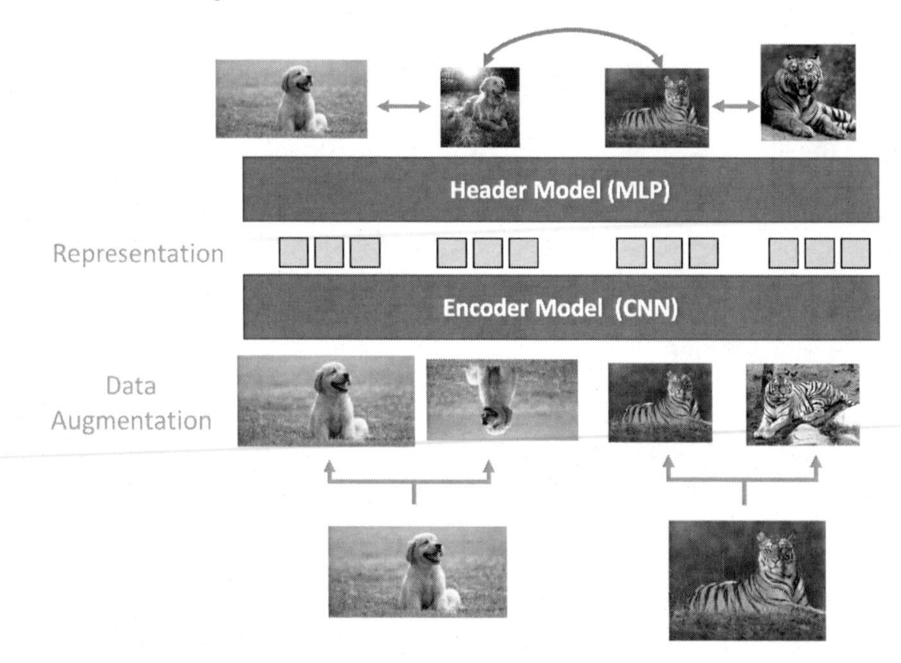

Figure 8.5 – How SimCLR works (Note: the architecture is executed from the bottom up)

The architecture consists of the following building blocks:

1. As a first step, **data augmentation** is performed on the group of random images. Various data augmentation tasks are performed. Some of them are standard ones, such as rotating the images, cropping them, and changing the color by making them grayscale. Other more complex data augmentation tasks, such as Gaussian Blur, are also performed. You will find that the more complex or sophisticated the augmentation transforms, the more useful it is for the model.

This data augmentation step is very important since we want to make the model learn the true representation reliably and consistently. Another, and rather important, reason is that we don't have labels in the dataset. So, we have no way of knowing which images are actually similar to each other and which are dissimilar. And thus, having various augmented images from a single image creates a "true" set of similar images for the model that we can be *apriori* sure of.

2. The next step is then to create a batch of images that contains similar and dissimilar images. As an analogy, this can be thought of as a batch that has some positive ions and some negative ions, and we want to isolate them by moving a magical magnet over them (SimCLR).
3. This process is followed by an encoder that is nothing but a CNN architecture. **ResNet** architectures such as ResNet-18 or ResNet-50 are most commonly used for this operation. However, we strip away the last layer and use the output after the last average pool layer. This encoder helps us learn the image representations.
4. This is followed by the header module (also known as projection head), which is a **Multi-Layer Perceptron** (**MLP**) model. This is used to map contrastive loss to the space where the representations from the previous step are applied. Our MLP can be a single hidden layer neural network (as in SimCLR) or a 3-layer network (as it is in SimCLR2). You can even experiment with larger neural networks. This step is used to balance alignment (keeping similar images together) and uniformity (preserve the maximum amount of information).
5. The key in this step is the contrastive loss function that is used for contrastive prediction. Its job is to identify other positive images in a dataset. The specialized loss function used for this is **NT-Xent** (the normalized temperature-scaled, cross-entropy loss). This loss function helps us measure how the system is learning in subsequent epochs.

These steps describe the SimCLR architecture and, as you may have noted, it works purely on unlabeled images. The magic of SimCLR is realized when you fine-tune it for a downstream task such as image classification. This architecture can learn features for you, and then you can use those features for any task.

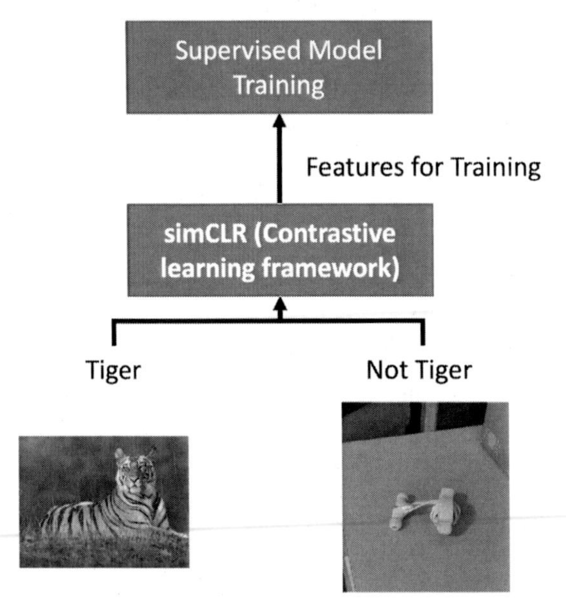

Figure 8.6 – Semi-supervised approach for finding relevant images

The task could be to find whether images in your dataset are relevant to your objective. Imagine you want to save tigers by creating an image recognition model for tigers and you only want tiger images. Any camera traps may include other animals (and even unrelated objects). But not all your images will be labeled. You can build a **Semi-Supervised Learning** model by using SimCLR architecture followed by a supervised classifier for whatever small number of labels you have and get your data cleaned. It can also be thought of as transfer learning by transferring the weights learned through the representation learning of the SimCLR model to subsequent classification tasks.

Another more basic task could be to classify images by supplying very few labels and features from the SimCLR architecture. The question that may occur to you is "just how little?" Experiments have shown that for a downstream task that is just 10% or even 1% labeled, we can get nearly 95% accuracy.

SimCLR model for image recognition

We have seen that SimCLR can do the following:

- Learn feature representations (unit hypersphere) by grouping similar images together and pushing dissimilar images apart.
- Balance **alignment** (keeping similar images together) and **uniformity** (preserving the maximum information).
- Learn on unlabeled training data.

The primary challenge is to use the unlabeled data (that comes from a similar but different distribution from the labeled data) to build a useful prior, which is then used to generate labels for the unlabeled set. Let's look at the architecture we will implement in this section.

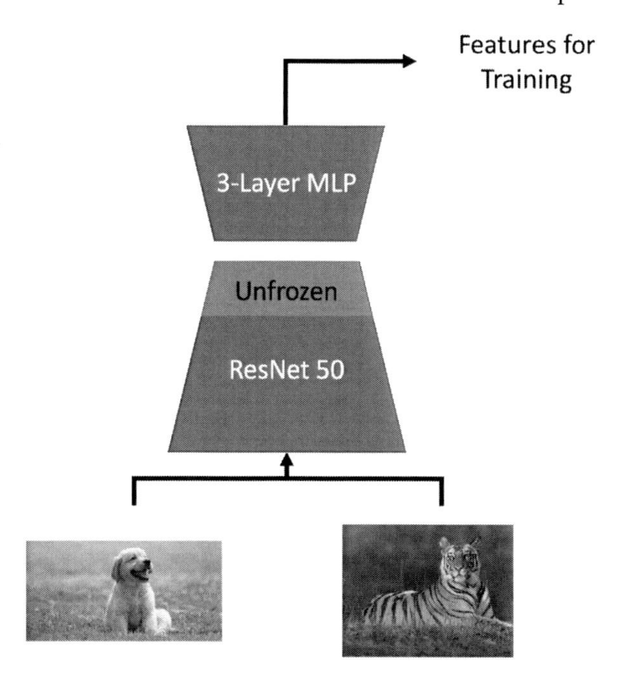

Figure 8.7 – SimCLR architecture implementation

We will use the ResNet-50 as the **Encoder**, followed by a three-layer MLP as the projection head. We will then use logistic regression, or MLP, as the supervised classifier to measure the accuracy.

The SimCLR architecture involves the following steps, which we implement in code:

1. Collecting the dataset
2. Setting up data augmentation
3. Loading the dataset
4. Configuring training
5. Training the SimCLR model
6. Evaluating the performance

Collecting the dataset

We will use the STL-10 dataset from `https://cs.stanford.edu/~acoates/stl10/`.

As described on the dataset web page, the STL-10 dataset is an image recognition dataset for developing Self-Supervised Learning algorithms. It consists of the following:

- 10 classes: airplane, bird, car, cat, deer, dog, horse, monkey, ship, and truck.
- Images are 96x96 pixels and in color.
- 500 training images (10 pre-defined folds) and 800 test images per class.
- 100,000 unlabeled images for unsupervised learning. These examples are extracted from a similar but broader distribution of images. For instance, it contains other types of animals (bears, rabbits, and so on) and vehicles (trains, buses, and so on) in addition to the ones in the labeled set.

The binary files are split into data and label files with suffixes `train_X.bin`, `train_y.bin`, `test_X.bin`, and `test_y.bin`.

You can download the binary files directly from `http://ai.stanford.edu/~acoates/stl10/stl10_binary.tar.gz` and put them in your data folder. Or, to work on a cloud instance, execute the full Python code available at `https://github.com/mttk/STL10`. The STL-10 dataset is also available in the `torchvision` module under `https://pytorch.org/vision/stable/datasets.html#stl10` and can also be directly imported into the notebook.

Since the STL-10 dataset is scraped from ImageNet, any pre-trained model on ImageNet can be used to accelerate training by using pre-trained weights.

The SimCLR model depends on three packages: `pytorch`, `torchvision`, and `pytorch_lightning`. As a first step, please install and import these packages into your notebook. Once the packages are installed, we will go about importing them:

```
import os
import urllib.request
from copy import deepcopy
from urllib.error import HTTPError

import matplotlib
import matplotlib.pyplot as plt
import pytorch_lightning as pl
import seaborn as sns
import torch
import torch.nn as nn
import torch.nn.functional as F
import torch.optim as optim
import torch.utils.data as DataLoader

from IPython.display import set_matplotlib_formats
from pytorch_lightning.callbacks import LearningRateMonitor,
ModelCheckpoint
from pytorch_lightning.callbacks import ModelCheckpoint
from pytorch_lightning.callbacks import Callback

import torchvision
from torchvision import transforms
import torchvision.models as models
from torchvision import datasets
from torchvision.datasets import STL10
from tqdm.notebook import tqdm

from torch.optim import Adam

import numpy as np
from torch.optim.lr_scheduler import OneCycleLR
```

```
import zipfile
from PIL import Image
import cv2
```

After the necessary packages are imported, we have to collect the images in STL-10 format. We can download the data from the Stanford repository into our local data path to be used for further processing. You should add the path of the folder where you have downloaded the STL-10 files.

Setting up data augmentation

The first step that we need to do is to create a data augmentation module. This is an extremally important step in SimCLR architecture, and the final result is greatly affected by the richness of the transformations undertaken in this step.

> **Important Note**
>
> PyTorch Lightning also includes various SimCLR transforms out of the box using Bolts. We are, however, manually defining it here. You can also refer to out-of-the-box transforms here for various approaches: `https://pytorch-lightning-bolts.readthedocs.io/en/latest/transforms.html#simclr-transforms`. Please be careful about your PyTorch Lightning version and the `torch` version to use them.

Our goal is to create a positive set that can easily be achieved by creating multiple copies of a given image and applying various augmentation transformations to it. As a first step, we can create as many image copies as we want:

```
class DataAugTransform:
    def __init__(self, base_transforms, n_views=4):
        self.base_transforms = base_transforms
        self.n_views = n_views

    def __call__(self, x):
        return [self.base_transforms(x) for i in range(self.n_
views)]

```

In the preceding code snippet, we are creating four copies of the same image.

We will now go ahead and apply four key transforms to the images. As per the original paper and further research, the cropping and resizing of images are crucial transforms and help the model to learn better:

```
augmentation_transforms = transforms.Compose(
    [
        transforms.RandomHorizontalFlip(),
        transforms.RandomResizedCrop(size=96),
        transforms.RandomApply([transforms.
ColorJitter(brightness=0.8, contrast=0.8, saturation=0.8,
hue=0.1)], p=0.8),
        transforms.RandomGrayscale(p=0.2),
        transforms.ToTensor(),
        transforms.Normalize((0.5,), (0.5,)),
    ]
)
```

In the preceding code snippet, we augment the image and perform the following transforms:

- Random resize and crop
- Random horizontal flip
- Random color jitter
- Random grayscale

Please note that the data augmentation step can take a considerable amount of time to finish for a reasonably large dataset.

> **Important Note**
>
> One of the heavier transforms that is mentioned in the SimCLR paper but not performed here is a Gaussian Blur. It blurs images by adding noise using the Gaussian function by giving more weight to the center part of the image than other parts. The final average effect is to reduce the detail of the image. You can optionally perform a Gaussian Blur transform as well on the STL-10 images. In the new version of `torchvision`, you can use the following option to perform it: `#transforms.GaussianBlur(kernel_size=9)`.

Loading the dataset

Now, we will define the path to download the dataset and collect it:

```
DATASET_PATH = os.environ.get("PATH_DATASETS", "bookdata/")

CHECKPOINT_PATH = os.environ.get("PATH_CHECKPOINT", "booksaved_
models/")
```

In the preceding code snippet, we defined the dataset and checkpoint path.

We will now apply the transforms to the STL-10 dataset and create two views of it:

```
unlabeled_data = STL10(
    root=DATASET_PATH,
    split="unlabeled",
    download=True,
    transform=DataAugTransform(augmentation_transforms, n_
views=2),
)
train_data_contrast = STL10(
    root=DATASET_PATH,
    split="train",
    download=True,
    transform=DataAugTransform(augmentation_transforms, n_
views=2),
)
```

It then transforms into a torch tensor for model training by applying the data augmentation process. We can verify the output of the preceding process by visualizing some of the images:

```
pl.seed_everything(96)
NUM_IMAGES = 20
imgs = torch.stack([img for idx in range(NUM_IMAGES) for img in
unlabeled_data[idx][0]], dim=0)
img_grid = torchvision.utils.make_grid(imgs, nrow=8,
normalize=True, pad_value=0.9)
```

```
img_grid = img_grid.permute(1, 2, 0)

plt.figure(figsize=(20, 10))
plt.imshow(img_grid)
plt.axis("off")
plt.show()
```

In the preceding code snippet, we print the original image along with the augmented one. This should show the following result:

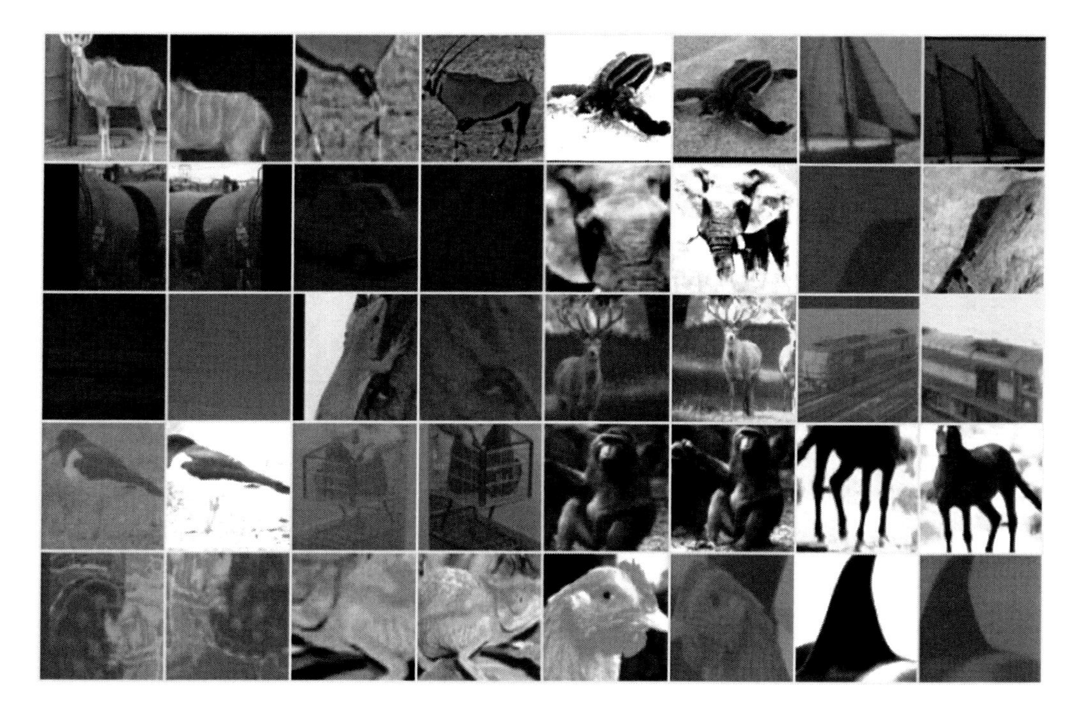

Figure 8.8 – STL-10 augmented images

As you can see, various image transforms have been applied successfully. The multiple copies of the same image will serve as a positive set of pairs for the model to learn.

Training configuration

Now we will set up the configuration of the model training, which includes hyperparameters, the loss function, and the encoder.

Setting hyperparameters

We will use the YAML file to pass on various hyperparameters to our model training. Having a YAML file makes it easy to create various experiments:

```
weight_decay: 10e-6
out_dim: 256

dataset:
  s: 1
  input_shape: (96,96,3)
  num_workers: 4

optimizer:
  lr: 0.0001

loss:
  temperature: 0.05
  use_cosine_similarity: True

lr_schedule:
  max_lr: .1
  total_steps: 1500

model:
  out_dim: 128
  base_model: "resnet50"
'''
config = yaml.full_load(config)
```

The preceding code snippet will load the YAML file and set the following hyperparameters:

- `batch_size`: The batch size to use for training.
- `Epochs`: The number of epochs to run the training for.
- `out_dim`: The output dimensions of the embedding layer.

- `s`: The brightness, contrast, saturation, and hue level of the color jitter transformation.
- `input_shape`: The input shape to the model after the final image transformation. All raw images will be resized to this shape (H, W, color channels).
- `num_workers`: The number of workers to use for the data loader. It can increase training speed by pre-fetching and processing data.
- `lr`: The initial learning rate to use for training.
- `temperature`: The temperature-tuning parameter to smooth the probabilities of the loss function.
- `use_cosine_similarity`: A Boolean indicator of whether to use cosine similarity in the loss function.
- `max_lr`: The maximum learning rate for the 1cycle learning rate scheduler.
- `total_steps`: The total number of training steps for the 1cycle learning rate scheduler.

> **Important Note on Batch Size**
>
> The batch size plays a very important role in contrastive learning models. In SimCLR, it has been observed that having a large batch size is associated with better results. However, a large batch size also requires much more compute in the form of GPU.

Defining the loss function

The purpose of the loss function is to help distinguish between positive and negative pairs. The original paper describes the **NTXent** loss function.

We will now go ahead and implement this loss function in the code:

```
import yaml # Handles config file loading
# Load config file
config = '''
batch_size: 128
epochs: 100
class NTXentLoss(torch.nn.Module):
    def __init__(self, device, batch_size, temperature, use_
cosine_similarity):
        super(NTXentLoss, self).__init__()
```

```
        self.batch_size = batch_size
        self.temperature = temperature
        self.device = device
        self.softmax = torch.nn.Softmax(dim=-1)
        self.mask_samples_from_same_repr = self._get_
correlated_mask().type(torch.bool)
        self.similarity_function = self._get_similarity_
function(use_cosine_similarity)
        self.criterion = torch.
nn.CrossEntropyLoss(reduction="sum").cuda()
    def _get_similarity_function(self, use_cosine_similarity):
        if use_cosine_similarity:
            self._cosine_similarity = torch.
nn.CosineSimilarity(dim=-1)
            return self._cosine_simililarity
        else:
            return self._dot_simililarity
    def _get_correlated_mask(self):
        diag = np.eye(2 * self.batch_size)
        l1 = np.eye((2 * self.batch_size), 2 * self.batch_size,
k=-self.batch_size)
        l2 = np.eye((2 * self.batch_size), 2 * self.batch_size,
k=self.batch_size)
        mask = torch.from_numpy((diag + l1 + l2))
        mask = (1 - mask).type(torch.bool)
        return mask.to(self.device)
    @staticmethod
    def _dot_simililarity(x, y):
        v = torch.tensordot(x.unsqueeze(1), y.T.unsqueeze(0),
dims=2)
        return v
    def _cosine_simililarity(self, x, y):
        v = self._cosine_similarity(x.unsqueeze(1),
y.unsqueeze(0))
        return v
    def forward(self, zis, zjs):
        representations = torch.cat([zjs, zis], dim=0)
        similarity_matrix = self.similarity_
```

```
function(representations, representations)
        # filter out the scores from the positive samples
        l_pos = torch.diag(similarity_matrix, self.batch_size)
        r_pos = torch.diag(similarity_matrix, -self.batch_size)
        positives = torch.cat([l_pos, r_pos]).view(2 * self.
batch_size, 1)
        negatives = similarity_matrix[self.mask_samples_from_
same_repr].view(2 * self.batch_size, -1)
        logits = torch.cat((positives, negatives), dim=1)
        logits /= self.temperature
        labels = torch.zeros(2 * self.batch_size).to(self.
device).long()
        loss = self.criterion(logits, labels)
        return loss / (2 * self.batch_size)

```

In the preceding code snippet, we implemented the NTXtent loss function, which will measure the loss for the positive pairs. Do remember that the task of the model is to minimize the loss between positive pairs and, hence, this loss function.

Defining the encoder

We can use any encoder architecture (such as VGGNet, or AlexNet, or ResNet, and so on). Since the original paper has ResNet, we will also use ResNet as our encoder:

```
class ResNetSimCLR(nn.Module):

    def __init__(self, base_model, out_dim, freeze=True):
        super(ResNetSimCLR, self).__init__()

        # Number of input features into the last linear layer
        num_ftrs = base_model.fc.in_features
        # Remove last layer of resnet
        self.features = nn.Sequential(*list(base_model.
children())[:-1])
        if freeze:
            self._freeze()

```

In the preceding code block, we have removed the last softmax layer of ResNet and passed on the feature to the next module. We can follow this up with a header projection code block using an MLP model. While SimCLR1 has a single-layer MLP, SimCLR2 has a 3-layer MLP, which is what we will use here. Others have also got good results with a 2-layer MLP model. (Please note that this code is part of the same class as above:)

```
        # header projection MLP - for SimCLR
        self.l1 = nn.Linear(num_ftrs, 2*num_ftrs)
        self.l2_bn = nn.BatchNorm1d(2*num_ftrs)
        self.l2 = nn.Linear(2*num_ftrs, num_ftrs)
        self.l3_bn = nn.BatchNorm1d(num_ftrs)
        self.l3 = nn.Linear(num_ftrs, out_dim)

    def _freeze(self):
        num_layers = len(list(self.features.children())) # 9
layers, freeze all but last 2
        current_layer = 1
        for child in list(self.features.children()):
            if current_layer > num_layers-2:
                for param in child.parameters():
                    param.requires_grad = True
            else:
                for param in child.parameters():
                    param.requires_grad = False
            current_layer += 1

    def forward(self, x):
        h = self.features(x)
        h = h.squeeze()

        if len(h.shape) == 1:
            h = h.unsqueeze(0)

        x_l1 = self.l1(h)
        x = self.l2_bn(x_l1)
        x = F.selu(x)
```

```
        x = self.l2(x)
        x = self.l3_bn(x)
        x = F.selu(x)
        x = self.l3(x)
        return h, x_l1, x

```

In the preceding code snippet, we have defined the convolutional layers for the ResNet and then frozen the last layer and used that feature as an input to a projection head model, which is a 3-layer MLP.

Now, we can extract the features from either the last layer of ResNet or from the last layer of the 3-layer MLP model and use it as a true representation of the images that the model has learned.

> **Important Note**
>
> While ResNet with SimCLR will be available as a pre-trained model for STL-10, if you are trying SimCLR architecture for another dataset, this code will be useful for training it from scratch.

SimCLR pipeline

Now that we have put in place all the building blocks for the SimCLR architecture, we can finally construct the SimCLR pipeline:

```
class simCLR(pl.LightningModule):

    def __init__(self, model, config, optimizer=Adam, 
loss=NTXentLoss):
        super(simCLR, self).__init__()
        self.config = config

        # Optimizer
        self.optimizer = optimizer

        # Model
        self.model = model

        # Loss
```

```
        self.loss = loss(self.config['batch_size'], **self.
config['loss'])

    # Prediction/inference
    def forward(self, x):
        return self.model(x)

    # Sets up optimizer
    def configure_optimizers(self):
        optimizer = self.optimizer(self.parameters(), **self.
config['optimizer'])
        scheduler = OneCycleLR(optimizer, **self.config["lr_
schedule"])
        return [optimizer], [scheduler]
```

In the preceding code snippet, we have used the config file (`dictionary`) to pass on parameters to each module: `optimizer`, `loss`, and `lr_schedule`. We are using the Adam optimizer and calling the NTXtent loss function that we constructed previously.

Now we can add training and validation loops to the same class:

```
    # Training loops
    def training_step(self, batch, batch_idx):
        x, y = batch
        xis, xjs = x
        ris, _, zis = self(xis)
        rjs, _, zjs = self(xjs)

        zis = F.normalize(zis, dim=1)
        zjs = F.normalize(zjs, dim=1)

        loss = self.loss(zis, zjs)
        return loss

    # Validation step
    def validation_step(self, batch, batch_idx):
        x, y = batch
```

```
        xis, xjs = x
        ris, _, zis = self(xis)
        rjs, _, zjs = self(xjs)

        zis = F.normalize(zis, dim=1)
        zjs = F.normalize(zjs, dim=1)

        loss = self.loss(zis, zjs)
        self.log('val_loss', loss)
        return loss

    def test_step(self, batch, batch_idx):
        loss = None
        return loss

def _get_model_checkpoint():
    return ModelCheckpoint(
        filepath=os.path.join(os.getcwd(),"checkpoints","best_
val_models"),
        save_top_k = 3,
        monitor="val_loss"
    )
```

In the preceding code snippet, we have created a model class that takes the following inputs:

- Hyperparameters from the config file
- NTXtent as a loss function
- Adam as the optimizer
- An encoder as a model (can be changed to any model other than ResNet if desired)

We further define the training and validation loops to calculate the loss and finally save the model checkpoint.

Important Note

It is advisable that you should construct a callback class, which will save the model checkpoint and resume the model training from the saved checkpoint. It can also be useful for passing preconfigured weights of the encoder. Please refer to GitHub or Chapter 10 for more details.

Model training

Now that we have defined the model configuration, we can move on to model training.

We will first use a data loader to load the data:

```
train_loader = DataLoader.DataLoader(
                unlabeled_data,
                batch_size=128,
                shuffle=True,
                drop_last=True,
                pin_memory=True,
                num_workers=NUM_WORKERS,
        )
val_loader = DataLoader.DataLoader(
                train_data_contrast,
                batch_size=128,
                shuffle=False,
                drop_last=True,
                pin_memory=True,
                num_workers=NUM_WORKERS,
        )
```

We will use the ResNet-50 architecture as the encoder. You can play with other ResNet architectures, such as ResNet-18 or ResNet-152, and compare the results:

```
resnet = models.resnet50(pretrained=True)

simclr_resnet = ResNetSimCLR(base_model=resnet, out_
dim=config['out_dim'])
```

In the preceding code snippet, we import the ResNet CNN model architecture and use `pretrained=True` to use the pre-trained weights of the model to speed up the training. Since the PyTorch ResNet model is trained on the ImageNet dataset and our STL-10 dataset is also scraped from ImageNet, using the pre-trained weights is a reasonable choice.

We will now initiate the training process:

```
model = simCLR(config=config, model=simclr_resnet)
trainer = pl.Trainer()
```

You should see the following information, depending on the hardware you are using:

```
GPU available: True, used: False
TPU available: False, using: 0 TPU cores
IPU available: False, using: 0 IPUs
```

Figure 8.9 – GPU available for model training

In the preceding code snippet, we create the SimCLR model from the architecture mentioned and use the trainer to fit the model by passing the dataset from the data loader:

```
trainer.fit(model, train_loader, val_loader)
```

This should show you the following initiation of the training process:

```
# Fits the model
trainer.fit(model, train_loader, val_loader)

LOCAL_RANK: 0 - CUDA_VISIBLE_DEVICES: [0]

  | Name  | Type         | Params
---------------------------------------
0 | model | ResNetSimCLR | 40.8 M
1 | loss  | NTXentLoss   | 0
---------------------------------------
32.3 M    Trainable params
8.5 M     Non-trainable params
40.8 M    Total params
163.313   Total estimated model params size (MB)
Validation sanity check: 0%
Global seed set to 96
Epoch 99: 100% 820/820
```

Figure 8.10 – SimCLR training process

The sharp-eyed among you may have noticed that it is using the NTXent loss function.

> **Important Note**
>
> Depending on the hardware you have access to, you can use various options in the PyTorch Lightning framework to speed up the training process. As shown in *Chapter 7, Semi-Supervised Learning*, if you are using a GPU, then you can use the `gpu=-1` option and also enable 16-bit precision for mixed-mode precision training. Refer to Chapter 10 for more details on options for scaling up the training process.

Once the model is trained, you can save the model weight

```
torch.save(model.state_dict(), 'weights_only.pth')
torch.save(model, 'entire_model.pth')
```

This will save the model weights as `weights_only.pth and the entire model as `entire_model.pth'

Model evaluation

While the SimCLR model architecture will learn the representation of the unlabeled images, we still need a method to measure how well it learned those representations. In order to do this, we use a supervised classifier that has some labeled images (from the original STL-10 dataset), and then we use the features learned in the SimCLR model to apply the feature map for images learned via representation learning and then compare the results.

Model evaluation therefore consists of three steps:

1. Extracting the features from the SimCLR model
2. Defining a classifier
3. Predicting accuracy

We can try to compare the results by passing a very limited number of labels, such as 500 or 5,000 (or 1 to 10%), and then also compare the results with the supervised classifier, which has been trained with 100% of the labels. This will help us to compare how well our self-supervised model was able to learn representations from unlabeled images.

Feature extraction from the SimCLR model

We first need to extract the features learned from the model. To do so, we load the model

```
def _load_resnet_model(checkpoints_folder):
    model = torch.load('entire_model.pth')
    model.eval()
    state_dict = torch.load(os.path.join(checkpoints_folder,
'weights_only.pth'), map_location=torch.device(device))
    model.load_state_dict(state_dict)
    model = model.to(device)
    return model
```

This code snippet will load the pre-trained SimCLR model weights from weights_only.pth and the entire model from entire_model.pth.

Now we can use the data loader to instantiate the training and test split:

def get_stl10_data_loaders(download, shuffle=False, batch_size=128):

```
    train_dataset = datasets.STL10('./data', split='train',
    download=download,
    transform=transforms.
    ToTensor())
    train_loader = DataLoader.DataLoader(train_dataset, batch_
size=batch_size,num_workers=4, drop_last=False,
    shuffle=shuffle)
    test_dataset = datasets.STL10('./data', split='test',
    download=download,
    transform=transforms.
    ToTensor())
    test_loader = DataLoader.DataLoader(test_dataset, batch_
size=batch_size,
    num_workers=4, drop_last=False,
    shuffle=shuffle)
    return train_loader, test_loader

```

In this code snippet, the training and test datasets are instantiated.

We can now define the feature extractor class:

```
class ResNetFeatureExtractor(object):
  def __init__(self, checkpoints_folder):
    self.checkpoints_folder = checkpoints_folder
    self.model = _load_resnet_model(checkpoints_folder)

  def _inference(self, loader):
    feature_vector = []
    labels_vector = []
    for batch_x, batch_y in loader:

      batch_x = batch_x.to(device)
```

```
        labels_vector.extend(batch_y)
        features, _ = self.model(batch_x)
        feature_vector.extend(features.cpu().detach().numpy())

      feature_vector = np.array(feature_vector)
      labels_vector = np.array(labels_vector)

      print("Features shape {}".format(feature_vector.shape))
      return feature_vector, labels_vector

    def get_resnet_features(self):
      train_loader, test_loader = get_stl10_data_
loaders(download=True)
      X_train_feature, y_train = self._inference(train_loader)
      X_test_feature, y_test = self._inference(test_loader)

      return X_train_feature, y_train, X_test_feature, y_test
```

In the preceding code snippet, we get the features extracted from the ResNet model we have trained. We can validate this by printing the shapes of the file:

```
checkpoints_folder = ''
resnet_feature_extractor = ResNetFeatureExtractor(checkpoints_
folder)
X_train_feature, y_train, X_test_feature, y_test = resnet_
feature_extractor.get_resnet_features()
```

You should see the following output, which shows the shapes of the training and test files:

```
Files already downloaded and verified
Files already downloaded and verified
Features shape (5000, 2048)
Features shape (8000, 2048)
```

Now that we are ready, we can define the supervised classifier to train the supervised model on top of the **Self-Supervised** features.

Supervised classifier

We can use any supervised classifier for this task, such as MLP or logistic regression. In this module, we will choose logistic regression. In this section, we are using the scikit-learn module to implement logistic regression.

We start by defining the `LogisticRegression` class:

```
import torch.nn as nn

class LogisticRegression(nn.Module):

    def __init__(self, n_features, n_classes):
        super(LogisticRegression, self).__init__()
        self.model = nn.Linear(n_features, n_classes)

    def forward(self, x):
        return self.model(x)
```

The preceding step will instantiate the class. This is followed by defining the configuration for the logistic regression model:

```
class LogiticRegressionEvaluator(object):
  def __init__(self, n_features, n_classes):
    self.log_regression = LogisticRegression(n_features, n_
classes).to(device)
    self.scaler = preprocessing.StandardScaler()

  def _normalize_dataset(self, X_train, X_test):
    print("Standard Scaling Normalizer")
    self.scaler.fit(X_train)
    X_train = self.scaler.transform(X_train)
    X_test = self.scaler.transform(X_test)
    return X_train, X_test

  def _sample_weight_decay():
    weight_decay = np.logspace(-7, 7, num=75, base=10.0)
    weight_decay = np.random.choice(weight_decay)
    print("Sampled weight decay:", weight_decay)
```

```
        return weight_decay

    def eval(self, test_loader):
        correct = 0
        total = 0

        with torch.no_grad():
            self.log_regression.eval()
            for batch_x, batch_y in test_loader:
                batch_x, batch_y = batch_x.to(device), batch_y.
to(device)
                logits = self.log_regression(batch_x)

                predicted = torch.argmax(logits, dim=1)
                total += batch_y.size(0)
                correct += (predicted == batch_y).sum().item()

            final_acc = 100 * correct / total
            self.log_regression.train()
            return final_acc
```

In the preceding code snippet, we are defining the logistic regression parameters:

- We first normalize the dataset.
- Then we define L2 regularization parameters from a range of 75 logarithmically spaced values between 10–7 and 107. This is a setting that you can tune.
- We also define how we measure the accuracy in the `final_acc` parameter.

We can now feed the classifier with data loaders and ask it to pick up the model:

```
    def create_data_loaders_from_arrays(self, X_train, y_train,
X_test, y_test):
        X_train, X_test = self._normalize_dataset(X_train, X_test)
        train = torch.utils.data.TensorDataset(torch.from_numpy(X_
train), torch.from_numpy(y_train).type(torch.long))
        train_loader = torch.utils.data.DataLoader(train, batch_
size=128, shuffle=False)
        test = torch.utils.data.TensorDataset(torch.from_numpy(X_
test), torch.from_numpy(y_test).type(torch.long))
```

```
    test_loader = torch.utils.data.DataLoader(test, batch_
size=128, shuffle=False)
    return train_loader, test_loader

```

You can also define `test_loader` as we have defined `train_loader` here. We will now define the hyperparameters for the optimizers:

```
  def train(self, X_train, y_train, X_test, y_test):
    train_loader, test_loader = self.create_data_loaders_from_
arrays(X_train, y_train, X_test, y_test)
    weight_decay = self._sample_weight_decay()
    optimizer = torch.optim.Adam(self.log_regression.
parameters(), 3e-4, weight_decay=weight_decay)
    criterion = torch.nn.CrossEntropyLoss()
    best_accuracy = 0
    for e in range(200):

      for batch_x, batch_y in train_loader:

        batch_x, batch_y = batch_x.to(device), batch_y.
to(device)
        optimizer.zero_grad()
        logits = self.log_regression(batch_x)
        loss = criterion(logits, batch_y)
        loss.backward()
        optimizer.step()
      epoch_acc = self.eval(test_loader)
      if epoch_acc > best_accuracy:
        #print("Saving new model with accuracy {}".
format(epoch_acc))
        best_accuracy = epoch_acc
        torch.save(self.log_regression.state_dict(), 'log_
regression.pth')
```

In the preceding code snippet, we use a logistic regression model to train the classifier using Adam as the optimizer and cross entropy loss as the loss function and only save the model with the best accuracy. We are now ready to perform model evaluation.

Predicting accuracy

We can now use the logistic regression model to predict accuracy:

```
log_regressor_evaluator = LogiticRegressionEvaluator(n_
features=X_train_feature.shape[1], n_classes=10)

log_regressor_evaluator.train(X_train_feature, y_train, X_test_
feature, y_test)
```

The logistic regression model should tell you how accurately the model is performing on the features that have been learned from the self-supervised architecture:

```
Standard Scaling Normalizer
Sampled weight decay: 5.623413251903491e-06
--------------
Done training
Best accuracy: 73.5375
```

Figure 8.11 – Accuracy results

As you can see, we are getting 73% accuracy on the logistic regression model.

The accuracy reflects the features that were learned in a completely unsupervised manner and without any labels. We have compared those learned features to a traditional classifier as if labels were present. And then, by passing a fraction of the labels, we can achieve an accuracy that is comparable to having the labelled dataset. As mentioned previously, with a better training capacity, you can achieve the results mentioned in the original paper, that is, 95% accuracy with just 1% of the labels.

You are strongly encouraged to repeat the evaluation steps by varying the number of labeled training sets and comparing that with the full training of all labels. That would help demonstrate the immense power of Self-Supervised Learning.

Next steps

While we have only built a supervised classifier to use the features learned from the SimCLR model, the SimCLR model utility does not have to be limited to it. You can use representations learned from unlabelled images in various other fashions:

- You can compare the features learned by using a dimensionality reduction technique. By using **Principal Component Analysis** (**PCA**), you can map the features to a higher dimensional space and compare them.
- You can also use some anomaly detection methods, such as One-Class SVM, to find outliers in the images.

Apart from these, you can also try tweaking the SimCLR architecture code and building new models. Here are some ways to tweak the architecture:

- You can try another supervised classifier to fine-tune, such as MLP, and compare the results.
- Try the model training with other encoder architectures, such as ResNet-18, ResNet-152, or VGG, and see whether that gives a better representation of the features.
- You can also try training from scratch, especially if you are using it for another dataset. Finding a set of images that is unlabelled should not be a challenge. You can always use ImageNet labels for some similar classes as your validation labels for your fine-tuned evaluation classifier, or manually label a small number and see the results.
- Currently, the SimCLR architecture uses the NTXent loss function. If you are feeling confident, you could play with a different loss function.
- Trying some loss functions from **Generative Adversarial Networks** (**GANs**) to mix and match GANs with self-supervised representation can be an exciting research project.

Finally, don't forget that SimCLR is just one of the many architectures for contrastive learning. PyTorch Lightning also has built-in support for other architectures, such as CPC, SWAV, and BYOL. You should try them out, too, and compare the results with SimCLR as well.

Summary

Most of the image datasets that exist in nature or industry are unlabeled image datasets. Think of X-ray images generated by diagnostic labs, or MRI or dental scans, and many more. Pictures generated on Amazon reviews or images from Google Street View or e-commerce websites like EBay are also mostly unlabelled; also a large proportion of Facebook, Instagram, or WhatsApp images are never tagged and are therefore unlabelled as well. A lot of these image datasets remain unused with untapped potential due to current modelling techniques requiring large amounts of manually labelled sets. Removing the need for large, labelled datasets and expanding the realm of what is possible is **Self-Supervised Learning**.

We have seen in this chapter how PyTorch Lightning can be used to quickly create **Self-Supervised Learning** models such as contrastive learning. In fact, PyTorch Lightning is the first framework to provide out-of-the-box support for many **Self-Supervised Learning** models. We implemented a SimCLR architecture using PyTorch Lightning and, using built-in functionalities, easily created a model that would have taken a lot of effort on TensorFlow or PyTorch. We have also seen that the model performs quite well with a limited number of labels. With as little as 1% of the dataset labelled, we achieved results that are comparable to using a 100% labeled set. We can distinguish the unlabelled images from each other purely by learning their representations. This representation learning method enables the additional methods to identify anomalous images in the set or automatically cluster the images together. Self-Supervised Learning methods such as SimCLR are currently considered to be among the most advanced methods in Deep Learning.

So far, we have seen all the popular architectures in Deep Learning, starting with CNNs, moving on to GANs, and then to Semi-Supervised Learning, and finally to Self-Supervised Learning. We will now shift our focus from training the models to deploying them. In the next chapter, we will see how we can take models to production and familiarize ourselves with the techniques to deploy and score models.

Section 3: Advanced Topics

In this section, we will focus on advanced users who need to train Deep Learning models on massive amounts of data using distributed training or deploy and score it.

This section comprises the following chapters:

- *Chapter 9, Deploying and Scoring Models*
- *Chapter 10, Scaling and Managing Training*

9
Deploying and Scoring Models

Without knowing it, you may have already experienced some of the models we have covered so far in this book. Recall how your photos app can automatically detect *faces* in your picture collections or group all your pictures with a particular friend together. That is nothing more than an image recognition Deep Learning model in action (the likes of **Convolutional Neural Networks** (**CNNs**)), or you might be familiar with Alexa listening to your voice or Google autocompleting your text while searching for a query. Those are NLP-based Deep Learning models making things easier for us. Or you might have seen some e-shopping apps or social media sites suggesting captions for a product; that is semi-supervised learning in its full glory! But how do you take a model that you have built in a Python Jupyter notebook and make it consumable on devices, be it a speaker, a phone, an app, or a portal? Without application integration, a trained model remains a statistical object with little practical significance.

In order for a model to be consumed and be used in a production environment, we have to make the model available in a manner such that it can be integrated with various end user applications. A popular way of consuming a model is via a REST API endpoint. Once an API endpoint is created, a model can be plugged into any application server and be served for a variety of end applications or edge devices. The deployment of a model involves converting the model into an object file and loading that object file later for scoring purposes. Scoring a model means getting a predicted output against given input. To score a model, we should be able to integrate the model into the application, that is, deploy it. In this chapter, we will primarily cover how to perform these activities using the PyTorch Lightning framework and how we can easily take a PyTorch Lightning model to production. We will use Flask – a popular web development framework – to create a simple API endpoint in order to deploy the model.

Another challenge facing the consumption of models is that there are so many frameworks to train the model, such as PyTorch Lightning (Of course!), Caffe, and TensorFlow. All these frameworks have their own file formats and often data scientists are required to integrate the output of one model with another. While deploying in a production environment, models may need to be consumed in a framework-agnostic fashion. In this chapter, we will contrast methods to deploy and score a model natively within the PyTorch Lightning framework using checkpoints, with the **ONNX** (**Open Neural Network Exchange**) format, which is a portable and interoperable format that enables Deep Learning models to be transferred across frameworks.

We will cover the following topics in this chapter:

- Deploying and scoring a Deep Learning model natively
- Deploying and scoring inter-portable models

Technical requirements

The code for this chapter has been developed and tested on macOS with Anaconda or in Google Colab with Python. If you are using another environment, please make the appropriate changes to your `env` variables. Please ensure you have the correct version before running the code.

In this chapter, we will primarily be using the following Python modules, mentioned with their versions:

- `pytorch-lightning` (version 1.5.10)
- `torch` (version 1.11.0)
- `requests` (version 2.27.1)

- `torchvision` (version 0.12.0)
- `flask` (version 2.0.2)
- `pillow` (version 8.2.0)
- `numpy` (version 1.21.3)
- `json` (version 2.0.9)
- `onnxruntime` (version 1.10.0))

Working examples for this chapter can be found at this GitHub link: `https://github.com/PacktPublishing/Deep-Learning-with-PyTorch-Lightning/tree/main/Chapter09`.

In order to make sure that these modules work together and not go out of sync, we have used the specific version of torch, torchvision, torchtext, torchaudio with PyTorch Lightning 1.5.2. You can also use the latest version of PyTorch Lightning and torch compatible with each other. More details can be found on the GitHub link: `https://github.com/PacktPublishing/Deep-Learning-with-PyTorch-Lightning`

```
!pip install torch==1.10.0 torchvision==0.11.1
torchtext==0.11.0 torchaudio==0.10.0 --quiet
!pip install pytorch-lightning==1.5.2 --quiet
```

The source dataset link is as follows:

- Kaggle – Histopathological cancer detection dataset: `https://www.kaggle.com/c/histopathologic-cancer-detection`

This is the same dataset that we have used in *Chapter 2, Getting off the Ground with the First Deep Learning Model*, for creating our first Deep Learning model. This is the dataset that contains images of cancer tumor images and images labeled with positive and negative identification. It consists of 327,680 color images, each with a size of 96x96 pixels, and extracted from scans of lymph nodes. The data is provided under the CC0 License. The original link for the original dataset is `https://github.com/basveeling/pcam`. However, in this chapter, we will make use of the Kaggle source since it has been de-duplicated from the original set.

Deploying and scoring a Deep Learning model natively

Once a Deep Learning model is trained, it basically contains all the information about its structure, that is, its model weights, layers, and so on. For us to be able to use this model later in the production environment on new sets of data, we need to store this model in a suitable format. The process of converting a data object into a format that can be stored in memory is called **serialization**. Once a model is serialized in such a fashion, it's an autonomous entity and can be transmitted or transferred to a different operating system or a different deployment environment (such as staging or production).

However, once a model is transferred to a production environment, we must reconstruct the model parameters and weights in their original format. This process of recreation from the serialized format is called **de-serialization**.

There are some other ways to productionalize ML models as well, but the most commonly used method is to first serialize the model using "some" format after training is finished and then de-serialize the model in the production environment.

The serialized ML model can be saved in various file formats, such as JSON, `pickle`, ONNX, or **Predictive Model Markup Language** (**PMML**). PMML is perhaps the oldest file format that was used to productionalize models in the SPSS days of packaged software for data science. In recent years, however, formats such as `pickle` and ONNX are more widely used.

We will see some of these in action in this chapter.

The pickle (.PKL) model file format

Most of the current training is done using Python environments, and `pickle` is an easy and quick format to serialize the model. It is also natively available in most frameworks. The `pickle` file format is also used by many frameworks, such as `scikit-learn`, to store their models by default. The `pickle` file format converts a model into byte form, which is not human-readable, and stores the model in an object-oriented way in its special format.

The ML community often calls the process of serialization using the `pickle` file format **pickling,** and de-serialization **un-pickling**. We can pickle objects with the following data types: Booleans, integers, floats, complex numbers, strings, tuples, lists, sets, dictionaries, classes, and functions. Un-pickling converts the byte stream into a Python hierarchy so that the model can be consumed.

`pickle` has some advantages; for example, it keeps track of objects previously serialized, has many in-built methods in Python, which makes de-serialization easy and fast, and has easy import functionality by storing classes separately.

The main disadvantage of `pickle` is that it is native to Python and does not provide cross-language support. Even different versions of Python (such as 2.x and 3.x) may have compatibility issues.

Deploying our Deep Learning model

We first looked at Deep Learning models in *Chapter 2, Getting off the Ground with the First Deep Learning Model*. We built an image recognition model using CNN architecture. It was a three-layer convolution CNN model (with five fully connected layers) that used the Adam optimizer. You can find the model here on the GitHub page: `https://github.com/PacktPublishing/Deep-Learning-with-PyTorch-Lightning/tree/main/Chapter02`.

The dataset we used was the histopathological cancer detection dataset, and the model could predict whether an image contains metastatic cancer using a binary classifier.

As we have trained this model, the next logical step is to understand how we can take it to production and integrate it into an application.

We will start our process from where we left off last time with a trained model and see how we can deploy and score it.

Saving and loading model checkpoints

When we train a Deep Learning model, we go on updating model parameters during each epoch. In other words, the state of the model keeps changing throughout the training. Although the state is in memory while the training is in progress, the PyTorch Lightning framework automatically saves the model state to a **checkpoint** periodically. This is an important feature because a saved checkpoint can be used to resume model training if it is interrupted for some reason. Also, after a model is fully trained, we can use its final checkpoint to instantiate the model's final state and use the model for scoring; this is done using the aptly named `load_from_checkpoint` method of the `LightningModule` class.

By default, the PyTorch Lightning framework stores a checkpoint after every epoch in the current working directory under `lightning_logs/version_<number>`. Specifically, the default checkpoint file is named `epoch=<number>-step=<number>.ckpt`, and it is saved in the `lightning_logs/version_<number>/checkpoints` directory.

The first step here is to re-train the model by executing `Cancer_Detection.ipynb` (which can be found at `https://github.com/PacktPublishing/Deep-Learning-with-PyTorch-Lightning/tree/main/Chapter09`, using Google Colab).

Figure 9.1 – Training output of CNNImageClassifier

Once our model is trained, it can be found in Google Drive under the same directory that you provided as an argument while training the model as shown here:

```
ckpt_dir = "/content/gdrive/MyDrive/Colab Notebooks/cnn"
ckpt_callback = pl.callbacks.ModelCheckpoint(every_n_epochs=25)

model = CNNImageClassifier()
trainer = pl.Trainer(
    default_root_dir=ckpt_dir,
                        gpus=-1,
                      #  progress_bar_refresh_rate=30,
                        callbacks=[ckpt_callback],
                        log_every_n_steps=25,
                        max_epochs=500)
trainer.fit(model, train_dataloaders=train_dataloader)
```

From the preceding code, we can check under the `'/Colab Notebooks/cnn'` directory. We will download this folder and save it in our local directory for working on throughout this chapter.

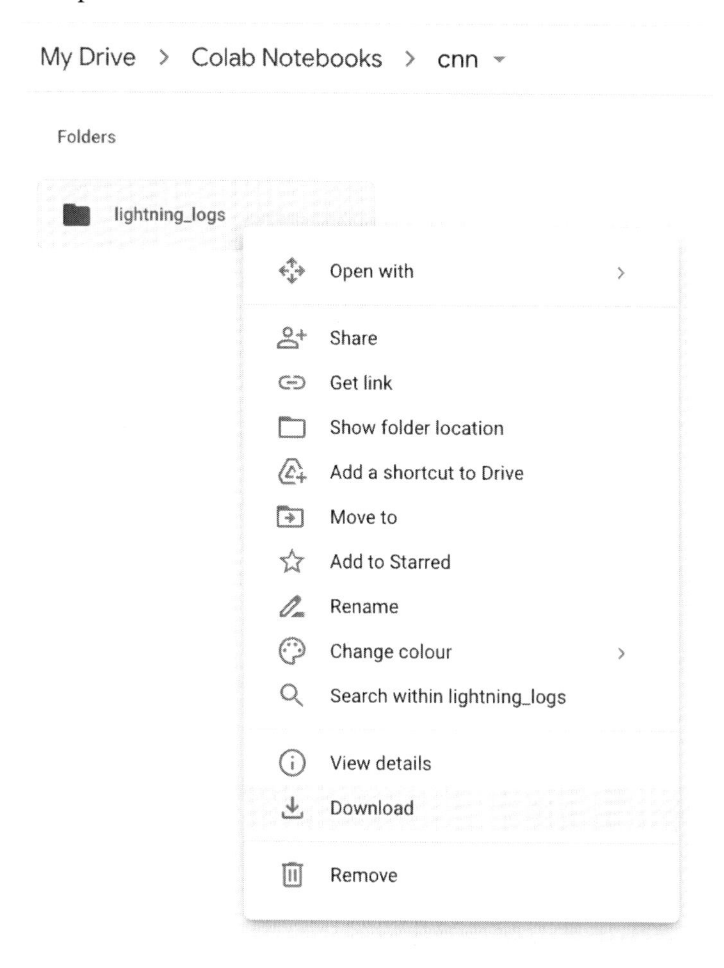

Figure 9.2 – Checkpoint directory

Once downloaded, we will save it in the `Chapter09` directory and use the right path for the checkpoint to load the model in subsequent sections; for example:

```
model = CNNImageClassifier.load_from_checkpoint("./lightning_
logs/version_0/checkpoints/epoch=499-step=15499.ckpt")
```

You can also have the following `import` block, which will import the `torch.randn` model into the local directory:

```
from image_classifier import CNNImageClassifier
```

> **Important Note**
>
> Our CNN model is defined in the `CNNImageClassifier` class, which, as usual, extends the `LightningModule` class provided by the PyTorch Lightning framework. This class definition needs to be accessible during the training processes when the model is saved, as well as during deployment and scoring when the model is loaded and used. So, we make the class definition reusable by defining it in its own file, named `image_classifier.py`.

Deploying and scoring a model using Flask

Flask is a popular web development framework. In this section, we'll create a simple web application using Flask to make our model accessible via an API named `predict`. The API uses an HTTP `POST` method. Our application has two main components:

- A Flask server that takes an input image of a histopathological scan of tissue, transforms the image, scores the image using the model, and returns a response of whether the image contains tumor tissue.
- A Flask client that sends a histopathological scan of tissue to the server and displays the response it receives from the server:

1. We'll describe the implementation details of the server. First, we import all the tools that we will need:

```
import torch.nn.functional as functional
import torchvision.transforms as transforms

from PIL import Image

from flask import Flask, request, jsonify

from image_classifier import CNNImageClassifier
```

We use the `SoftMax` function in the `torch.nn.functional` module to get the probability distribution and the `torchvision.transforms` module to transform the image. **PIL** stands for **Python Imaging Library**, which we use to load the image received from the client. Of course, as stated earlier, the Flask framework is the backbone of our server application; we import `request`, which provides a mechanism for processing HTTP requests, and `jsonify`, which provides JSON representation that is sent back to the client. The `ImageClassifier` class is defined in `image_classifier.py`, so we import that as well.

> **Important Note**
>
> Functions from `torchvision.transforms` that we use to resize and center-crop the image expect a `PIL` image, which is why we use the `PIL` module to load the image.

2. Then, we load our fully trained CNN model:

```
model = ImageClassifier.load_from_checkpoint("./
lightning_logs/version_0/checkpoints/epoch=499-
step=15499.ckpt")
```

We instantiate the model outside of the API definition so that the model will be loaded only once, rather than with each and every API invocation.

3. Next, we define helper functions used by our implementation of the API:

```
IMAGE_SIZE = 64
def transform_image(img):
    transform = transforms.Compose([
      transforms.Resize(IMAGE_SIZE),
      transforms.CenterCrop(IMAGE_SIZE),
      transforms.ToTensor()
    ])
    return transform(img).unsqueeze(0)

def get_prediction(img):
    result = model(img)
    return functional.softmax(result, dim=1)[:,
1].tolist()[0]
```

The `transform_image` function takes an image named `img` as input. It resizes the image and center-crops it to `a size of 32` (defined using the `IMAGE_SIZE` variable). It then converts the image to a tensor and calls `unsqueeze(0)` on the tensor to insert a dimension of `size 1` at the `0` position, as required by our CNN model.

The `get_prediction` function takes the transformed image as input. It passes the input to the model to get the result and then calls `functional.softmax` on it to get the probability.

4. Then, we instantiate the Flask class and define a POST API named `predict`:

```
app = Flask(__name__)

@app.route("/predict", methods=["POST"])
def predict():
    img_file = request.files['image']
    img = Image.open(img_file.stream)
    img = transform_image(img)
    prediction = get_prediction(img)
    if prediction >= 0.5:
        cancer_or_not = "cancer"
    else:
        cancer_or_not = "no_cancer"
    return jsonify({'cancer_or_not': cancer_or_not})
```

The `predict` function has all the logic to execute the following operations in sequence: retrieve the image file from the request, load the image, transform the image, and get the prediction. The client is expected to upload a file named `image` to the `predict` API, so we use that name in `request.files['image']` to retrieve the file. After we get the prediction from the model, we use `0.5` as the probability threshold for outputting `cancer` or `no_cancer` (you can adjust the threshold based on your application needs). The `jsonify` call takes care of converting the dictionary into JSON representation and sending it back to the client in the HTTP response.

5. Finally, we start our Flask application:

```
if __name__ == '__main__':
    app.run()
```

By default, the Flask server starts listening to requests sent to localhost on the `5000` port, as shown in the following output:

```
* Serving Flask app 'server_ckpt' (lazy loading)
* Environment: production
  WARNING: This is a development server. Do not use it in a production deployment.
  Use a production WSGI server instead.
* Debug mode: off
* Running on http://127.0.0.1:5000/ (Press CTRL+C to quit)
```

Figure 9.3 – Starting the Flask server

6. Next, we describe the implementation of the client. The client sends an HTTP `POST` request to the server on localhost's `5000` port. We will work in the `client.ipynb` notebook for this section:

```
import requests

server_url = 'http://localhost:5000/predict'
path = './00006537328c33e284c973d7b39d340809f7271b.tif'
files = {'image': open(path, 'rb')}
resp = requests.post(server_url, files=files)
print(resp.json())
```

We define the URL of the server's POST API using a variable named `server_url` and the location of the image file using a variable named `path`.

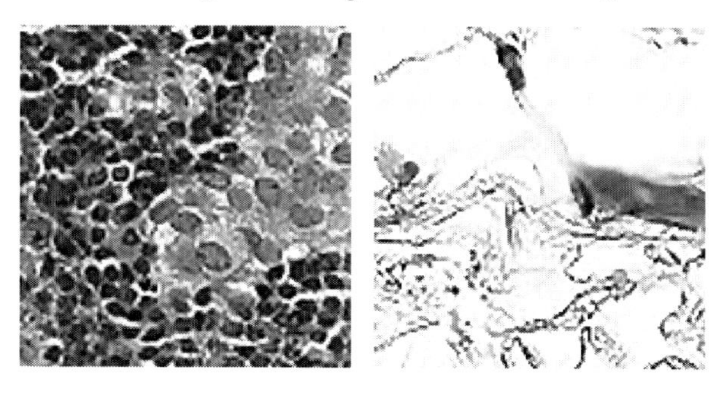

Figure 9.4 – Images used for scoring the model (from the Kaggle dataset)

Note that we have copied these two images from the dataset to this GitHub repository, so you don't need to download a complete dataset from Kaggle.

We also define the `files` dictionary in which we load the image file, with `image` as the key name as expected by the server API implementation. We then send the files to the server using an HTTP `POST` request and display the JSON response.

The following screenshot shows the client output:

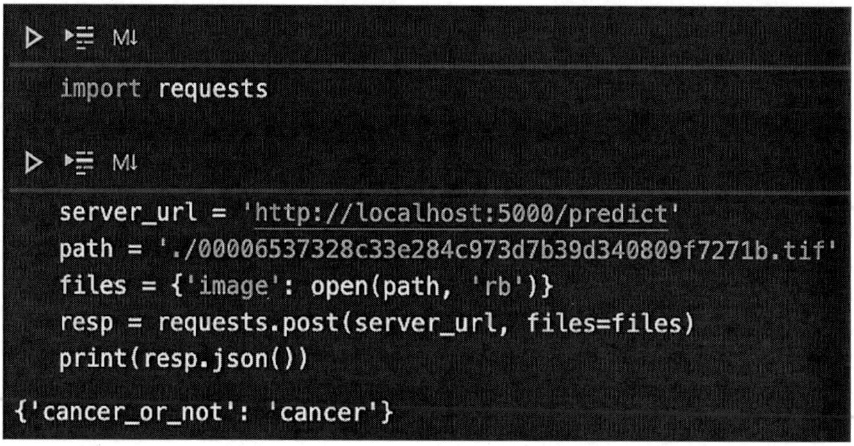

```
import requests
```

```
server_url = 'http://localhost:5000/predict'
path = './00006537328c33e284c973d7b39d340809f7271b.tif'
files = {'image': open(path, 'rb')}
resp = requests.post(server_url, files=files)
print(resp.json())
{'cancer_or_not': 'cancer'}
```

Figure 9.5 – JSON response output

The server output displays the timestamp when it processed an HTTP `POST` request received by the `/predict` API, as well as the `200` status code, indicating that the processing was successful:

```
127.0.0.1 - - [<timestamp>] "POST /predict HTTP/1.1" 200 -
```

We can also use the **Client URL** (**cURL**) command-line tool, or other API testing tools such as **Postman**, to send the request to the server. The following code snippet shows the `curl` command:

```
curl -F 'image=@000020de2aa6193f4c160e398a8edea95b1da598.tif'
http://localhost:5000/predict -v
```

Here is the output of the `curl` command:

```
*   Trying ::1...
* TCP_NODELAY set
* Connection failed
* connect to ::1 port 5000 failed: Connection refused
*   Trying 127.0.0.1...
* TCP_NODELAY set
* Connected to localhost (127.0.0.1) port 5000 (#0)
> POST /predict HTTP/1.1
> Host: localhost:5000
> User-Agent: curl/7.64.1
> Accept: */*
> Content-Length: 28172
> Content-Type: multipart/form-data; boundary=------------------------8d6c0537f5ecef88
> Expect: 100-continue
>
< HTTP/1.1 100 Continue
* We are completely uploaded and fine
* HTTP 1.0, assume close after body
< HTTP/1.0 200 OK
< Content-Type: application/json
< Content-Length: 30
< Server: Werkzeug/2.0.2 Python/3.9.7
< Date: Wed, 23 Mar 2022 15:45:27 GMT
<
{"cancer_or_not":"no_cancer"}
* Closing connection 0
```

Figure 9.6 – Prediction from the server

Most of the preceding output is about the operation of the `curl` command because we ran it with the `-v` option (for verbose). We have highlighted the server response to the end of the output in the preceding screenshot.

Deploying and scoring inter-portable models

There are so many Deep Learning frameworks available at the doorstep of a data scientist. The PyTorch Lightning framework is just the latest in a series of frameworks that includes TensorFlow, PyTorch, and even older ones such as Caffe and Torch. Each data scientist (based on what they first studied or their comfort level) normally prefers one framework over the others. Some frameworks are in Python while others are in C++. It's hard to standardize a framework in one project, let alone one department or one company. It is possible that you may train a model first in PyTorch Lightning and then, after some time, have a need to refresh it in Caffe or TensorFlow. Having a model transferred between different frameworks or an *inter-portable* model across frameworks and languages thus becomes essential. ONNX is one such format designed for this purpose.

In this section, we will see how we can achieve inter-portability in deployment using the ONNX format.

What is the ONNX format? Why does it matter?

ONNX is a cross-industry model format first introduced by Microsoft and Facebook in 2007. Its goal is to enhance Deep Learning and framework-agnostic hardware and promote inter-operability. It has been increasingly adopted by many frameworks, such as PyTorch and Caffe. The following is a visualization of the latest frameworks supported by the ONNX format:

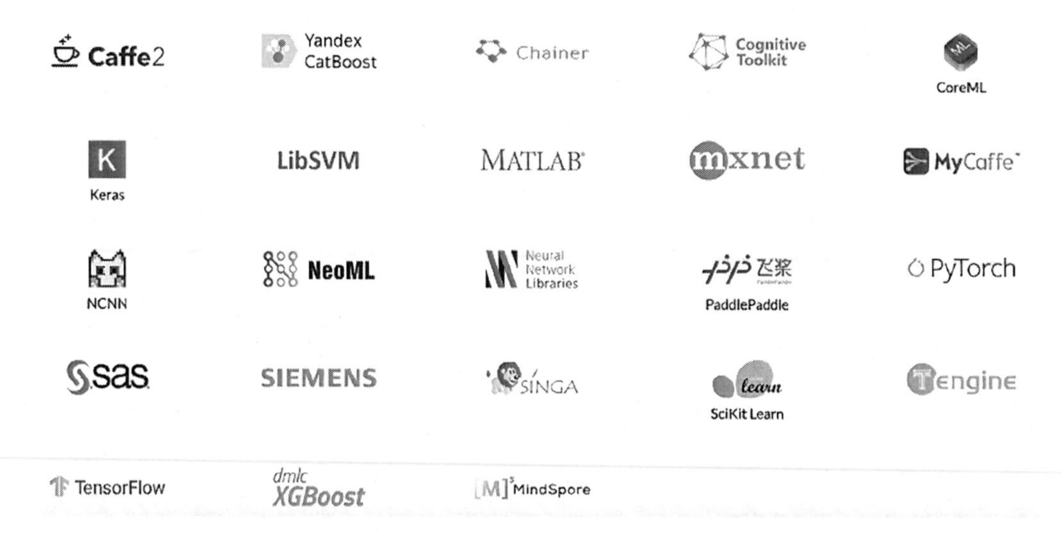

Figure 9.7 – Various Deep Learning frameworks

The thing that makes ONNX stand out from the rest of the many model formats is that it is designed specifically for Deep Learning models (while also supporting traditional models). It includes a definition for an extensible computation graph model along with built-in operators. It aims to free data scientists from being locked into any single framework. Once a model is in ONNX format, it can run on a platform, hardware, or devices (GPU or CPU), irrespective of whether it has an NVIDIA or Intel processor.

ONNX thus simplifies the whole productionalization process by taking a load off the ML engineering team to ensure that the framework supports the respective hardware. ONNX also works really well with Linux, Windows, and Macintosh environments, and has an API in Python, C, and Java, which makes it a truly versatile and unifying model framework across all platforms. It is no surprise that ONNX has become popular in recent years and also has an in-built function in the PyTorch Lightning framework. It should be noted that while many frameworks support ONNX, it's not yet supported by *all* frameworks (but it is evolving fast).

Saving and loading the ONNX model

As we described earlier, the PyTorch Lightning framework saves the state of the model using a checkpoint file. A checkpoint file is a very PyTorch-specific way of loading and deploying a model, but it's not the only means of deploying a model. We can export a model to the ONNX format using the `to_onnx` method of the model:

1. First, we import the `torch` module and `image_classifier`, where the `ImageClassifier` class is defined:

```
import torch

from image_classifier import CNNImageClassifier
```

2. Then, we load our fully trained CNN model:

```
model = ImageClassifier.load_from_checkpoint("./
lightning_logs/version_0/checkpoints/epoch=499-
step=15499.ckpt")
```

   Please ensure that the path for the checkpoint is correct to load the model. Please note that your path will change based on the name and location of your checkpoint folder

3. The `to_onnx` method requires the path of the ONNX file to be created, named `filepath` in the following code, as well as a sample input named `input_sample`. Our CNN model expects an input of size `(1, 3, 32, 32)`; we use `torch.randn` to create the sample:

```
filepath = "model.onnx"
input_sample = torch.randn((1, 3, 32, 32))
model.to_onnx(filepath, input_sample, export_params=True)
```

   This saves an ONNX file named `model.onnx` in the current working directory.

4. We use `onnxruntime` to load the model. `onnxruntime.InferenceSession` loads the model and creates a `session` object:

```
session = onnxruntime.InferenceSession("model.onnx",
None)
```

We describe how the ONNX model is loaded and used for scoring in the next section.

Deploying and scoring the ONNX model using Flask

The Flask client-server application that we use for demonstrating the ONNX format is very similar to the one we used for the checkpoint format:

1. First, we import all the tools that we will need:

```
import onnxruntime
import numpy as np

import torchvision.transforms as transforms
from PIL import Image

from flask import Flask, request, jsonify
```

   Note that we don't need to import `image_classifier` here because the `ImageClassifier` class is no longer required now that we have already converted our PyTorch model into the ONNX format.

2. Next, we use `onnxruntime` to create a session object by loading `model.onnx`:

```
session = onnxruntime.InferenceSession("model.onnx",
None)
input_name = session.get_inputs()[0].name
output_name = session.get_outputs()[0].name
```

   `input_name` and `output_name` are needed when scoring the model. We instantiate `session` and define the `input_name` and `output_name` variables outside of the API definition so that the logic is executed only once, rather than on every API invocation.

3. Next, we define helper functions used by our implementation of the API:

```
IMAGE_SIZE = 32
def transform_image(img):
    transform = transforms.Compose([
      transforms.Resize(IMAGE_SIZE),
      transforms.CenterCrop(IMAGE_SIZE),
      transforms.ToTensor()
    ])
    return transform(img).unsqueeze(0)

```

The `transform_image` function takes an image named `img` as input. It resizes the image and center-crops it to a `size of 32` (defined using the `IMAGE_SIZE` variable). It then converts the image to a tensor and calls `unsqueeze(0)` on the tensor to insert a dimension of size `1` at the `0` position because we have just one image in our batch:

```
def get_prediction(img):
    result = session.run([output_name], {input_name:
img})
    result = np.argmax(np.array(result).squeeze(),
axis=0)
    return result
```

The `get_prediction` function takes the transformed image as input. It passes the input to the model to get the result. The result is an array of logits for the two classes. We need to find the maximum of the logits and the class it belongs to in order to predict the class of the image. Therefore, we use the `numpy argmax` function on the squeezed array to ascertain the index of the maximum logits. This gives us the class of the image having maximum logits, which is again stored in the `result` variable.

> **Important Note**
> Although `torchvision.transforms` is PyTorch-specific, we still need to continue to use it in this ONNX example because that is how we have trained our model. We cannot use other image-processing libraries such as OpenCV because they have their own peculiarities, so images transformed using those libraries won't be exactly the same as what we used during training.

Moreover, although the ONNX model requires a NumPy array as input, we use `transforms.ToTensor()` because that is how we normalized the images during training. Refer to the documentation that says, *"Converts a PIL image or numpy.ndarray (H x W x C) in the range [0, 255] to a torch.FloatTensor of shape (C x H x W) in the range [0.0, 1.0]."*

As mentioned in an earlier note, functions from `torchvision.transforms` that we use to resize and center-crop the image expect a `PIL` image, which is why we use the `PIL` module for loading the image, as described next.

4. Then, we instantiate the Flask class and define a POST API named `predict`:

```
app = Flask(__name__)

@app.route("/predict", methods=["POST"])
def predict():
    img_file = request.files['image']
    img = Image.open(img_file.stream)
    img = transform_image(img)
    prediction = get_prediction(img.numpy())
    if prediction == 0:
        cancer_or_not = "no_cancer"
    elif prediction == 1:
        cancer_or_not = "cancer"
    return jsonify({'cancer_or_not': cancer_or_not})
```

   The `predict` function has all the logic to execute the following operations in sequence: retrieve the image file from the request, load the image, transform the image, and get the prediction. The client is expected to upload a file named `image` to the `predict` API, so we use that name in `request.files['image']` to retrieve the file.

   We use `img.numpy()` to convert the tensor returned by the `transform_image` function into a NumPy array.

   After we get the prediction from the model that returns the class of the image, we define the rule that if the prediction is `0`, it belongs to the `no_cancer` class, and if it is `1`, it belongs to the `cancer` class. The `jsonify` call takes care of converting the dictionary into JSON representation and sending it back to the client in the HTTP response.

5. Finally, we start our Flask application:

```
if __name__ == '__main__':
    app.run()
```

As mentioned in the previous example, the Flask server starts listening to requests sent to localhost on the `5000` port by default, as shown in the following output:

```
* Serving Flask app 'server_ckpt' (lazy loading)
* Environment: production
  WARNING: This is a development server. Do not use it in a production deployment.
  Use a production WSGI server instead.
* Debug mode: off
* Running on http://127.0.0.1:5000/ (Press CTRL+C to quit)
```

Figure 9.8 – Flask server ready

> **Important Note**
>
> Make sure that you terminate the checkpoint server in the previous example before you launch the ONNX server; otherwise, you will get an error that says something such as "Address already in use" because that server is already listening to the `5000` port, where you are trying to launch a new server.

The client code is exactly the same (`client.ipynb`) because the client doesn't care about the server's internal implementation – whether the server uses a native checkpoint-based model instance or an ONNX-based model instance for scoring.

The following screenshot shows the client output:

```
import requests

server_url = 'http://localhost:5000/predict'
path = './00006537328c33e284c973d7b39d340809f7271b.tif'
files = {'image': open(path, 'rb')}
resp = requests.post(server_url, files=files)
print(resp.json())

{'cancer_or_not': 'cancer'}
```

Figure 9.9 – Model prediction

Similar to what we described in the previous example, the server output displays the timestamp when it processes an HTTP `POST` request received by the `/predict` API, as well as the `200` status code indicating that the processing was successful:

```
127.0.0.1 - - [<timestamp>] "POST /predict HTTP/1.1" 200 -
```

Of course, we can also use the cURL command-line tool to send the request to our ONNX server as well:

```
curl -X POST -F
'image=@00006537328c33e284c973d7b39d340809f7271b.tif' http://
localhost:5000/predict -v
```

Next steps

Now that we have seen how to deploy and score a Deep Learning model, feel free to explore other challenges that sometimes accompany the consumption of models:

- How do we scale the scoring for massive workloads, for example, serving 1 million predictions every second?
- How do we manage the response time of scoring throughput within a certain round-trip time? For example, the round-trip between a request coming in and the score being served cannot exceed 20 milliseconds. You can also think of ways to optimize such DL models while deploying, such as batch inference and quantization.
- Heroku is a popular option to deploy. You can deploy a simple ONNX model over Heroku under a free tier. You can deploy the model without the frontend or with a simple frontend to just upload a file. You can go a step further and use a production server, such as Uvicorn, Gunicorn, or Waitress, and try to deploy the model.
- It is also possible to save the model as a `.pt` file and use JIT to script the model, and then perform inference. You can try this option and compare the performance.

Such deployment challenges are typically handled by the machine learning engineering team with the help of cloud engineers. This process typically also involves creating replication systems that can scale automatically to account for incoming workloads.

Further reading

Here is a link to the *Inference in Production* page of the PyTorch Lightning website: `https://pytorch-lightning.readthedocs.io/en/latest/common/production_inference.html`.

To learn more about ONNX and ONNX Runtime, visit their websites: `https://onnx.ai` and `https://onnxruntime.ai`.

Summary

Data scientists often play a supporting role in the model deployment and scoring aspects. However, in some companies (or smaller data science projects where there may not be a fully staffed engineering or ML-Ops team), data scientists may be asked to do such tasks. This chapter should be helpful in preparing you for doing both test and experimental deployments, as well as integration with end user applications.

We have seen in this chapter how PyTorch Lightning can be easily deployed and scored to be consumed via a REST API endpoint with the help of a Flask application. We have seen how we can do so both natively via checkpoint files or via a portable file format such as ONNX. We have seen how different file formats such as ONNX can be used to aid the deployment process in real-life production situations, where multiple teams may be using different frameworks for training the models.

Looking back, we started our journey with an introduction to our first Deep Learning model and then successively looked at more and more advanced algorithms to accomplish various tasks, such as GANs, semi-supervised learning, and self-supervised learning.

We have also seen how some of the objectives of training a large Deep Learning model can be achieved using either a pre-trained model or out-of-the-box models such as Flash.

In the next chapter, we will compile some important tips that will be helpful in troubleshooting as you practice your Deep Learning journey and guide you as a ready reckoner for scaling your model for massive workloads.

10
Scaling and Managing Training

So far, we have been on an exciting journey in the realm of **Deep Learning** (**DL**). We have learned how to recognize images, how to create new images or generate new texts, and how to train machines without fully labeled sets. It's an open secret that achieving good results for a DL model requires a massive amount of compute power, often requiring the help of a **Graphics Processing Unit** (**GPU**). We have come a long way since the early days of DL when data scientists had to manually distribute the training to each node of the GPU. PyTorch Lightning obfuscates most of the complexities associated with managing underlying hardware or pushing down training to the GPU.

In the earlier chapters, we have pushed down training via brute force. However, doing so is not practical when you have to deal with a massive training effort for large-scale data. In this chapter, we will take a nuanced view of the challenges of training a model at scale and managing the training. We will describe some of the common pitfalls and tips and tricks on how to avoid them. We will also describe how to set up your experiments, how to make model training resilient to issues in the underlying hardware, and how to leverage the hardware to improve training efficiency, among other things. Treat this chapter as a ready reckoner for your more complex training needs.

In this chapter, we will cover the following topics to aid in the training of DL models:

- Managing training
- Scaling up training
- Controlling training

Technical Requirements

In this chapter, we will be using version 1.5.2 of PyTorch Lightning. Please install this version using below command

```
!pip install pytorch-lightning==1.5.2
```

Managing training

In this section, we will go through some of the common challenges that you may encounter while managing the training of DL models. This includes troubleshooting in terms of saving model parameters and debugging the model logic efficiently.

Saving model hyperparameters

There is often a need to save the model's hyperparameters. A few reasons are reproducibility, consistency, and that some models' network architecture are extremely sensitive to hyperparameters.

On more than one occasion, you may find yourself being unable to load the model from the checkpoint. The `load_from_checkpoint` method of the `LightningModule` class fails with an error.

Solution

A checkpoint is nothing more than a saved state of the model. Checkpoints contain precise values of all parameters used by the model. However, hyperparameter arguments passed to the `__init__` model are not saved in the checkpoint by default. Calling `self.save_hyperparameters` inside `__init__` of the `LightningModule` class saves the arguments' names and values in the checkpoint as well.

Check whether you are passing additional arguments, such as the learning rate, to the `__init__` model of your `LightningModule` class. If you are, then you need to make sure that the values of those arguments are also captured in your checkpoint. To accomplish that, call `self.save_hyperparameters` inside `__init__` of the `LightningModule` class.

The following code snippet shows how we used `self.save_hyperparameters` in our **Convolutional Neural Network-Recurrent Neural Network** (**CNN-RNN**) cascaded model implemented as the CNN-**Long Short-Term Memory** (**LSTM**) architecture in Chapter 7:

```
def __init__(self, cnn_embdng_sz, lstm_embdng_sz, lstm_hidden_
lyr_sz, lstm_vocab_sz, lstm_num_lyrs, max_seq_len=20):
    super(HybridModel, self).__init__()
    """CNN"""
    resnet = models.resnet152(pretrained=False)
    module_list = list(resnet.children())[:-1]
    self.cnn_resnet = nn.Sequential(*module_list)
    self.cnn_linear = nn.Linear(resnet.fc.in_features,
                  cnn_embdng_sz)
    self.cnn_batch_norm = nn.BatchNorm1d(cnn_embdng_sz,
                       momentum=0.01)
    """LSTM"""
    self.lstm_embdng_lyr = nn.Embedding(lstm_vocab_sz,
                      lstm_embdng_sz)
    self.lstm_lyr = nn.LSTM(lstm_embdng_sz, lstm_hidden_lyr_sz,
                lstm_num_lyrs, batch_first=True)
    self.lstm_linear = nn.Linear(lstm_hidden_lyr_sz,
                   lstm_vocab_sz)
    self.max_seq_len = max_seq_len
    self.save_hyperparameters()
```

In the preceding code snippet, the last line in `__init__` calls `self.save_hyperparameters`.

Efficient debugging

Experimenting with and debugging a DL model written in PyTorch could turn out to be a very time-consuming process for the following reasons:

- DL models are trained using a large amount of data. The training process may take hours or days to run, even on high-performance hardware such as GPUs or **Tensor Processing Units** (**TPUs**). The training is performed iteratively using multiple batches of data and epochs. This unwieldy train-validate-test cycle may cause a delay in the manifestation of bugs in the programming logic.

- Python is not a compiled language; it is an interpreted language. Syntax errors such as typos and missing `import` statements are not caught beforehand, as in compiled languages such as C and C++. Such an error only surfaces when that particular line of code is run by the Python Virtual Machine.

Can PyTorch Lightning help in catching programming errors quickly to save time wasted in repeated reruns after correcting the errors?

Solution

The PyTorch Lightning framework provides different arguments that can be passed to the `Trainer` module during model training to reduce debugging time. Here are some of them:

- `limit_train_batches`: This argument can be passed to `Trainer` to control a subset of the data to be used for a training epoch. The following code snippet provides an example of this:

```
import pytorch_lightning as pl
...
# use only 10% of the training data for each epoch
trainer = pl.Trainer(limit_train_batches=0.1)
# use only 10 batches per epoch
trainer = pl.Trainer(limit_train_batches=10)
```

  This setting is useful for debugging some issues that happen after an epoch. It saves time because it accelerates the running time of an epoch.

  Note that there are similar arguments, named `limit_test_batches` and `limit_val_batches` for test and validation data, respectively.

- `fast_dev_run`: This argument limits train, validation, and test batches to quickly check for bugs. Unlike the `limit_train/val/test_batches` argument, this argument disables checkpoints, callbacks, loggers, and so on, and runs only one epoch. So, as the name suggests, this argument should only be used during development for quick debugging. You can see it in action in the following code snippet:

```
import pytorch_lightning as pl
...
# runs 5 train, val, test batches and then terminate
trainer = pl.Trainer(fast_dev_run=5)
```

```
# run 1 train, val, test batch and terminate
trainer = pl.Trainer(fast_dev_run=True)
```

- `max_epochs`: This argument limits the number of epochs, and training is terminated once the number of `max_epochs` arguments is reached.

  The following code snippet shows how we used this argument when training the CNN model to limit the training to 100 epochs:

```
trainer = pl.Trainer(max_epochs=100, gpus=-1)
```

Monitoring the training loss using TensorBoard

It is important to ensure throughout the training process that training loss is converging without getting stuck in local minima. If it doesn't converge, then you need to adjust parameters such as the learning rate, the batch size, or the optimizer and restart the training process. How can we visualize the loss curve to monitor that the loss is continuously decreasing?

Solution

By default, PyTorch Lightning supports the **TensorBoard** framework, which provides tracking and visualizing of metrics such as the training loss. You can save the loss calculated during execution of every batch and epoch by calling the `log()` method in your `LightningModule` code. For example, the following code snippet shows how we registered the loss in *Chapter 7, Semi-Supervised Learning* in the definition of the `training_step` method of the `HybridModel` class defined in `model.py`:

```
def training_step(self, batch, batch_idx):
    loss_criterion = nn.CrossEntropyLoss()
    imgs, caps, lens = batch
    outputs = self(imgs, caps, lens)
    targets = pk_pdd_seq(caps, lens, batch_first=True)[0]
    loss = loss_criterion(outputs, targets)
    self.log('train_loss', loss, on_epoch=True)
    return loss
```

The call to `self.log` saves the loss value internally, and for that, as mentioned earlier, PyTorch Lightning uses the TensorBoard framework by default. We also give a name to this loss metric: `train_loss`. The `on_epoch=True` argument instructs the PyTorch Lightning framework to log the loss not only for every batch but also for every epoch.

We have described **tracking** of the preceding loss metric. Next, we describe the **visualization** of the loss metric. We will work in the `tensorboard.ipynb` notebook for the remainder of this section. As can be seen in the notebook, we simply need to point TensorBoard to the location of the `lightning_logs` directory created by the PyTorch Lightning framework during model training. So, launch the `tensorboard.ipynb` notebook from the parent directory of `lightning_logs`. Here is the code that does the visualization trick:

```
%load_ext tensorboard
%tensorboard --logdir "./lightning_logs"
```

In the preceding code snippet, we first load the `tensorboard` extension, and then we provide the location of the `lightning_logs` directory to it using the `--logdir` command-line argument.

Upon execution of the notebook cell, the TensorBoard framework gets launched below the cell, as shown in the following screenshot:

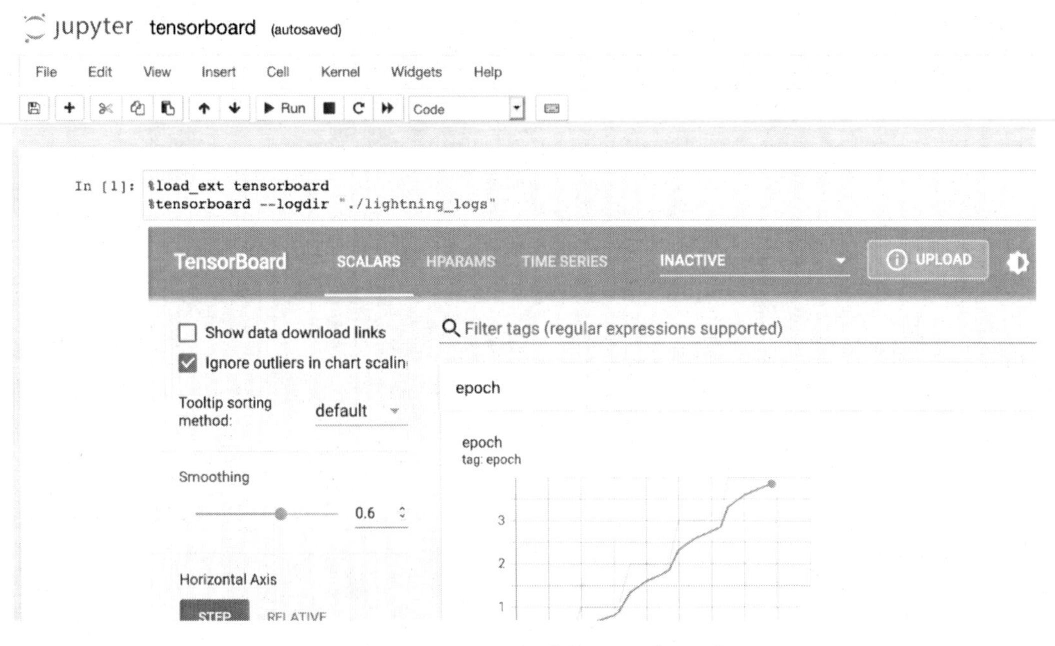

Figure 10.1 – TensorBoard for Visualizing loss

Important Note

It might take a couple of seconds for the TensorBoard framework to get displayed, especially if you have run thousands of epochs during your model training. It takes a bit more time for TensorBoard to load all that metrics data.

Coming back to the name, `train_loss`, that we used for the loss metric when we called `self.log` in the definition of the `training_step` method in the preceding code snippet, TensorBoard displays two loss charts. Scroll down below the `epoch` and `hp_metric` charts in TensorBoard, then expand the `train_loss_epoch` and `train_loss_step` tabs shown in the following screenshot:

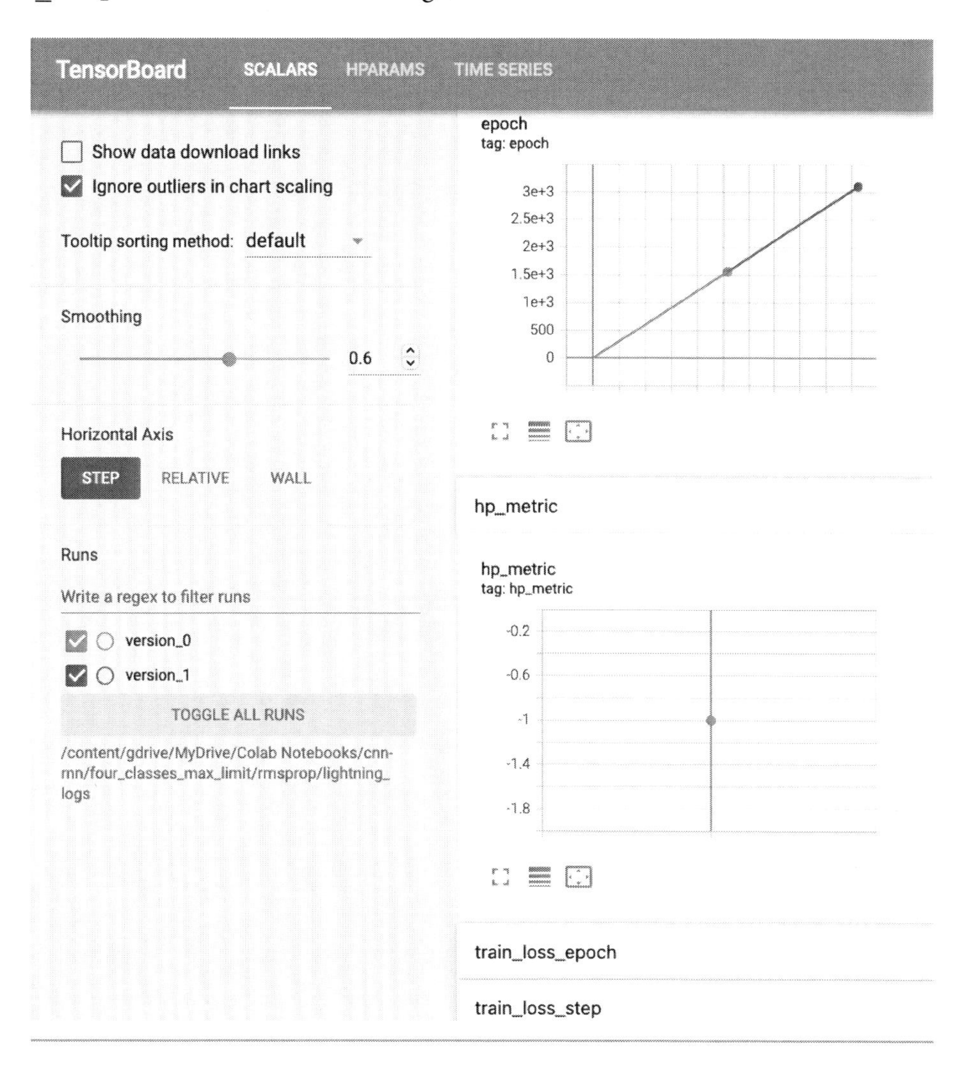

Figure 10.2 – TensorBoard loss chart tabs

Note that the PyTorch Lightning framework automatically appends `_epoch` and `_step` to the name `train_loss` that we provided in the code in order to differentiate between epoch metrics and step metrics. This is because we asked the framework to record the loss for every epoch in addition to the loss for every step in the preceding code snippet by passing the `on_epoch=True` argument to `self.log`.

The following screenshot shows both loss charts:

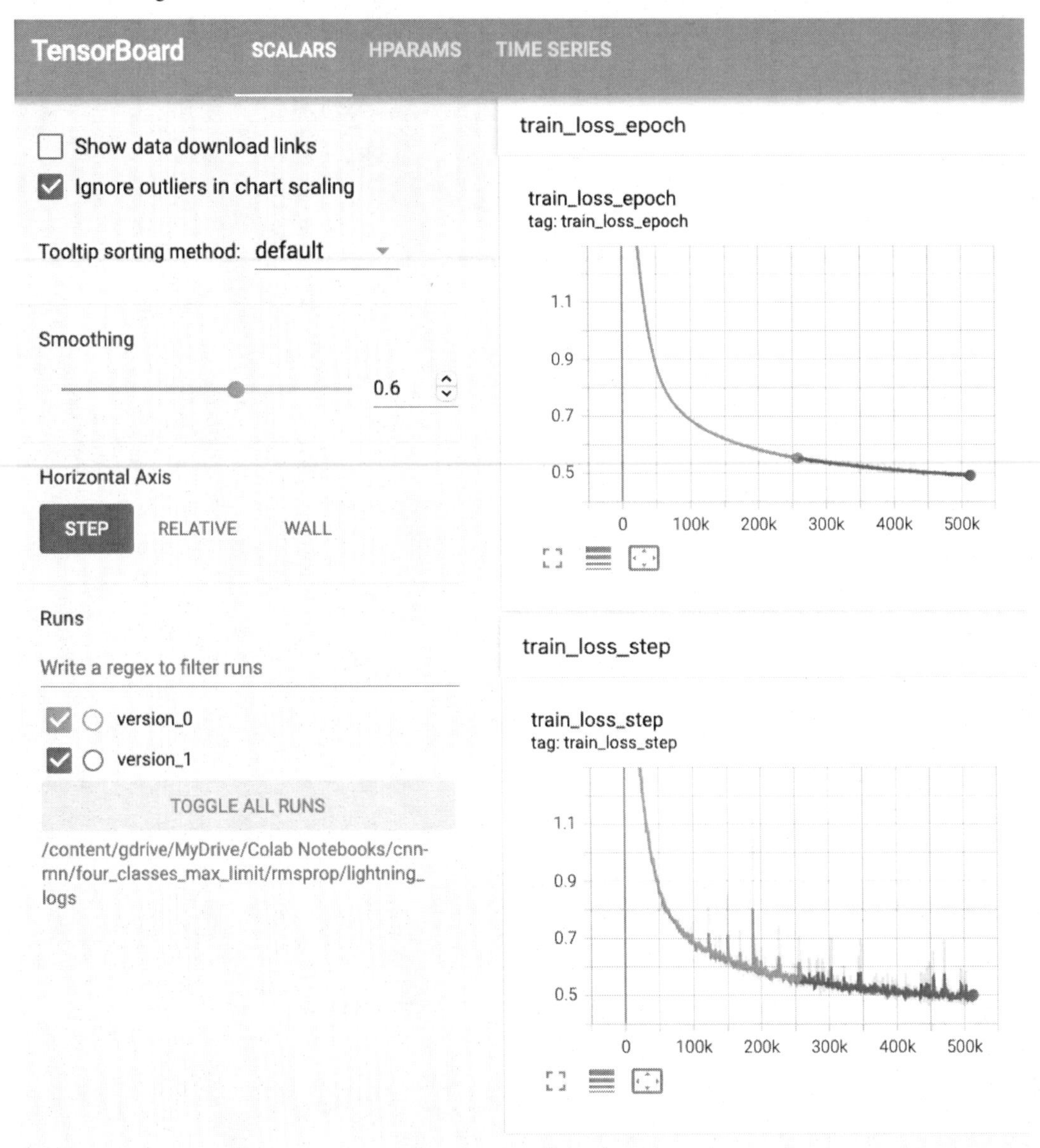

Figure 10.3 – TensorBoard loss charts

Finally, note that different colors are automatically used for different versions. As can be seen on the bottom left-hand side of the preceding screenshot, orange has been used for `version_0` and blue has been used for `version_1`. If your training process is spanned across many versions, then you may choose to display metrics for one or more of those versions by selecting the checkboxes or radio buttons next to those version numbers. For example, training in the following screenshot has a total of 8 versions. We used the learning rate value of `0.001` for versions 0 through 5, but since the training did not converge, we then lowered the learning rate value to `0.0003` and restarted the training, as a result of which subsequent versions were created. We selected just 6, 7, and 8 in the following screenshot to visualize the loss curve for the learning rate value of `0.0003`:

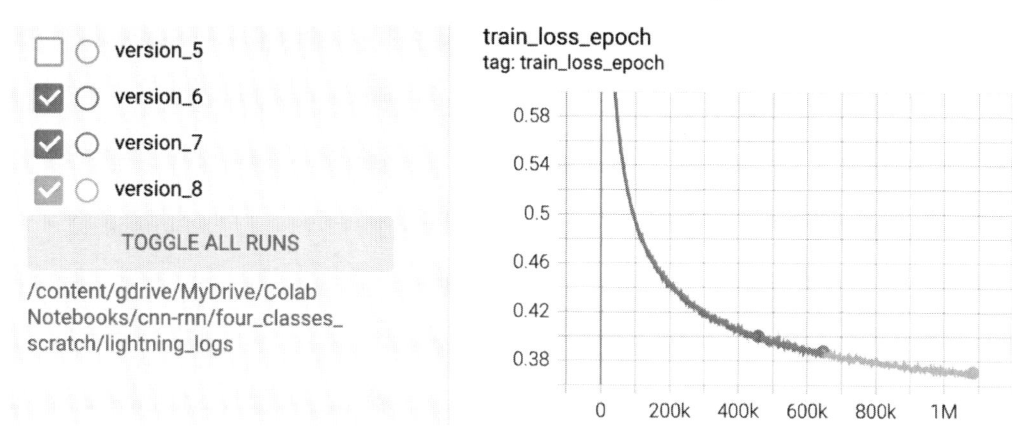

Figure 10.4 – TensorBoard select versions

Scaling up training

Scaling up training requires us to speed up the training process for large amounts of data and utilize GPUs and TPUs better. In this section, we will cover some of the tips on how to efficiently use provisions in PyTorch Lightning to accomplish this.

Speeding up model training using a number of workers

How can the PyTorch Lightning framework help speed up model training? One useful parameter to know is `num_workers`, which comes from PyTorch, and PyTorch Lightning builds on top of it by giving advice about the number of workers.

Solution

The PyTorch Lightning framework offers a number of provisions for speeding up model training, such as the following:

- You can set a non-zero value for the `num_workers` argument to speed up model training. The following code snippet provides an example of this:

```
import torch.utils.data as data
...
dataloader = data.DataLoader(num_workers=4, ...)
```

  The optimal `num_workers` value depends on the batch size and configuration of your machine. A general guideline is to start at a number equal to the number of **Central Processing Unit** (**CPU**) cores on your machine. As mentioned in the documentation found at `https://pytorch-lightning.readthedocs.io/en/stable/guides/speed.html#num-workers`, "*the best thing to do is to increase the* `num_workers` *slowly and stop once you see no more improvement in your training speed.*"

Note that PyTorch Lightning gives advice about `num_workers`, as shown in the following screenshot of output emitted when the model training was run with a `num_workers=1` argument on `DataLoader`:

```
6.4 M     Trainable params
0         Non-trainable params
6.4 M     Total params
25.643    Total estimated model params size (MB)
/usr/local/lib/python3.7/dist-packages/pytorch_lightning/trainer/data_loading.py:106: UserWarning: The dataloader, train
  f"The dataloader, {name}, does not have many workers which may be a bottleneck."
```

Figure 10.5 – Output of model training run with num_workers=1 argument

As shown in the highlighted text in the preceding screenshot, the framework gives a warning. Here is the full text next to the user warning seen in the preceding screenshot:

```
"UserWarning: The dataloader, train dataloader, does not have
many workers which may be a bottleneck. Consider increasing the
value of the `num_workers` argument` (try 4 which is the number
of cpus on this machine) in the `DataLoader` init to improve
performance."
```

Note that Jupyter notebook environments such as **Google Colaboratory** (**Google Colab**), Amazon SageMaker, and IBM Watson Studio allow you to set the configuration of the underlying hardware for your Jupyter notebook.

For example, in Google Colab, in the **Change Runtime Type** setting, you can set the **Runtime shape** field to **High-RAM** instead of **Standard** so that you can increase the value of the `num_workers` argument to `DataLoader`.

GPU/TPU training

A CPU is often insufficient to achieve the speed required for model training. Making use of a GPU is one option. If you are on Google Cloud or a notebook-based service such as Colab, then a TPU is also an option. This is a processing unit specially designed for DL models. Let's now see how the PyTorch Lightning framework can help take advantage of GPU/TPU hardware.

Solution

If the underlying hardware of the machine where you are running your Jupyter notebook has a GPU/TPU, then you should use this to accelerate the training. The PyTorch Lightning framework makes it very easy to switch to a GPU/TPU through a simple changing of flags passed as arguments to `Trainer`. An example of this is provided in the following code snippet:

```
import pytorch_lightning as pl
...
# use 2 gpus
trainer = pl.Trainer(gpus=2)
# use all gpus
trainer = pl.Trainer(gpus=-1)
```

You can use the `gpus` argument passed to `Trainer` to specify the number of GPUs. You can set it to `-1` to specify that you want to use all GPUs. The following code snippet shows how we used this argument when training our CNN model:

```
trainer = pl.Trainer(max_epochs=100, gpus=-1)
```

For TPU training, use the `tpu_cores` argument for `Trainer`, as follows:

```
# use 1 TPU core
trainer = Trainer(tpu_cores=1)
# use 4 TPU cores
trainer = Trainer(tpu_cores=4)
```

Note that in Google Colab, you can change the runtime type to set the hardware accelerator to `GPU` or `TPU` instead of `None`.

The following screenshot shows the **Notebook settings** pop-up dialog in Google Colab:

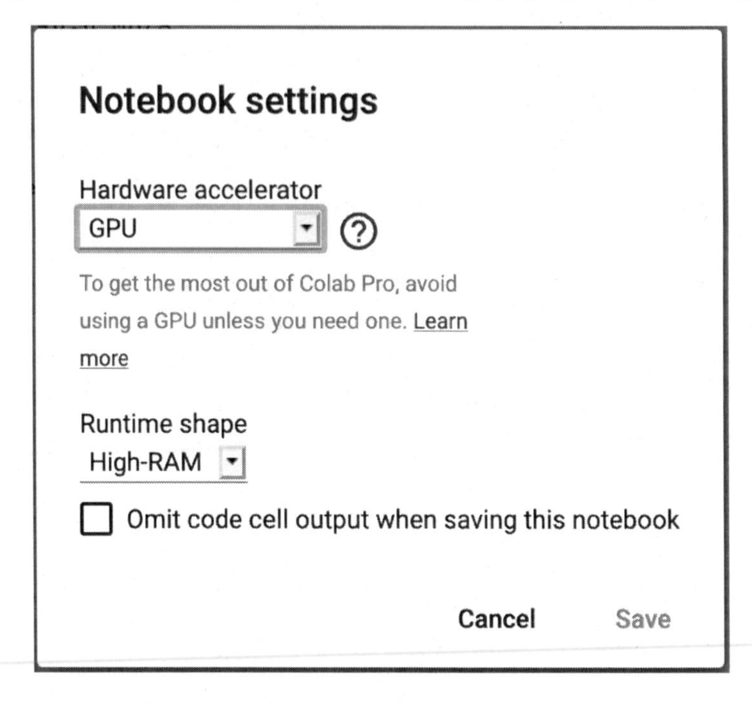

Figure 10.6 – Notebook settings in Google Colab

This will help you enable the GPU services on Google Colab.

Mixed precision training/16-bit training

DL models such as CNNs convert a higher-dimensional object such as an image into a lower-dimensional object, such as a Tensor. In other words, we don't need precise calculations, and if we can sacrifice a little bit of precision then can we get a lot of improvement in speed. One of the ways TPUs improve performance is by using this concept. However, for non-TPU environments, this facility is not available.

Making use of a better processing unit such as GPU or multi-CPU significantly improves training performance, as we discussed in the previous section. But we can additionally enable the lower precision at the framework level? PyTorch Lightning allows you to use mixed precision training by simply passing an additional argument named `precision` to the `Trainer` module.

Solution

Mixed precision training makes use of two different numbers of bits for floating-point numbers—the higher 32 bits as well as the lower 16 bits. This reduces the memory footprint during the model training and in turn, improves training performance.

PyTorch Lightning supports mixed precision training for CPUs and GPUs, as well as TPUs. The following example shows how the `precision` option can be used along with the `gpus` option:

```
import pytorch_lightning as pl
...
trainer = pl.Trainer(gpus=-1, precision=16)
```

This allows the model to train faster, and a performance boost can be as big as reducing epoch training time by half. In chapter 7 we have seen that by using 16 bit precision we improved CNN model training speed by about 30-40%.

Controlling training

There is often a need to have an audit, balance, and control mechanism during the training process. Imagine you are training a model for 1,000 epochs and a network failure causes an interruption after 500 epochs. How do you resume training from a certain point while ensuring that you won't lose all your progress, or save a model checkpoint from a cloud environment? Let's see how to deal with these practical challenges that are often part and parcel of an engineer's life.

Saving model checkpoints when using the cloud

Notebooks hosted in cloud environments such as Google Colab have resource limits and idle timeout periods. If these limits are exceeded during the development of a model, then the notebook is deactivated. Owing to the inherently elastic nature of the cloud environment, (which is one of the value propositions of the cloud) the underlying compute and storage resources are decommissioned when a notebook is deactivated. If you refresh the browser window of the deactivated notebook, the notebook is typically restarted with brand new compute/storage resources.

The checkpoint directory and files are no longer accessible after notebooks hosted in a cloud environment are deactivated due to resource limits or idle timeout periods. One way to solve this problem is to use a mounted drive.

Solution

As we have mentioned previously, PyTorch Lightning automatically saves the state of the last training epoch in a checkpoint, which is saved in the current working directory by default. However, the current working directory of the machine where notebooks are launched is not a good choice for saving checkpoints in cloud notebooks owing to the transient nature of their underlying infrastructure, as described in the preceding section. In such environments, the cloud provider typically offers persistent storage that can be accessed from the notebook.

Next, we will describe how Google Drive persistent storage can be used in Google Colab, which is nothing but a cloud notebook. We'll proceed as follows:

1. First, we import Google Drive into our notebook, as follows:

```
from google.colab import drive
drive.mount('/content/gdrive')
```

2. Then, we can refer to a directory in Google Drive using a path that starts with `/content/gdrive/MyDrive`. Note that, during the execution of the preceding `drive.mount()` statement, you will be prompted to authenticate as shown in the following screenshot:

Permit this notebook to access your Google Drive files?
This notebook is requesting access to your Google Drive files. Granting access to Google Drive will permit code executed in the notebook to modify files in your Google Drive. Make sure to review notebook code prior to allowing this access.
No thanks
Connect to Google Drive

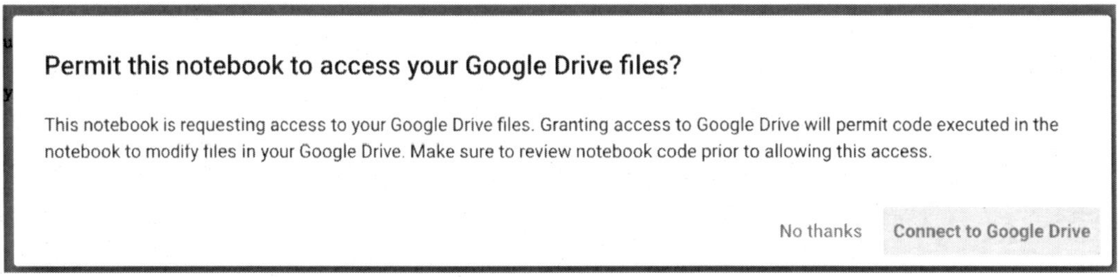

Figure 10.7 – Entering authorization code

3. Click on the Connect to Google Drive button. Select your account on the next popup. Then, click Allow on the next popup, as shown here:.

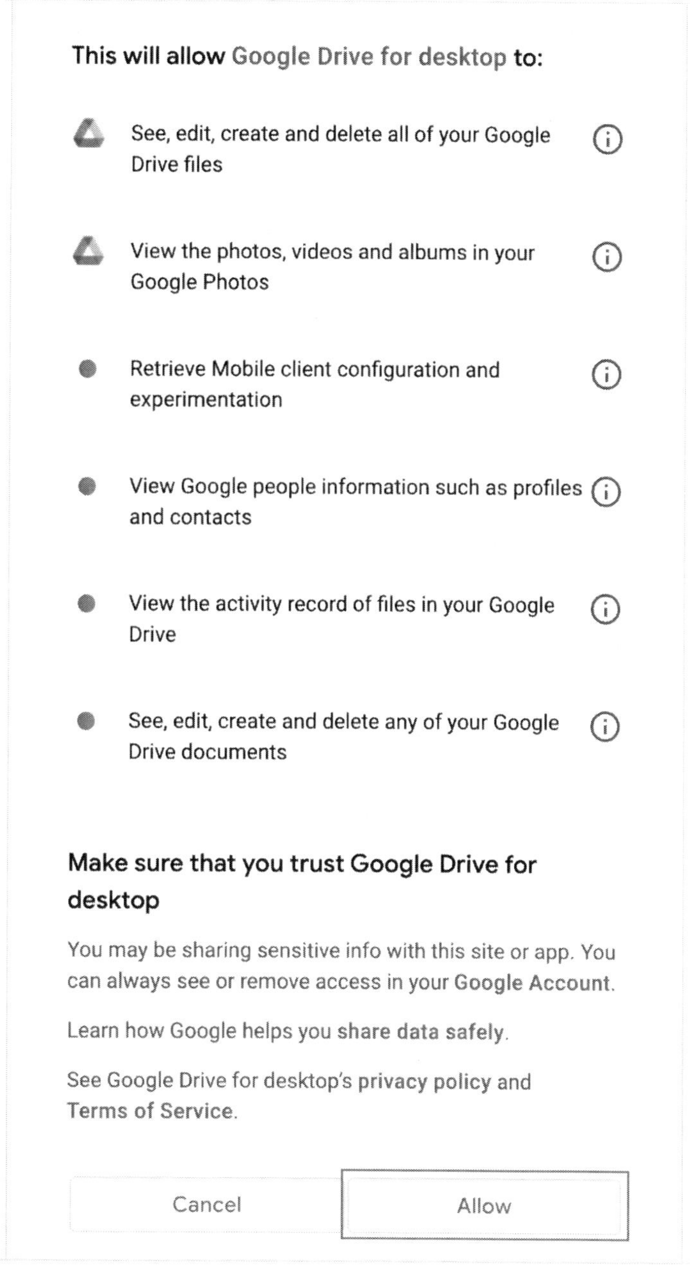

This will allow Google Drive for desktop to:

See, edit, create and delete all of your Google Drive files

View the photos, videos and albums in your Google Photos

Retrieve Mobile client configuration and experimentation

View Google people information such as profiles and contacts

View the activity record of files in your Google Drive

See, edit, create and delete any of your Google Drive documents

Make sure that you trust Google Drive for desktop

You may be sharing sensitive info with this site or app. You can always see or remove access in your Google Account.

Learn how Google helps you share data safely.

See Google Drive for desktop's privacy policy and Terms of Service.

Cancel Allow

Figure 10.8 – Allowing access to Google Drive

4. Then, use the `default_root_dir` argument of the PyTorch Lightning `Trainer` module to change the checkpoint path to your Google Drive. For example, the following code stores the checkpoint in the `Colab Notebooks/cnn` directory in Google Drive. Its full path is `/content/gdrive/MyDrive/Colab Notebooks/cnn`, as shown in the following code snippet:

```
import pytorch_lightning as pl
...
ckpt_dir = "/content/gdrive/MyDrive/Colab Notebooks/cnn"
trainer = pl.Trainer(default_root_dir=ckpt_dir,
                     max_epochs=100)
```

Inside the `/content/gdrive/MyDrive/Colab Notebooks/cnn` directory, the checkpoint is stored under the `lightning_logs/version_<number>/checkpoints` directory structure.

Changing the default behavior of the checkpointing feature

How do you go about changing the default behavior of the checkpointing feature of the PyTorch Lightning framework?

Solution

The PyTorch Lightning framework automatically saves the state of the last training epoch to the current working directory by default. In order for users to change this default behavior, the framework provides a class named `ModelCheckpoint` in `pytorch_lightning.callbacks`. We will describe a couple of examples of such customizations in this section, as follows:

- First, instead of saving the state of the last training epoch, you can choose to save every *n*th epoch, as follows:

```
import pytorch_lightning as pl
...
ckpt_callback = pl .callbacks.ModelCheckpoint(every_n_
epochs=10)
trainer = pl.Trainer(callbacks=[ckpt_callback],
                     max_epochs=100)
```

- The every_n_epochs argument passed to ModelCheckpoint specifies the periodicity for saving the checkpoint. We use the value 10 for the every_n_epochs argument in the preceding code snippet. ModelCheckpoint is then passed to Trainer using the callbacks array argument. The preceding code will save the checkpoint in the current working directory, but of course, you can change that location using the default_root_dir argument passed to Trainer, as shown here:

```
import pytorch_lightning as pl
...
ckpt_dir = "/content/gdrive/MyDrive/Colab Notebooks/cnn"
ckpt_callback = pl .callbacks.ModelCheckpoint(every_n_
epochs=10)
trainer = pl.Trainer(default_root_dir=ckpt_dir,
                     callbacks=[ckpt_callback],
                     max_epochs=100)
```

- This customization stores only the latest checkpoint after an epoch that is a multiple of 10—that is, it saved a checkpoint after the 10th epoch, then replaced that with the checkpoint after the 20th epoch, and then replaced that after the 30th epoch, and so on.
- But what if you want to save the five most recent checkpoints instead of just one, or what if you want to save all the checkpoints?
- You might want to save more than one checkpoint in order to perform some comparative analysis on the checkpoints later. You can accomplish this by using the save_top_k argument of ModelCheckpoint. The framework only stores the latest checkpoint by default because the default value of the save_top_k parameter is 1.
- You can set save_top_k to -1 to save all checkpoints. When it is used along with the every_n_epochs=10 argument, all checkpoints that are multiples of 10 will be saved, as shown here:

```
import pytorch_lightning as pl
...
ckpt_dir = "/content/gdrive/MyDrive/Colab Notebooks/cnn"
ckpt_callback = pl .callbacks.ModelCheckpoint(every_n_
epochs=10,
                                               save_top_k=-1)
trainer = pl.Trainer(default_root_dir=ckpt_dir,
```

```
                        callbacks=[ckpt_callback],
                        max_epochs=100)
```

The following screenshot shows that all checkpoints that are multiples of 10 have been saved to Google Drive. Note that epoch numbering starts at `0`, so the checkpoint that starts with `epoch=9` is for the 10th epoch, the checkpoint that starts with `epoch=19` is for the 20th epoch, and so on:

Name ↑	Owner	Last modified	File size
epoch=9-step=319.ckpt	me	12:27 PM me	73.4 MB
epoch=19-step=639.ckpt	me	12:29 PM me	73.4 MB
epoch=29-step=959.ckpt	me	12:30 PM me	73.4 MB
epoch=39-step=1279.ckpt	me	12:32 PM me	73.4 MB
epoch=49-step=1599.ckpt	me	12:34 PM me	73.4 MB
epoch=59-step=1919.ckpt	me	12:36 PM me	73.4 MB
epoch=69-step=2239.ckpt	me	12:38 PM me	73.4 MB
epoch=79-step=2559.ckpt	me	12:40 PM me	73.4 MB
epoch=89-step=2879.ckpt	me	12:41 PM me	73.4 MB
epoch=99-step=3199.ckpt	me	12:43 PM me	73.4 MB

Figure 10.9 – All checkpoints in multiples of 10

Note that you can also use the `best_model_path` and `best_model_score` attributes of the `ModelCheckpoint` object to access the best model checkpoint.

Resuming training from a saved checkpoint

One of the nagging aspects of DL models is that they take a really long time—often days—to complete the training process. During this time, how can any intermediate results be viewed? Or, if the training process is interrupted due to failures, how can training be resumed from a saved checkpoint?

Solution

As mentioned in this chapter, notebooks hosted in cloud environments such as Google Colab have resource limits and idle timeout periods. If these limits are exceeded during the development of a model, then the notebook is deactivated and its underlying filesystem becomes inaccessible. In such cases you should use a cloud provider's persistent storage to save the checkpoint; for example, use Google Drive to store the checkpoint when using Google Colab.

But even then, training may be interrupted due to a timeout period or due to some issue in the underlying infrastructure, an issue in the program logic, and so on. In such cases, the PyTorch Lightning framework allows you to resume training using the `ckpt_path` argument of `Trainer`. This is important for DL algorithms because they typically require prolonged training on lots of data, therefore it helps to avoid wasting time spent retraining the model.

The following code uses a saved checkpoint to resume model training:

```
import pytorch_lightning as pl
...
ckpt_dir = "/content/gdrive/MyDrive/Colab Notebooks/cnn"
latest_ckpt = "/content/gdrive/MyDrive/Colab Notebooks/cnn/
lightning_logs/version_4/checkpoints/epoch=39-step=1279.ckpt"
ckpt_callback = pl .callbacks.ModelCheckpoint(every_n_
epochs=10, save_top_k=-1)
trainer = pl.Trainer(default_root_dir=ckpt_dir,
callbacks=[ckpt_callback], ckpt_path=latest_ckpt, max_
epochs=100)
```

This code snippet uses the `default_root_dir` argument of `Trainer` to specify a location in Google Drive for saving the checkpoints. Also, the `ModelCheckpoint` class is given `every_n_epochs` and `save_top_k` arguments so that checkpoints corresponding to all epochs that are multiples of 10 will be saved. And last but not least, the code uses `epoch=39-step=1279.ckpt` (which corresponds to the 40th epoch because epoch numbering starts at 0) as the value of the `ckpt_path` argument to `Trainer`.

The following screenshot shows how the PyTorch Lightning framework is restoring states from the checkpoint file—as highlighted in the first line of the output—so that training can be resumed beyond the 40th epoch:

```
Restoring states from the checkpoint file at /content/gdrive/MyDrive/Colab Notebooks/cnn/lightning_logs/version_4/checkpoints/epoch=39-step=1279.ckp
LOCAL_RANK: 0 - CUDA_VISIBLE_DEVICES: [0]
Restored all states from the checkpoint file at /content/gdrive/MyDrive/Colab Notebooks/cnn/lightning_logs/version_4/checkpoints/epoch=39-step=1279.

  | Name              | Type             | Params
-------------------------------------------------------
0 | conv_layer1       | Conv2d           | 84
1 | relu1             | ReLU             | 0
2 | pool              | MaxPool2d        | 0
3 | conv_layer2       | Conv2d           | 168
4 | relu2             | ReLU             | 0
5 | fully_connected_1 | Linear           | 6.1 M
6 | fully_connected_2 | Linear           | 250 K
7 | fully_connected_3 | Linear           | 15.1 K
8 | fully_connected_4 | Linear           | 122
9 | loss              | CrossEntropyLoss | 0
-------------------------------------------------------
6.4 M     Trainable params
0         Non-trainable params
6.4 M     Total params
25.643    Total estimated model params size (MB)
/usr/local/lib/python3.7/dist-packages/pytorch_lightning/trainer/data_loading.py:327: UserWarning: The number of training samples (32) is smaller th
  f"The number of training samples ({self.num_training_batches}) is smaller than the logging interval"
Epoch 40: 62%                                        20/32 [00:09<00:05, 2.33it/s, loss=0.21, v_num=10, train_accuracy=0.9
```

Figure 10.10 – Resuming the training

As displayed on the last line in the screenshot before the start of the progress bar, the training resumed at epoch 40 (again, it is really the 41st epoch because epoch numbering starts at 0).

Notice the location of the checkpoint that we use for resuming the training: `lightning_logs/version_4/checkpoints/epoch=39-step=1279.ckpt`. It is `version_4`. As a result, subsequent checkpoints 50 through 100 will be saved under the `version_5` directory, as shown in the following screenshot:

Name ↑	Owner	Last modified	File size
epoch=49-step=1599.ckpt	me	Sep 24, 2021 me	73.4 MB
epoch=59-step=1919.ckpt	me	Sep 24, 2021 me	73.4 MB
epoch=69-step=2239.ckpt	me	Sep 24, 2021 me	73.4 MB
epoch=79-step=2559.ckpt	me	Sep 24, 2021 me	73.4 MB
epoch=89-step=2879.ckpt	me	Sep 24, 2021 me	73.4 MB
epoch=99-step=3199.ckpt	me	Sep 24, 2021 me	73.4 MB

Figure 10.11 – Checkpoints 50 through 100 saved under version_5 directory

This helps us track all the saved checkpoints as a fail-safe mechanism and use models at various timeframes to compare model training results.

Saving downloaded and assembled data when using the cloud

The downloading and assembling of data used for training a DL model is typically a one-time processing step. Granted that sometimes you may realize that you need to further clean the data you have already processed or get more data in order to create a better model, but the data doesn't change beyond a certain point—it has to be frozen.

On the other hand, model training may take days or even weeks to complete. It involves iterating over the data thousands or hundreds of thousands of times, tuning the model's hyperparameters, and restarting or resuming the training to achieve convergence by avoiding local minima. How can we ensure that data processing steps are not redone unnecessarily? How can we make the same copy of processed data available throughout the training process?

Solution

You can bundle processed data and save it, then unbundle and use the data throughout model training. This is especially important in cloud notebook environments owing to the transient nature of their underlying infrastructure, as described in a previous section. Let us learn with an example; here is how you can modify the notebooks we used in *Chapter 7, Semi-Supervised Learning*:

- We used three different notebooks for data processing in *Chapter 7, Semi-Supervised Learning*: `download_data.ipynb`, `filter_data.ipynb`, and `process_data.ipynb`. The second and third notebooks start and pick up from the point where their previous notebook ends. They assume that data from the previous notebook is in the current working directory. In other words, the current working directory acts as the common context between the three notebooks, which certainly is not the case if the notebooks are launched in a cloud environment. All three notebooks will be assigned their own separate compute and storage infrastructure. The following bullet points describe how you can solve this problem.
- You can combine the three notebooks together. Start with the contents of the `download_data.ipynb` notebook, then append cells from the `filter_data.ipynb` notebook, and then append cells from the `process_data.ipynb` notebook. Let's call this synthesized notebook simply `data.ipynb`; it downloads the COCO 2017 data, filters it, resizes the images, and creates the vocabulary.

- Append the following code cell to the `data.ipynb` notebook to bundle the processed data:

```
!tar cvf coco_data_filtered.tar coco_data
!gzip coco_data_filtered.tar
```

The preceding code creates a bundle named `coco_data_filtered.tar.gz` and stores it in the current working directory.

- Finally, append the following code cell to the `data.ipynb` notebook to store the `coco_data_filtered.tar.gz` bundle in persistent storage outside of the cloud infrastructure where the `data.ipynb` notebook is run. The code uses a mounted Google Drive to save the data bundle, but you can instead use any other persistent storage supported by a cloud provider:

```
from google.colab import drive
drive.mount('/content/gdrive')
!cp ./coco_data_filtered.tar.gz /content/gdrive/MyDrive/
Colab\ Notebooks/cnn-rnn
```

The code first mounts Google Drive at `/content/gdrive`. Then, it saves the data bundle in a folder named `cnn-rnn` inside the `Colab\ Notebooks` folder.

> **Important Note**
>
> During the execution of the preceding `drive.mount()` statement, you will be prompted to authenticate with Google and enter the authorization code, as described in a previous section of this chapter.

Further reading

We have mentioned some key tips and tricks that we have found useful for common troubleshooting. You can always refer to the *Speed up model training* documentation for more details on how to speed up training or on other topics. Here is a link to the documentation: `https://pytorch-lightning.readthedocs.io/en/latest/guides/speed.html`.

We have described how PyTorch Lightning supports the TensorBoard logging framework by default. Here is a link to the TensorBoard website: `https://www.tensorflow.org/tensorboard`.

Additionally, PyTorch Lightning supports CometLogger, CSVLogger, MLflowLogger, and other logging frameworks. You can refer to the *Logging* documentation for details of how those other logger types can be enabled. Here is a link to the documentation: `https://pytorch-lightning.readthedocs.io/en/stable/extensions/logging.html`.

Summary

We began this book with just a curiosity for what DL and PyTorch Lightning are. Anyone new to the Deep Learning or a curious beginner to PyTorch Lightning can get their feet wet by trying simple image recognition models and then continue to raise their game by learning skills such as **Transfer Learning** (**TL**) or how to make use of other pre-trained architectures. We continued to leverage the PyTorch Lightning framework for doing not just image recognition models but also **Natural Language Processing** (**NLP**) models, time series, and other traditional **Machine Learning** (**ML**) challenges. Along the way, we learned about RNN, LSTM, and Transformers.

In the next section of the book, we explored exotic DL models such as **Generative Adversarial Networks** (**GANs**), Semi-supervised learning, and Self-Supervised Learning that expand the art of what is possible in the domain of ML and these are not just advanced models but super cool ways to create art and lots of fun to work with. We wrapped up this book in the last section by giving a primer on taking DL models into production and common troubleshooting techniques to scale and manage large training workloads.

While the objective of the book is to get someone who is embarking on their journey in DL up and running, we hope that those who come from other frameworks also found this a quick and easy way to make the transition to PyTorch Lightning.

While our journey may be coming to an end with this chapter, your journey into DL has just begun!! We still have many unanswered questions in **Artificial Intelligence** (**AI**) that need new algorithms to be developed and many unsolved problems that need new architectures to be designed. The next few years will be the most exciting time to be a Data Scientist focusing on DL! With tools such as PyTorch Lightning, you can focus on doing cool things such as researching new methods or building new models while letting the framework do the hard work for you. Despite all the glitz and glamour and hype over the last few years associated with DL, the ML community has barely reached the base camp. We are still in the early stages of summitting the mountain of **AGI (Artificial General Intelligence)**, and the view from the top of AGI will be that of a machine truly comparable to human intelligence & intellectual capabilities. Being part of the DL community will make you part of the adventure that will transform humanity!

So, while we have come to the end of this book, we welcome you to the as-yet unexplored dimensions of AI that you will hopefully discover as part of your journey and leave an impact on humanity. Welcome aboard!!!

Index

A

B

C

D

K

L

M

N

O

P

R

S

T

U

V

W

X

Other Books You May Enjoy

If you enjoyed this book, you may be interested in these other books by Packt:

Deep Learning with fastai Cookbook

ISBN: 9781800208100

- Prepare real-world raw datasets to train fastai Deep Learning models
- Train fastai Deep Learning models using text and tabular data
- Create recommender systems with fastai
- Find out how to assess whether fastai is a good fit for a given problem
- Deploy fastai Deep Learning models in web applications
- Train fastai Deep Learning models for image classification

Machine Learning Engineering with MLflow

ISBN: 9781800560796

- Develop your machine learning project locally with MLflow's different features
- Set up a centralized MLflow tracking server to manage multiple MLflow experiments
- Create a model life cycle with MLflow by creating custom models
- Use feature streams to log model results with MLflow
- Develop the complete training pipeline infrastructure using MLflow features
- Set up an inference-based API pipeline and batch pipeline in MLflow
- Scale large volumes of data by integrating MLflow with high-performance big data libraries

Packt is searching for authors like you

If you're interested in becoming an author for Packt, please visit `authors.packtpub.com` and apply today. We have worked with thousands of developers and tech professionals, just like you, to help them share their insight with the global tech community. You can make a general application, apply for a specific hot topic that we are recruiting an author for, or submit your own idea.

Share Your Thoughts

Now you've finished *Deep Learning with PyTorch Lightning*, we'd love to hear your thoughts! Scan the QR code below to go straight to the Amazon review page for this book and share your feedback or leave a review on the site that you purchased it from.

`https://packt.link/r/180056161X`

Your review is important to us and the tech community and will help us make sure we're delivering excellent quality content.

Made in United States
North Haven, CT
23 March 2024